Public Work and the Academy

Public Work and the Academy

An Academic Administrator's Guide to Civic Engagement and Service-Learning

Editors

Mark Langseth
Minnesota Campus Compact

William M. Plater
Indiana University-Purdue University Indianapolis

Assistant Editor

Scott Dillon

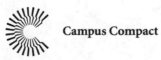

Campus Compact

ANKER PUBLISHING COMPANY, INC.
Bolton, Massachusetts

Public Work and the Academy
An Academic Administrator's Guide to Civic Engagement and
Service-Learning

ISBN 1-882982-73-8

Composition by Beverly Jorgensen/Studio J Graphic Design
Cover design by Tepperman/Ray Associates

Anker Publishing Company, Inc.
176 Ballville Road
P.O. Box 249
Bolton, MA 01740-0249 USA

www.ankerpub.com

Dedication

To our spouses,
Kate and Gail

About the Authors

The Editors

Mark Langseth has served as founding executive director of Minnesota Campus Compact (1994-present) and founding director of the Minnesota Campus Service Initiative (1987-1994), the nation's first such statewide effort. He initiated Minnesota Campus Compact's groundbreaking Chief Academic Officers' Initiative for Service-Learning and Civic Engagement in 1999.

William M. Plater has served as the chief academic officer at Indiana University-Purdue University Indianapolis (IUPUI) since 1987 and as interim president in 2002-2003. He has also served as dean of liberal arts and professor of English at IUPUI. He has written extensively on the changing nature of faculty work and, more broadly, higher education.

Scott Dillon is an undergraduate student in the College of Liberal Arts at the University of Minnesota and production assistant for the University of Minnesota Press. He is currently researching the importance of the written word in both literature and journalism.

The Contributors

Louis S. Albert is president of the West Campus of Pima Community College. He served as vice chancellor for educational services for the San Jose/Evergreen Community College District from 1998 to 2003, and as vice president of the American Association for Higher Education from 1982 to 1998. He chairs the Board of the International Partnership for Service-Learning.

Victor Bloomfield has served as professor of biochemistry, molecular biology, and biophysics at the University of Minnesota since 1970, teaching and doing research on DNA biophysics. He was chair of the Faculty Consultative Committee in 1997-1998. He is currently interim dean of the graduate school and vice provost for research.

Dale A. Blyth is the associate dean for youth development at the University of Minnesota. He has authored articles on adolescent development and service-learning and serves as a consultant to the Kellogg Foundation in designing the National Learning in Deed Initiative.

Harry C. Boyte is founder and codirector of the Center for Democracy and Citizenship at the Humphrey Institute at the University of Minnesota. He has written eight books on citizenship, community organizing, and politics, and is coauthor with Elizabeth Hollander of the *Wingspread Declaration on Civic Responsibility in Higher Education.*

Robert G. Bringle is Chancellor's Professor of psychology and philanthropic studies and director of the Center for Service and Learning at Indiana University-Purdue University Indianapolis. His programmatic and research interests include developing ways to implement and institutionalize service-learning and civic engagement.

Robert Bruininks is president of the University of Minnesota, where he has contributed nearly 35 years of service as professor, dean, and most recently, executive vice president and provost. As a researcher, he has authored or coauthored nearly 90 journal articles and more than 70 book chapters, as well as training materials and several nationally standardized tests. He is strongly committed to the University of Minnesota's responsibilities as a public land-grant university in service to the state and its citizens.

Barry Checkoway is professor of social work and urban planning and founding director of the Ginsberg Center for Community Service and Learning at the University of Michigan, where his research and teaching focuses on community organization, social planning, and neighborhood development.

Amy Driscoll is the director of teaching, learning, and assessment at California State University-Monterey Bay and was formerly director of community/university partnerships at Portland State University. She is codirector of the Clearinghouse and National Review Board for the Scholarship of Engagement. She is coauthor of *Making Outreach Visible: A Guide* to *Documenting Professional Service and Outreach* (AAHE, 1999) and has published in the *Michigan Journal of Community Service-Learning* and the *Journal of Higher Education Outreach and Engagement.*

Susan Engelmann is program coordinator in the Office of the Executive Vice President and Provost, and has provided program management for the Civic Engagement Task Force and the Council on Public Engagement at the University of Minnesota.

Robert J. Exley presently serves as vice president for academic affairs at Iowa Western Community College. He received his associate of arts from San Jacinto College in Houston, Texas, his B.A. and M.S. from the University of Houston-Clear Lake, and his Ph.D. from the University of Texas-Austin. Prior to joining Iowa Western Community College in July of 2000, he served as chairperson for the Wolfson Campus' Department of Community Education. At Miami-Dade Community College, he was the program director for the college's nationally recognized service-learning program.

Edwin Fogelman is professor of political science and chair of the University of Minnesota's Council on Public Engagement. In spring 2002, he received a special Provost's Award for Leadership in Civic Engagement.

Barbara S. Frankle is dean of faculty and professor of history at LeMoyne-Owen College, a liberal arts historically black college in Memphis, Tennessee. She helped develop service-learning at the college, directing the program from its inception until it became an integral part of the curriculum. She was the principal investigator for significant grants to design, develop, and implement the program from the Ford Foundation, the Council for Independent Colleges, and the National Corporation for National Service.

Andrew Furco is director of the Service-Learning Research and Development Center at the University of California-Berkeley, where he serves on the Graduate School of Education faculty. His research has focused on investigating the effects of service-learning and civic engagement in K-12 and higher education, as well as explorations of strategies to institutionalize service-learning practice. He has served as a Campus Compact Engaged Scholar and currently is a member of the National Review Board for the Scholarship of Engagement, the Campus Compact/AAHE Service-Learning Consulting Corps, and the National Service-Learning Partnership Board of Directors.

Donald W. Harward served as president of Bates College from 1989 to 2002, where he was a strong advocate for campus civic engagement. Before taking office at Bates, he served as vice president for academic affairs at The College of Wooster, Ohio; preceding his tenure there, he taught and served in the Department of Philosophy at the University of Delaware, and subsequently designed and led the university honors program.

Julie A. Hatcher is associate director of the Center for Service and Learning at Indiana University-Purdue University Indianapolis and adjunct faculty in philanthropic studies. Her programmatic and research interests include service-learning, the philosophical work of John Dewey and its implications for undergraduate education, and the role of higher education in a democracy.

Myron S. Henry is professor of mathematical sciences at the University of Southern Mississippi (USM). He served as provost of USM from August 1998 to January 2001, as provost of Kent State University in Northeast Ohio, and as provost at Old Dominion University in Norfolk, Virginia. He was also dean of arts and sciences at Central Michigan University, and served as interim dean and a faculty member at Montana State University. He spent a professional leave at North Carolina University, and for a brief time, taught high school mathematics in Alexandria, Indiana.

Barbara A. Holland is director of the National Service-Learning Clearinghouse, based at ETR Associates in California and funded by the Corporation for National and Community Service as a comprehensive web-based resource for enhancing the quality of service-learning programs. She is also a senior scholar in the Center for Service and Learning at Indiana University-Purdue University Indianapolis and executive editor of *Metropolitan Universities* journal. Her research interests focus on organizational change in higher education with special attention to the development of civic missions, and the implementation and assessment of civic engagement strategies.

Robert J. Jones is vice president and executive vice provost for faculty and academic programs, as well as a professor of plant physiology in the Department of Agronomy and Plant Genetics at the University of Minnesota. As vice president and executive provost, he serves as the deputy academic and administrative officer of the executive vice president and provost.

Rosalyn J. Jones is dean of the College of Arts and Sciences at Johnson C. Smith University in Charlotte, North Carolina. She is also a member of the Campus Compact/AAHE Service-Learning Consulting Corps.

Francis M. Lazarus is vice president for academic affairs and provost of the University of San Diego (USD). He began his position at USD in 1996, after serving as vice president for academic affairs at Marquette University in Milwaukee, Wisconsin.

Richard J. Meister is professor of history, specializing in American urban and social history. He came to DePaul University as dean of the College of Liberal Arts and Sciences in 1981 and became executive vice president for academic affairs in 1993.

Jim Ostrow is vice president for academic affairs at Lasell College and a sociologist. Previously he served as director of the Service-Learning Center at Bentley College and as chief academic officer at the Fayette Campus of Pennsylvania State University.

Joseph Paul is vice president for student affairs and assistant professor of educational leadership at the University of Southern Mississippi. He has served as a student affairs administrator in higher education for 26 years, and as vice president since 1993. He earned a Ph.D. in administration of higher education from the University of Alabama in 1984.

Judith S. Rauner, director of the University of San Diego Office for Community Service-Learning from 1986 to 2002, initiated the office that facilitates outreach to the community through cocurricular service and service-learning integrated into the curriculum. She has extensive program development and administrative experience in nonprofit organizations and schools. She has an Ed.D. in educational leadership and an M.A. in human resources administration.

John Saltmarsh is project director of Integrating Service with Academic Study at the national office of Campus Compact. He taught American history for over a decade at Northeastern University. He has written widely on service-learning and civic engagement, including contributions to *Connecting Past and Present: Concepts and Models for Service-Learning in*

History (AAHE, 2000) and *Learning to Serve: Promoting Civil Society Through Service-Learning* ([with Elizabeth Hollander and Edward Zlotkowski] Kluwer Academic Publishers, 2001).

Lorilee R. Sandmann is currently on the faculty of the University of Georgia's School of Leadership and Lifelong Learning in the College of Education. Previously, she served as associate vice president for public service and outreach at the university, vice provost for institutional effectiveness and strategic partnerships at Cleveland State University and the University of Minnesota. In those positions, she has provided leadership to major institutional change processes to promote extension and application of knowledge and defining and evaluating faculty scholarship. She is also codirector of the Clearinghouse and National Review Board for the Scholarship of Engagement.

Thomas J. Schnaubelt is executive director of Wisconsin Campus Compact and former director of the Mississippi Center for Community and Civic Engagement at the University of Southern Mississippi. His involvement in service-learning began ten years ago and spans student and academic affairs. He earned his Ph.D. at the University of Mississippi in higher education administration, an M.A. from the University of Michigan in social foundations and policy, and a B.S. in physics from the University of Wisconsin-Stevens Point.

Catherine A. Solheim is associate dean for outreach in the College of Human Ecology at the University of Minnesota. She received her Ph.D. in family social science from the University of Minnesota in 1990.

Charles R. Strain is professor of religious studies at DePaul University. He became associate vice president of academic affairs in 1999. He recently published "Creating the Engaged University: Service-Learning, Religious Studies, and Institutional Mission" in *From Cloister to Commons: Concepts and Models for Service-Learning in Religious Studies* edited by Richard Devine, Joseph A. Favazza, and F. Michael McLain (AAHE, 2002).

Craig Swan is professor of economics and currently serves as vice provost for undergraduate education at the University of Minnesota. He was an ex-officio member of the university's Task Force on Civic Engagement and serves as a member of the University of Minnesota's Council on Public Engagement.

Cynthia Villis is associate provost at the University of San Diego (USD), where she oversees its Pre-College Institute and develops academic outreach programs and proposals to foundations, among other responsibilities. From 1987 to 1997, she was USD's dean of academic services and director of its Counseling Center. She is licensed as a psychologist in California.

Billie Wahlstrom is vice provost for distributed education and instructional technology at the University of Minnesota. She coordinates efforts at the university to use instructional technology strategically and effectively to enhance teaching, learning, and outreach activities. She is a professor in the Department of Rhetoric and teaches in the areas of message design and new media.

Joshua B. Young currently serves as the director of Miami-Dade Community College's Center for Community Involvement, where he oversees all service-learning and America Reads activities. He possesses a bachelor's degree in sociology from the University of Virginia and master's degrees in social work and public administration from Florida State University. He served two tours with the Peace Corps in Mali, West Africa, and Paraguay, South America, and has directed summer community service programs for youth for four summers in the Dominican Republic with Visions International. He has been with Miami-Dade Community College since 1994.

Steven R. Yussen became dean of the College of Education and Human Development at the University of Minnesota in 1998. He is a faculty member in the university's Institute of Child Development, where he earned a Ph.D. in 1973.

Edward Zlotkowski is Senior Faculty Fellow at Campus Compact. He teaches English at Bentley College in Waltham, Massachusetts, where he founded the Bentley College Service-Learning Project in 1990. He is the author of *Successful Service-Learning Programs* (Anker, 1998) and is the series editor for the American Association for Higher Education 19-volume series on service-learning in the disciplines.

Table of Contents

Preface

As Bill Plater and I see it, editors of books like this one have three primary jobs: to clearly communicate a rationale and outline for the work; to recruit, select, and guide exemplary contributors; and to introduce and provide a sense of coherence for the book as a whole. It is toward this last goal that we offer some introductory words here and in the first chapter. In this section, I offer some larger context and a summary of each chapter; in the introductory chapter, Bill provides more specific context, including definitions and rationales for the burgeoning service-learning/civic engagement movement in higher education.

As this manuscript is completed, small towns, cities, and states throughout the U.S. prepare to commemorate the second anniversary of September 11, 2001. Though no memorial can remove the national and global reverberations of pain that emanated from that tragic day, as has often been the case in U.S. history, such a horrific event has provided a powerful opportunity to reflect on who we are as members of a national and global society. For example, just what are the ties that bind us—locally, nationally, and globally—and how might those ties be better nurtured?

As evidenced by recent aggressive proposals by congressional Republicans and Democrats to expand "national service," many Americans have been reminded of what de Tocqueville observed about the U.S. in our early days: that our propensity to roll up our sleeves through voluntary association with others to get things done is one of our greatest strengths. Perhaps the most hopeful glimmer from 9/11 is that we might rediscover the power and responsibility of such citizen action that has distinguished us from our very beginning.

Notably, U.S. colleges and universities have been engaged in similar soul-searching processes spanning at least the last decade. Much of this reflection has been prompted by a growing concern that the public no longer views higher education with the carte blanche reverence we once enjoyed. One need only witness disturbingly consistent declines in the percentage of state and federal dollars spent on higher education over the past 15 years to find evidence of plummeting public interest in academe.

While much of higher education's soul searching has focused on concerns about proprietary institutions and technology-based education supplanting more traditional forms, a growing movement of service-learning and civic engagement advocates has insisted upon even deeper reflections about who we are, where we've been, and where we're going in higher education. Indeed, many such advocates, along with higher education historians, have concluded that at the dawn of the 21st century, higher education finds itself in the midst of a historic identity crisis—a crisis that will not be resolved by trumpeting louder our traditional arguments about the value of liberal learning or our contribution to workforce development and economic vitality. We must do more.

Fortunately, much like the nation's post-9/11 rediscovery of the importance of civic connectedness, colleges and universities—two-year and four-year, public and private, urban, suburban, and rural—have begun to rediscover their roots in civic engagement. Even more promising, many institutions have made great strides toward enhancing their community connectedness in ways—importantly—that also significantly enhance teaching, research, and outreach missions. Could civic engagement be more intentionally and publicly linked with workforce/economic development and liberal learning at the core of higher education's collective identity? Might such a link provide an antidote to the public's perception that higher education has become more about private gain than public good?

Certainly, in order to embed civic engagement as a more fundamental element of higher education's identity, more intentional leadership will be required by those who shape our institutions. Thus, as service-learning/civic engagement's potential to address higher education's identity crisis has grown, so too has the need for related resources targeted specifically at academic leaders.

Navigating the Book

The purpose of this book is to provide academic leaders with a resource to increase their fluency with and ability to lead service-learning and civic engagement efforts on their campuses, with their peers, and throughout U.S. higher education. It is written specifically for academic leaders—chief academic officers, provosts, deans, division and department chairs—who have significant responsibility for their campus's academic programs.

We have deliberately included a wide variety of topical essays and case studies so that readers might gravitate toward specific issues or types of institutions most applicable to their college or university. Concurrently, we have attempted to provide insights in every chapter that are applicable across institution types and that transcend specific issue concerns. Indeed, one of the great strengths of the civic engagement movement is its ability to engage very different types of institutions in discussions on a wide range of topics yielding highly productive exchanges of ideas and experiences. We have attempted to replicate this strength in the book and expect that the reader will discover insights in unexpected places. Each chapter is briefly outlined below.

In Chapter 1, Bill Plater discusses a range of issues, including definitions, links with larger institutional concerns, the critical role of the academic leader, and international efforts to move service-learning and civic engagement deeper into the educational mainstream. Chapters 2–5 include important topical essays on issues most relevant to academic leaders. In Chapter 2, Andrew Furco and Barbara Holland draw on their groundbreaking research on institutionalization and sustainability of service-learning efforts, including helpful summaries of the role of service-learning in meeting larger institutional priorities and of key dimensions of service-learning institutionalization. In Chapter 3, Edward Zlotkowski and John Saltmarsh posit service-learning as one of the most comprehensive responses to addressing reform concerns in higher education, citing a variety of highly regarded contemporary scholars of education. In Chapter 4, Amy Driscoll and Lorilee Sandmann adeptly outline the important role of academic leaders in creating incentives and removing disincentives for faculty participation in service-learning, including references to the National Review Board on the Scholarship of Engagement, helpful tools for faculty interested in documenting their work for promotion and tenure, and related resources. In Chapter 5, Jim Ostrow offers a strong philosophical argument for service-learning, focusing on its potential for generating greater educational depth and drawing heavily on the teachings of John Dewey.

Chapters 6–16 provide case studies from a wide variety of institutions that have significantly embraced service-learning and/or civic engagement as central to advancing their institutional missions. Many have also applied service-learning and civic engagement to addressing a variety of larger institutional concerns—from bridging academic and student affairs to enhancing community relations to promoting multiculturalism to increasing student retention. In each case, the institution's developmental path and the role of the academic leader is discussed in significant detail.

In Chapter 6, Donald Harward, President Emeritus at Bates College, describes significant advancements in action research and community development partnerships between Bates and its surrounding area that occurred prior to his retirement in 2002. In Chapter 7, Richard Meister and Charles Strain outline DePaul University's process for embracing civic engagement as core to its institutional identity, including the development of an endowed center and their innovative "ladder of social engagement" model for building active citizens. In Chapter 8, Robert Bringle and Julie Hatcher outline the multifaceted, highly collaborative approach toward advancing civic engagement through service-learning at Indiana University-Purdue University Indianapolis, including Bill Plater's role in advancing these ideas. In Chapter 9, Rosalyn Jones provides an overview of Johnson C. Smith University's path to service-learning, including strong links to that institution's concept of excellence as an historically black university. In Chapter 10, Barbara Frankle draws on the distinctive history of Historically Black Colleges' and Universities' (HBCUs) relationship with their surrounding communities, describing the many processes she initiated to weave service-learning into larger curriculum change efforts.

In Chapter 11, Robert Exley and Joshua Young chronicle the evolution of service-learning at Miami-Dade Community College, drawing lessons useful to other community colleges, large and small. In Chapter 12, Louis Albert describes San Jose City College's journey to service-learning, highlighting nine factors that have contributed significantly to their success. In Chapter 13, Barry Checkoway examines a number of unique dilemmas faced by Research I institutions such as his University of Michigan, as they grapple with advancing civic engagement. Chapter 14 chronicles another Research I example—the University of Minnesota—in which former provost, now president, Robert Bruininks and several colleagues elaborate on their multiple efforts to create a more "engaged university." In Chapter 15, Francis Lazarus, Judith Rauner, and Cynthia Villis describe the University of San Diego's highly collaborative approach to service-learning, including strong links with their campus diversity efforts. Similarly, in Chapter 16, Myron Henry, Joseph Paul, and Thomas Schnaubelt elaborate on their collaborative approach between academic and student affairs toward advancing service-learning and civic engagement at the University of Southern Mississippi.

The book concludes with a resources section to guide the reader to other helpful publications, web sites, consultants, and networks.

A Work in Progress

Finally, as with any book, Bill and I had to make choices about who might contribute, and others made choices in their responses to our invitations. As a result, not all perspectives we would have liked to include are represented here. It is important to note, then, that we view this book not as a definitive volume on its topic, but rather as a beginning point for encouraging deeper reflection and action on the part of academic leaders about how service-learning and civic engagement fit within their unique campus contexts.

Fortunately, many other helpful resources exist toward this end. The resources section includes helpful referrals for all types of campuses—for rural, suburban, and urban campuses; for HBCUs, Tribal, and Hispanic-serving institutions; for large and small, public and private, two-year and four-year institutions. Where the book does not provide what you need, we strongly encourage you to pursue these resources. They are bountiful and helpful.

Ultimately, our aim in assembling this collection of reflections was to provide a number of ideas and inspirations that help spur action and leadership. Again, we hope the book also serves as a launching pad from which the reader pursues further resources to help advance the most noble goals of service-learning and civic engagement in higher education.

Mark Langseth
July 2003

Acknowledgements

We are grateful for the generous contributions of a number of people. First and foremost, we acknowledge the contributors who submitted the always thoughtful, sometimes challenging, chapters that comprise the heart of the book. These contributors include many recognized leaders in the civic engagement "movement" in higher education, along with other academic leaders who have made service-learning and civic engagement priorities at their institutions. Without their contributions, the book simply would not have been possible.

Second, we want to acknowledge Leah Harvey from Metropolitan State University, Maria Hesse from Chandler-Gilbert Community College, Rob Hollister from Tufts University, and Chris Kimball from Augsburg College for their immensely helpful reviews of an early manuscript. Likewise, we especially want to recognize Edward Zlotkowski from Bentley College and Campus Compact, and John Saltmarsh from Campus Compact. They provided feedback on the early manuscript, gave helpful advice toward developing the outline for the book, and assisted in identifying potential contributing authors.

Third, Scott Dillon-a junior at the University of Minnesota-completed much of the copyediting and a variety of other tasks critical to the completion of the book as part of a service-learning assignment in a writing course. We are particularly pleased to have engaged a service-learner in the process of producing the book. Scott performed tremendously well in this role, and he learned a great deal.

Fourth, we want to acknowledge Lori Coutts-Fraase, office manager at Minnesota Campus Compact, who helped facilitate communication between the editors and contributors for the book. Lori's always generous spirit allowed for efficient and consistent communication that contributed significantly to the book's completion.

Fifth, we want to acknowledge The Atlantic Philanthropies, whose generous support of Minnesota Campus Compact's work with chief academic officers contributed significantly to the knowledge base upon which this book was assembled.

Finally, we want to acknowledge Campus Compact and Anker Publishing for initiating the idea for the book. It was their vision and passion for producing an important new resource for academic leaders that propelled us to our coediting roles.

Mark Langseth and Bill Plater

Part I: Topical Essays

1 | Civic Engagement, Service-Learning, and Intentional Leadership

William M. Plater

Academic officers at all levels—from president or provost to department chair or director—can play major transformative roles in their colleges and universities if they become intentional about both the mission of their institutions and the way they will engage with the community personally and as the symbolic representative of the academic community. Leadership is a matter of choice, and those who decide to lead have a wide range of tools and assets to use in advancing civic engagement, especially through the development of service-learning. This chapter outlines many of the ways academic officers can provide leadership, even in the absence of money, a mandate from the governing board, or a prior tradition of service.

For colleges and universities, civic engagement emerges at the intersection of institutional mission and academic leadership. While some institutions and some leaders may avoid crossing this intersection for a brief period, the separate pathways of tradition and new possibilities inevitably bring leaders to a crossing point where they must decide how their institutions—and they personally—will be involved with society as a result of their location in a particular place and time and as a deliberate reflection of institutional purpose. Academic leaders cannot long ignore either the real-life interactions of their campuses with their local communities or the philosophical and moral purposes that underlie their institutions' avowed intentions with regard to societal engagement. At all levels of administration, academic leaders who affirmatively accept the call to

1

engage also gain the advantage of distinguishing their service in memorable and enduring ways by acting instead of reacting.

Civic Engagement and Academic Leadership

In placing civic engagement within a context of overall institutional mission, academic leaders play the critical role of defining, interpreting, articulating, and manifesting the way in which their colleges and universities will engage with their several communities, usually those of the places where they are located but sometimes those that transcend geographic boundaries. With rare exception, leaders join an academic institution with its mission already well established and with the programs and activities that reflect that mission in full flower. But they give shape, identity, and value to the ever-changing symbolic manifestations of mission in the way they lead, modify, or renew these programs.

Even though missions change but little over decades or even centuries, there is always opportunity for leaders to give energy, purpose, and optimism to mission in new ways as they adapt colleges and universities to meet changing social, economic, technological, and global conditions. In taking up the particular way in which their own institution relates to the larger society, academic leaders at all levels—center directors, department chairs, school deans, provosts, presidents, chancellors—make civic engagement more or less important by their own intention. No college or university is so narrowly focused, so vocationally oriented, or so committed to a particular belief that it does not have an obligation to account for its contribution to sustaining a civil society, contributing to the common good, or improving the human condition through the discovery, dissemination, or application of knowledge.

No matter how weak the institution's principles of civic engagement, no matter how restrictive the trustees' commitment, no matter how constrained the resources, academic leaders must necessarily speak—even in their silence—to the issues of how their institutions are engaged with a larger society. Teaching and learning, at their core, are acts of civic engagement because they profoundly affect society and the course of history. It is one of the clichés of the new century that education—teaching and learning—is the most important vehicle of social change. If this aspect of teaching is not fully understood, however, students are left to make the connections on their own. Service-learning and other forms of reflective engagement are thus a particular responsibility of academic leaders. As a microcosm, civil society is the citizen learning and thus engaging with what others know, believe, imagine, and hope. Every college and university is thus civically engaged. The important questions, however, are how well, to what purpose, and with what results?

In this book, a variety of academic leaders and scholars take up the intentionality of leadership with regard to civic engagement. Intention may evolve and expand with experience and growing confidence, but without intention—and eventually a plan—leadership will seldom rise above administration. *Administrators* may accept responsibility for civic engagement because it is the right thing to do, but *leaders* claim civic engagement as a manifestation of their own values and as a responsibility to make their community—their world—better. Leaders intend to change the communities of which they are a part, both their civil communities and their academic communities. What is the responsibility of leaders for the involvement of themselves, their constituents, and the institutions they serve in the communities of which they are a part? Who are the leaders? What is the role of service-learning, and why does it seem to have a privileged place among all the possible civic responses leaders might make? What have been the experiences of leaders across the spectrum of institutional types? How does changing global interdependence affect leadership?

While institutional organization and even campus politics may play the determining role, the chief academic officer ordinarily carries the burden of defining the parameters and importance of service-learning for the institution through advocacy, resource allocation, and intentionality in making service-learning an institutional priority. Important as this role of leadership is, however, the provost's or chief academic officer's greatest impact may come in more quiet and persistent ways by supporting deans and departmental leaders in their work to make service-learning meaningful within the academic culture of specific disciplines. When a community of scholars and teachers embraces service-learning as an important pedagogy that achieves its disciplinary objectives, the dean or chair has been effective. When two or more units make service-learning a routine part of their work, the dean or provost has succeeded. And when several units, divisions, or schools have accepted service-learning, the provost has probably affected, if not changed, the culture of the institution in such a way that its overall mission has a new immediacy and currency for students and the community as well as the faculty.

The chapters in this book address these questions directly, both in broad institutional terms and in highly individual responses. There are analytical chapters that apply our current knowledge to understanding these issues, and there are reflective chapters in the form of case studies that provide personal examples. The book itself is an attempt to create a renewable context of individual action within the social setting of a dialog among peers and advocates—to provide signposts of reflection on how to ascribe meaning to actions already taken and also to offer insights on how to provide leadership in the future. This is a book that can be sampled or read in its entirety, but it is also a resource to which leaders can return as their circumstances and experiences change.

From philosophical to practical, there are chapters to facilitate reflection on every aspect of academic leadership. By definition, academic leaders have a responsibility for translating the civic engagement mission of their respective institutions into specific programs and plans for action. Their responsibility for civic engagement is as broad as their colleges' or universities' involvement in teaching, research, and service. Other administrative officers may be involved in aspects of leading the institution, but only academic leaders have responsibility for teaching and learning. At the center of this academic work is service-learning. It is the principal, sustainable means for leaders to give form to their civic ideals.

Civic Engagement as Learning

For all but a small number, colleges and universities have student learning at the top of their priorities when implementing mission. This pervasive, underlying principle of academic mission creates the common ground of intentional academic leadership. Academic officers at all levels have both the occasion and the responsibility for translating mission into specific programs with expected results that can be evaluated and thus continuously improved. Despite problems of language and an ingrained resistance to jargon and to externally imposed terminology, most faculty have come to recognize service-learning as the primary means of enacting civic engagement in the classroom, across the major, and throughout the degree. As the term becomes more familiar and thus more accepted, faculty who have long engaged in practice-based learning, community-based learning, active learning, experiential learning, and learning under other names that combines practice with theory or action with reflection can accept the value of a widely shared understanding of what is expected for learning that enacts civic engagement. The precepts of service-learning thus have value even for those who cringe when the phrase is uttered.

Defining Service-Learning

There are—and should be—as many definitions of service-learning as there are institutions that explicitly combine service with learning as a goal. In fact, it is the ability to articulate the role, purpose, and form of service-learning that gives an academic officer an important, perhaps principal, opportunity to lead the institution—by intention—toward the larger goals of civic engagement. Despite the inherent importance of localized articulation of the concept, there are nonetheless emerging and converging definitions of what should be expected as a part of a legitimate service-learning experience. Campus Compact has provided a service to academic officers through its publications and its web site in setting forth alternative definitions. The Campus Compact web site, www.compact.org/faculty/definitions, offers a wide range of definitions. The definition posed by the American Association for Higher Education (AAHE) series on service-learning in the disciplines heads the Campus Compact (2003) listing:

> Service-learning means a method under which students learn and develop through thoughtfully-organized service that: is conducted in and meets the needs of a community and is coordinated with an institution of higher education, and with the community; helps foster civic responsibility; is integrated into and enhances the academic curriculum of the students enrolled; and includes structured time for students to reflect on the service experience. (¶ 1)

Campus Compact and the National Service-Learning Clearinghouse both cite the Corporation for National and Community Service's (n.d.) conception, which says service-learning promotes learning through active participation in thoughtfully organized service experiences; provides structured time for students to reflect by thinking, discussing, and/or writing about their service experience; provides an opportunity for students to use skills and knowledge in real-life situations; extends learning beyond the classroom and into the community; and fosters a sense of caring for others. The American Association of Community Colleges (n.d.) has a special program for service-learning, and it states that "service learning combines community service with classroom instruction, focusing on critical, reflective thinking as well as personal and civic responsibility" (¶ 1). The National Service-Learning Clearinghouse (2001) asserts that there is a common core upon which most seem to agree:

> Service-learning combines service objectives with learning objectives with the intent that the activity change both the recipient and the provider of the service. This is accomplished by combining service tasks with structured opportunities that link the task to self-reflection, self-discovery, and the acquisition and comprehension of values, skills, and knowledge content. (What is Service-Learning? section, ¶ 2)

Drawing on these definitions, extensive reports of other supporting organizations, and the research of specific individual authors, the Clearinghouse (2001) sets forth the most common characteristics of effective service-learning courses:

- They are positive, meaningful, and real to the participants.

- They involve cooperative rather than competitive experiences and thus promote skills associated with teamwork and community involvement and citizenship.

- They address complex problems in complex settings rather than simplified problems in isolation.

- They offer opportunities to engage in problem solving by requiring participants to gain knowledge of the specific context of their service-learning activity and community challenges, rather than only to draw upon generalized or abstract knowledge such as might come from a textbook; as a result, service-learning offers powerful opportunities to acquire the habits of critical thinking (i.e., the ability to identify the most important questions or issues within a real-world situation).

- They promote deeper learning because the results are immediate and uncontrived; there are no "right answers" in the back of the book.

- The immediacy of experience is more likely to generate emotional consequences, to challenge values and ideas, and to support personal development. (What are the Characteristics of Service-Learning? section, ¶ 5)

These overlapping ideas and guidelines provide enough of an orientation for most academic leaders to develop a concept of how service-learning can advance the mission of their own institution at their particular level of responsibility. There is flexibility in these concepts, because most experienced service-learning advocates and practitioners are committed to matching local talent and resources with local need and opportunity. Although there are no right answers for defining and implementing service-learning programs, there are clear best practice models and clear ethical standards—standards that invariably can be made compatible with the institution's mission and the academic officer's duties. As is the case with all forms of learning, thoughtful reflection and periodic assessment of results can help leaders adapt past experiences—including those that are less successful than imagined—into ever stronger, more effective programs.

Civic Engagement and Mission

The argument has already been made that any institution of learning is inherently engaged with society because of the results of learning. Other components of mission—research; professional, extension, economic, and clinical service; continuing education—all depend on a foundation of teaching and learning. Those institutions most open to difference and most tolerant of debate must understand the power of learning as the means to transform whole cultures and societies as well as individuals. Thus perceived, civic engagement is an explicit or implicit part of every institution's mission, and it is the role of academic leaders to explain this mission internally to their community of faculty, staff, and students and to their many external constituents, those recognized and claimed as well as those forgotten and ignored. Few colleges or universities ignore their geographic neighbors or fail to take into account the state and region of which they are a part, but some downplay their local addresses in favor of national or global recognition. Leaders ignore either learning or their local constituents at the peril of their own intentions.

While the missions of institutions range by degree from community colleges or specialized institutions to comprehensive research universities, all share a responsibility for learning, and few ignore research or service completely. This common mission and the related responsibilities of academic leadership provide a bond among administrators regardless of institutional size, location, or breadth of mission. Learning is the foundation on which civic leadership must be built, even as some leaders must also address vocational training, transfer education, remediation, and community or noncredit learning while others must deal with research in theoretical and applied contexts, clinical programs, and professional service that ranges from economic development to extension services. For the intentional leader, civic engagement becomes a unifying and integrating principle, resting on the foundation of learning but readily accommodating research and service.

With subtle cues or explicit directions from the president, chancellor, or chief executive officer, academic officers have the opportunity to relate nearly every dimension of academic work—the work of faculty—both to mission and to civic engagement. In turning inward and articulating to faculty and staff the civic context for their work, academic officers can use the higher, transcendent, and enduring qualities of mission to develop a context for civic engagement that can last beyond their terms in office and that can seize the imagination and hopes of colleagues, who then are empowered to act individually under the umbrella held by the provost or chief academic officer over the community of scholars. In turn, deans, chairs, heads, and directors can similarly act with authority derived from principle and precept.

For academic leaders, however, the unbroken chain of purpose and authority from mission to an articulated program of civic engagement to specific programs and practices—such as service-learning or faculty development or community-based research or promotion standards—must be both intentional and personally compelling. Leadership that is not based on understanding and conviction will not convince others or last long. Programs, projects, or investments of money and time must always be related to the larger purpose. Service-learning, for example, must be a means to an end, just as civic engagement itself is a means to a larger, more encompassing goal of the institution, such as sustaining a civil and just and pluralistic and democratic society.

Defining Civic Engagement

There are even more definitions of civic engagement than of service-learning. This rich pluralism of perspectives is a strength of American colleges and universities as they take a shared purpose and ideal grounded in service and give it an identity and vocabulary suited to the mission, type, level, and history of their particular campus. We are earnestly alike but richly different.

In many respects, John Dewey is the person most responsible for reawakening the responsibility of education to ensure the future of a democratic society. More recently, Ernest Boyer has stimulated deep thinking and a rich discourse centered around the civic role of colleges and universities in his concepts of a new American college and a scholarship of engagement. The American Association of State Colleges and Universities (AASCU), the Association of American Colleges and Universities (AAC&U), the American Association for Higher Education, and others have created commissions, study sections, and reports that define, refine, and advocate civic engagement, such as the National Association of State Universities and Land-Grant Colleges' (NASULGC) Kellogg Commission: "By engagement, we refer to institutions that have redesigned their teaching, research, and extension and service functions to become even more sympathetically and productively involved with their communities, however community may be defined" (2000, p. 13).

Foundations, governmental agencies, and professional societies that influence higher education have also tried their hand at defining civic engagement, with the added impetus of a carrot or a stick to privilege their particular iteration. Take, for example, the Pew Charitable Trusts' (2002) statement on its public policy initiatives: "A well-functioning democracy requires a healthy 'public sphere,' or set of institutions, processes and norms through which citizens can address issues of public concern. Democratic life is the interrelationship among citizens in this public sphere" (¶ 1).

By contrast, one of the more compelling explanations of the modern emergence of the engaged university comes from Ira Harkavy in his keynote address, "Honoring Community, Honoring Place," to the June 2002 National Gathering of Educators for Civic Engagement:

> How can the *idea* of the new type of university be credibly explained? In part, as a response to the growing concern for the state of democracy. And in part as a defensive response to the increasingly obvious, increasingly embarrassing, increasingly immoral contradiction between the increasing status, wealth, and power of American higher education— particularly its elite research university component—and the unnecessary poverty and deprivation afflicting millions of Americans, particularly those living within our cities. In short, the manifest contradiction between the *power* and the *performance* of American higher education sparked the emergence of the idea of the Democratic, Cosmopolitan, Community-Building, Engaged University. (p. 8)

From perspectives as diverse as history, principle, and guilt, there is a convergence around a few key ideas of civic engagement: social action for a public purpose in a local community. Academic leaders do not have to look long or far to find a compelling reason for civic engagement.

Enacting Civic Engagement

Indeed, academic officers can take encouragement from (and find safety in) the growing national recognition of the necessity of embracing the civic engagement components of every institution's mission. From groups as diverse as the NASULGC to the Wingspread Declaration on Renewing the Civic Mission of the American Research University (Campus Compact, 1999b) to the voluntary association of chief executive officers who signed the "Presidents' Fourth of July Declaration on the Civic Responsibility of Higher Education," (Campus Compact, 1999a) we have a growing consensus for the need to be explicit about a commitment to acting as a whole institution as a matter of purpose or intention. The definition of engagement cited above sets forth seven guiding principles for leadership that should be manifest in an engaged university. They apply equally well to independent colleges and universities as to their public counterparts, including community colleges:

1) **Responsiveness:** listening to the communities, states, and regions served.

2) **Respect for partners:** collaborating with communities based on an understanding of and respect for what they bring to a partnership.

3) **Academic neutrality:** taking up difficult, even divisive issues, while ensuring intellectual honesty and neutrality.

4) **Accessibility:** finding ways to make our complex disciplines and academic practices understood and useful to communities.

5) **Integration:** combining the discovery of knowledge and its dissemination through teaching and service as the whole and complete work of a university while bringing together disciplines to apply their expertise to issues and problems in their social context instead of the academic specialization exclusively.

6) **Coordination:** making sure that willing partners inside the university understand what each is doing and is capable of doing before inflicting narrow, unrelated activities on neighbors and communities.

7) **Resource partnerships:** committing sufficient institutional resources—along with community, corporate, and governmental partners—to ensure that the work can succeed. (NASULGC, 2000, p. 16)

The Presidents' Declaration and the Wingspread Declaration affirm similar principles for engagement while expressing urgency for action by leaders. Issued on July 4, 1999, the Presidents' Declaration, signed by almost 500 presidents, concludes with this strong statement:

> We believe that the challenge of the next millennium is the renewal of our own democratic life and reassertion of social stewardship. In celebrating the birth of our democracy, we can think of no nobler task than committing ourselves to helping catalyze and lead a national movement to reinvigorate the public purposes and civic mission of higher educa-

tion. We believe that now and through the next century, our institutions must be vital agents and architects of a flourishing democracy. (Campus Compact, 1999a, ¶ 11)

The point for academic officers is not to develop an ultimate, complete list of principles such as NASULGC offers or to issue proclamations, but to understand that there is widespread support for advocacy and thus to act out of individual and personal conviction that leadership matters. Taking an open and public stand on civic engagement is not only accepted, it is now expected.

Giving voice to civic engagement requires coordination between the levels of leadership, and the traditional hierarchy of leadership must be observed. Nonetheless, there is much room within any hierarchy for the academic officers to give voice to the importance of civic engagement and to propose, support, and model specific activities, whether these be service-learning, or voluntary student services, or scholarships for civic-learning, or standards for faculty advancement, or a new center for community engagement. At this time in our nation's—indeed, world's—history, the call to action for leaders has never been stronger or more prescient. Leaders need not act alone. But they must act if they are to lead.

Civic Engagement and Global Learning

The new century has ushered in a new awareness of the global interdependence of nations and peoples whose ethnic, religious, political, and economic ties transcend national borders. Even before the tragedy of September 11, 2001, the necessity of this interdependence was well understood as a function of global communication and interaction, if for no other reason. Just as learning is not limited by geographic or political or linguistic barriers, the principle and priority of civic engagement does not end with city limits, state boundaries, or national borders.

The rapid spread of service-learning and American-style civic engagement of universities to other nations offers an opportunity to build global understanding while providing specific tools to leaders of colleges and universities in the U.S. Within the past five years, educational institutions in Australia, the European Union, South Africa, and South Korea have developed service-learning programs in cooperation with Campus Compact and a number of American colleges and universities. It is now usual to find international participants in conferences and meetings; and faculty, presidents, provosts, deans, and directors of service-learning programs or community partnership offices have been invited as consultants to a number of countries. Educators abroad are eager to learn from the American model how to have direct engagement without the entanglements and dangers of political partisanship that have often characterized the "engagement" of universities in other nations with their communities or governments.

Through its web site (www.ipsl.org), the International Partnership for Service-Learning has articulated a set of principles about the value of joining study and service in worldwide settings. International service-learning

> is a powerful means of learning; addresses human needs that would otherwise remain unmet; promotes inter cultural/international literacy; advances the personal growth of students as members of the community; gives expression to the obligation of public and community service by educated people; and sets academic institutions in right relationship to the larger society. (The International Partnership for Service-Learning, n.d., (Beliefs section, ¶ 1)

From the Peace Corps to the specific programs of individual colleges, there are now hundreds of institutions and organizations developing service-learning within an international context.

This growing globalization of service-learning and local civic engagement offers academic leaders an opportunity to combine the deep involvement of students in their own American communities with a comparative perspective and a chance to experience other cultures. Whether through international service-learning arranged by a collaborating host institution in another country, through the exchange of reflective essays and scholarly papers via the Internet, or through participation in conferences, faculty and students alike have a new range of possible interactions across national boundaries that helps give meaning to concepts of democracy, pluralism, justice, and civility. Some universities have developed service-learning programs in local ethnic neighborhoods that include opportunities for travel to places of origin for immigrant communities, thus connecting all the dots of globalization.

World Community

Not all colleges and universities claim a global mission or perspective, but all exist within a global context and must adapt both their academic programs and their definition of community membership to global forces. Recent immigrants are now an even more significant portion of the U.S. population. The last census estimated that the number of immigrants grew by over 50% in the past decade, whereas in the period of the Great Migration of 1900 to 1910, the immigrant base grew only by a little over 30%. Moreover, many students from other countries seek higher education in this nation, and many American students study abroad. Community colleges and research universities alike share in a transnational diversity of students. Faculty are increasingly drawn from around the world. Research interests as varied as genetics, archeology, visualization, and semiotics draw people, institutions, and resources together for common purpose. As a community of scholars, we are more international than ever before.

Beyond the necessity of recognizing who we really are as the transcultural citizens of universities and colleges, we also must place our mission—research, learning, and related civic engagements—into the larger context of the world. Study-abroad programs are finding meaningful ways to build on service-learning pedagogies, and many disciplines—especially those related to professional practice—recognize the value of developing professional competence in cross-cultural if not transglobal contexts. For academic officers, the opportunity to relate domestic civic engagement to the international scene provides an occasion to consider the very sustainability of civil societies threatened by a growing array of environmental, political, religious, economic, technological, and similar broad forces. The ability to relate learning to civic engagement on a global scale belongs most clearly to academic officers, who command the essential concepts of mission, disciplines, and opportunity. The democratic life that is the subject of the Presidents' Declaration is threatened not so much by the armies of other nations or global terrorists as it is by the forces of ignorance, poverty, injustice, and intolerance that do not respect political boundaries and thus intrude into our consciousness and way of life. Academic leaders have a responsibility for helping students and faculty alike place themselves in this world that has become so intrusive, both around the corner and around the world.

The intellectual leap from a local community—whether it be as cosmopolitan as New York or as intentionally provincial as many college towns—to a global consciousness is not as great as it might appear. Intention creates context and thus the means to locate programs, activities, and plans within a global perspective. Leaders can make their programs of civic engagement as geographically encompassing and diverse as their mission, CEO or trustees, and resources will allow. For most, there are practical limits, even if they can be stretched from time to time. However, every academic leader has the prospect of global learning—and thus civic engagement—within reach because learning itself is global.

Intentional academic leaders can—and will—view their own place, time, and opportunity as part of a larger, global community and thus strive to put in place the values, ideas, and to the greatest extent possible the means to enact the belief that a civil, just, democratic, and pluralistic world begins on the campus with the students who cross the classroom threshold and the citizens who pass through figurative and literal gates—all in common pursuit of a better life for themselves and their community, no matter how far its boundaries may stretch. Academic leaders—unlike other educational administrators—have the power to bring the world home because they manage the intersection of knowledge and its use.

Civic Engagement and the Power of Individual Leadership

Without trying to draw overly refined distinctions, there are basically three levels of academic leadership: the department; the division, college or school; and the campus, with campus leadership typically distributed between an academic officer such as a provost and the executive officer such as the president or chancellor. For a smaller subset of institutions, there is also membership in a system and thus a fourth level of leadership; although only a small portion of colleges and universities are within systems, they account for a majority of the students enrolled in postsecondary education, and system leaders may play powerful roles when they are not merely managers.

With regard to enacting civic engagement at any level, individual academic leaders will more likely succeed if they are conscious of two transcendent roles that rise above resource allocation, personnel decisions, or even policy making. First, academic leaders at all levels are symbols of the academy, and they wield certain power as a result of their role. Unlike financial officers, student affairs officials, external affairs directors, alumni directors, or fundraising directors, academic leaders at all levels personify the overarching purpose of the institution. While symbolic power can be drained by inattention, stereotyping, or actions of administrators higher in the hierarchy, intentional leaders can use the symbolism of their office as chair, director, dean, or provost to great effect. Moral and principled leadership can have as great an impact as money or power, especially when the leader models desired behaviors by incorporating service-learning personally into teaching, by showing up at events to celebrate achievements in the community, by speaking or writing about the intrinsic rewards of service, and by protecting civic engagement from budget cuts. The office itself, like the title, empowers individuals with a capacity for leadership that should never be underestimated or undervalued.

The second role for academic officers is to manage intersections. Because every aspect of institutional work is derived from academic mission, academic officers alone have the authority to manage the intersection of resources with their proper use, of people with their assigned duties, of public statements of institutional priority with their legitimacy, or of future planning with tradition and mission. In part symbolic and in part personal, the ability to manage these intersections can give academic officers some of their most effective tools, even when they cannot act alone, even when they lack authority, or even when there is not enough money. Nowhere is this opportunity more apparent than recognizing one's role as the intermediary between the president or trustees and the deans, or between the provost and the chairs, or between the dean and the faculty. Explaining the intentions of one constituency to another is both a responsibility and a source of influence or even power. Most administrators understand the principle of managing up and managing down the chain of command, but academic leaders who use their moral authority as the caretaker of academic principles manage the intersection of policy with practice, rhetoric with reality. As with tenure, those who fail to use the reality of their status risk losing it. As with exercise, those who use their symbolic and practical authority grow stronger.

Civic Engagement and the Call to Action

Just as there is no standard mission that fits all institutions and no definition of service-learning that meets all needs, there is no list of steps for an effective leader to take in engaging an institution in society. Throughout this book, however, there will be examples and lessons learned that can give all academic leaders an opportunity to gain perspective on their own work. The critic Kenneth Burke describes the social use of literature as being equipment for living by giving readers the chance to see themselves in roles or places where they might not ordinarily be. The chapters in this volume offer a similar opportunity to gain perspective. Signposts to watch for are varied, but some of the following might prove useful when reading about others' experiences and reflecting on the possibilities for personal engagement and direct action:

- **Articulating** academic purposes and missions to constituencies inside and outside the academy belongs principally to academic officers. The ability to define specific work or projects allows the academic officer to use civic engagement as a rationale and purpose derived from mission and learning.

- Finding the **right language** for one's own institution is both pragmatic and a source of authority because few academic communities respond well to the definitions, terminology, jargon, and prescriptions of others. Academic leaders who can create the right language and terminology for their community can both inspire future action and deflect resistance or criticism. Communication is the basis of community, and language is the gateway of acceptance.

- **Relating** civic engagement and service-learning to other initiatives and to the overall agenda for the institution will broaden and deepen support. Most colleges and universities have specific priorities, some as often as each year. Retention, improvement of quality (or national rankings), external funding, philanthropy, or economic development are common priorities, and each of them can be supported by or even redefined as forms of civic engagement.

- In developing a personal agenda for leading the institution's civic engagement, the academic officer who is committed to change can be daunted and discouraged by the slow pace of acceptance or change among faculty or units. By focusing on the purpose of the institution—student learning—leaders can take certain comfort and even pride in the fact that **change among students is more immediate and more definite**; moreover, students themselves pass through the institution much more quickly than faculty or new ideas—leaving behind measurable evidence of success on an annual basis. Changing—that is, educating—a student through service-learning and civic engagement is inherently and tangibly rewarding, and it is reason enough to persist.

- Knowing **what is happening** at other institutions, especially peers, can give the academic officer effective arguments for motivating faculty and administrators to adopt proven strategies—and to keep up with the competition.

- **Planning** provides a well-tried means of incorporating the civic engagement agenda within a broader context, and it can be a means for moving the individual leader's intentions into a plan of action. Whether a part of a planning process or not, leaders must **continuously challenge** faculty and administrators to reflect on the purpose of the institution and to ensure that it practices what it advocates students learn.

- Most leaders have the ex officio capacity to **remove roadblocks** and barriers to some extent, and they need to be mindful of not creating others. When a problem is beyond unilateral action, leaders will know how to motivate others who can act to do so. Risk management issues related to community service, for example, typically instill fear in the minds of bureaucrats, lawyers, and accountants who see only liability without understanding that there are releases and contracts that can indemnify the institution. Only academic leaders can defend the necessity of such engagement as a matter of learning to create the framework for requiring other administrators to find solutions.

- **Modeling** civic engagement through personally using service-learning pedagogies in teaching or speaking about civic engagement in a consistent way or representing the faculty (if not the institution) at community events can all encourage and inspire others; actions often speak louder than words. When more highly placed leaders claim speaking roles, action and personal conduct can become equally effective as means of leading.

- Creating **leadership in others** reinforces and expands the leader's own authority. Making one's superior look good as a spokesperson for civic engagement is as useful as mentoring and supporting administrators who report to the academic officer. Nurturing faculty leadership by helping individuals discover civic engagement through conferences or meetings and then helping them with their own personal path of discovery can not only help with the immediate agenda but help sustain the agenda for the next generation.

- **Faculty development** more broadly should provide all faculty with ways to develop an understanding of the value of civic engagement for teaching, research, and service, as well as skills and knowledge about how to develop their own interests. Beyond workshops, conferences, grants for curriculum development, and mentoring, leaders need to ensure that the promotion, tenure, and salary **procedures, policies, and rewards for service** are commensurate with institutional rhetoric about the value of service. Whether making policies or interpreting them, academic leaders at all levels must develop a common purpose and consistency in the message they convey to faculty.

- **Hiring** new faculty and providing an **orientation** to the civic engagement agenda helps build future interest, especially as the faculty is becoming more diverse in its roles as well as in its ethnicity, gender, and ages. As more nontenure-track and part-time faculty assume responsibility for the institution's mission, they need to understand the importance of civic engagement as part of the underlying reason for their own appointments, and they need to acquire specific tools that will enable them to meet the responsibilities of their positions.

- Seeking new resources or **new energy for civic engagement through other opportunities** may take surprising forms. International civic engagement is one example that has become important in the past few years, and it will for the foreseeable future as nations become increasingly interdependent, even for the very continuation of a democratic and civil society in this nation. Technology offers other opportunities as the Internet makes distant resources available locally and dramatically increases the prospects for interaction. But collaboration with K–12 may offer the greatest opportunity as colleges and universities intentionally build on students' involvement with their communities in school and take advantage of a growing recognition that service is itself a form of service politics and contributes to an emerging redefinition of activism.

- **Resource management**—including the assignment of faculty and staff time—is, of course, the most important way to influence civic engagement, but in the absence of new resources to allocate for specific new activities, the management of resources with an eye to **sustainability, accountability,** and **ethical responsibility** (not all sources of money are appropriate even if more readily available, for example) will ensure the viability of civic engagement even in the absence of money. Leaders should never forget that time is money, either when allocating it to projects and committees or when accounting for investments. The hours of community service—especially through service-learning and other structured civic engagements—are worth millions of dollars in economic and **social development capital for local communities,** who need to be reminded of the benefit of having an engaged institution in town.

- **Expectation and envy management** are also important for academic leaders, who usually are in a position to hear multiple constituencies within the academy and within the community talk about other groups. When expectations are too high or too low, problems will ensue. When one group is envious of attention, resources, or the autonomy of others who may be engaged in civic engagement work, the seeds of competition and erosion may flower at unexpected times, especially just as the civic engagement work seems most secure.

- **Listening** to constituents and helping them locate themselves in civic engagement work or explain why they may not be included is important, but only when the academic leader really understands the different perspective.

- **Creating trust** among faculty, between faculty and the administration, between academic leaders and other administrators, and between the community and the institution is one of the most important things a leader can do to ensure success. Trust comes from many of the attributes noted here—listening to others yet leading by example, doing what leaders ask others to do. When there is trust, there is likely to be creativity and shared responsibility, both of which are necessary for sustainability.

- Leveraging **personal connections** inside the academy as well as in the community and across the nation can help colleagues at critical moments in their own development and their own work. Academic leaders should also not hesitate to meet people whom they do not know but should—by attending conferences, inviting guest speakers to campus, or initiating a conversation. Communities are built when people of common interests and values find each other, and effective leaders can accelerate the sometimes serendipitous process of making connections.

- Knowing that one has a personal **career path** with goals and ambitions can provide both a rationale and a context for engaging the institution in society. Without a sense of desired next steps in one's own career, some actions can be limiting, especially when the academic leader does not intend to move to a higher position or to a new institution. **Reflection and personal self-assessment** are undoubtedly the best ways to gain personal satisfaction and to develop one's own career.

In the absence of a formula for successful academic leadership, administrators who intend to change their institutions or who aspire to leave a legacy must keep their own counsel and take steps to create the means for periodic reflection and renewal. It is lonely at the top, but it is also lonely on the way to the top. It is difficult to express doubt or uncertainty to colleagues whom you would lead or to a superior in whom you wish to inspire confidence, yet every leader must have an opportunity to verbalize anxiety and to see one's own formative self in the careers and experiences of others.

This book addresses this fundamental need in part, and strategies for self-assessment as suggested above can help. However, in the end, in the office when the door is closed, academic leaders must recommit themselves daily to their own ideals and values and trust the choice they have made. They have agreed to lead by serving others within their community of shared values and purpose. Academic leadership itself is a form of service-learning, and wise leaders will expect to be changed by the process of leading just as they intend to change others. In the words of the National Service-Learning Clearinghouse's (2001) definition of service-learning—and service leadership: "This is accomplished by combining service tasks with structured opportunities that link the task to self-reflection, self-discovery, and the acquisition and comprehension of values, skills, and knowledge" (What is Serving-Learning? section, ¶ 2).

2 | Institutionalizing Service-Learning in Higher Education: Issues and Strategies for Chief Academic Officers

Andrew Furco
Barbara A. Holland

The institutionalization of service-learning in higher education is predicated on the presence of a number of interdependent factors, many of which are cultivated through the leadership and support of the campus's chief academic administrator. In this chapter, the authors identify these factors and present some of the potential pitfalls in institutionalizing service-learning. The authors conclude that service-learning is best sustained when it is not institutionalized for its own sake, but rather is used as a strategy to achieve other important institutional goals.

Each year, institutions of higher education adopt numerous educational programs, practices, and policies designed to assist, improve, and/or transform the academy. While some of these practices (e.g., grading systems, faculty tenure, academic calendars) are fully adopted and remain in place over many years, other practices (e.g., total quality management) are trends that fade away quickly, leaving behind few if any valuable vestiges. While interest in service-learning throughout the K–16 educational system has grown rapidly during the last decade, questions remain about whether service-learning will be a sustained practice or just another educational trend with limited impact.

Many institutions of diverse types are implementing service-learning, often in different ways, with different intentions, and with different levels of interest and commitment. Recent research is revealing the potential transforming effect of service-learning on academic organizations, and the conditions that must be present for its longevity and institutionalization. Like most educational initiatives, service-learning achieves institutionalization when it becomes an ongoing, expected, valued, and legitimate part of the institution's intellectual core and organizational culture. However, in comparison to other educational initiatives, service-learning presents some unique features that challenge traditional conceptions of what institutionalization means. Specifically, service-learning's multifaceted structure, multidisciplinary philosophical framework, and broad organizational impacts require institutional leaders to think differently about why and how to institutionalize this educational initiative.

These differences fall in two categories: 1) The institutionalization of service-learning is about much more than the acquisition of sustained funding; it is about defining academic culture and curricular philosophy, and 2) service-learning is not implemented with the goal of being a separate, distinctive program initiative and in fact cannot survive as such because it inspires and requires a complex web of internal and external relationships. As we will discuss, service-learning can be an effective strategy for accomplishing a variety of broader institutional goals. Because institutions have different missions, cultures, histories, and community contexts, the role, meaning, and value of service-learning varies from campus to campus. However, there are clear patterns across institutions that illustrate the impacts of service-learning and the components that are necessary to ensure its success and institutionalization (Furco, 2002a; Holland, 2000).

This chapter explains the distinctive nature of institutionalization of service-learning, key organizational factors and strategies, and the role of chief academic officers in monitoring and promoting its progress. It is written with the assumption that the reader has an interest in institutionalizing service-learning at some level deemed appropriate to the institution. We will argue that academic administrators must consider how the universality of service-learning makes it an effective strategy for achieving institutional goals within their institution's mission, and the degree to which that requires institutionalization of service-learning as a core element of the organization and culture.

A Different Conceptualization of Institutionalization

The stereotypical response to an identified campus concern is to create a separate, distinct program that is charged with addressing the issue. For example, to address a concern over faculty or student retention, a task force might be established to develop a plan on how to address this issue, or a special program might be put in place to support higher retention rates. This strategy works well when the issue at hand has clear programmatic demarcations. However, service-learning is less a *program* and more an *integrative strategy* that addresses multiple objectives and brings together a number of disparate units, structures, and programs on campus. Service-learning can often serve as a unifying agent that provides opportunities for faculty to work across disciplines, brings together the campus and community, promotes strong working relationships between students and their professors, and encourages student collaborations (Furco, 2002b).

Unlike many other educational programs and initiatives (freshman seminars, senior capstones, etc.) that target particular parts of the academy or serve a prescribed set of purposes, service-learning is a universal approach that is adaptable to the environment and needs of a particular campus. For example, service-learning can be adapted for all students regardless of their area of study or educational level. Service-learning can be integrated in any discipline and can engage students in a variety of service activities (tutoring, planting trees, water testing) that occur in all types of communities (urban, suburban, rural). The universality of service-learning gives it broad applicability to a variety of institutional intentions and can thus be used to achieve a variety of educational goals. This universality allows service-learning to be shaped in ways that best serve the objectives of the institution.

To be successful, service-learning requires the intentional integration of teaching, service, and research priorities within the context of each institution's mission and organizational goals; its quality and sustainability depend on such integration (Holland, 2001). Thus, service-learning permeates all three components of the academy's core mission, and its institutionalization is predicated on its connection to a wide variety of organizational components and academic objectives, many of which fall within the purview of the chief academic officer's responsibilities.

This connection to wider institutional agendas means that institutionalization of service-learning is not just about sustainable funding. Higher education has widespread traditions and stereotypes surrounding the introduction and sustainability of new academic endeavors that may lead academic administrators to overlook the programmatic elements that are essential to institutionalizing service-learning as an organizational strategy. Grants are a familiar method for supporting innovations in educational settings; they lend prestige and legitimacy. Grants are a mark of achievement and excellence, and give proponents of a new idea the time and resources to develop and implement their strategies, always with a hopeful eye toward institutionalization.

Therein lies the rub. Cultural and financial traditions in academia reinforce the notion that when the grant ends, the program ends unless it can raise more soft money. This tradition rises largely from the dominant model of sponsored research projects, which the institution has no expectation of moving to internal support after external funding ends. However, when the intent of a grant is to implement and institutionalize an organizational change initiative such as service-learning, public and private funders clearly expect that their investment will lead to an institutionalized program. Whether continued support is internal or external, the object of the initial investment was to support the startup of service-learning at an institution that professes commitment.

Funders are increasingly assertive about their expectation of sustainability and have learned what to look for from the research literature. Full institutionalization of service-learning is about commitment of faculty and academic leaders, the level of student and community involvement and the strength of campus-community partnerships, and the responsive involvement of key aspects of campus infrastructure and policy that ensures the connection of service-learning to key academic objectives of the institution. It is about capitalizing on its inherent, unifying nature and its potential to assist the academy in achieving important educational and institutional goals; it can be a force for promoting institutional change and collaboration on a wide variety of academic issues.

Thus, the goal of institutionalization of service-learning is not just sustainability of the activity; it is also about creating conditions where service-learning thrives and its potential for organizational impact is realized.

Connecting Service-Learning With Important Institutional Intentions

Service-learning, speaking broadly, is an academic strategy that seeks to engage students in activities that enhance academic learning, civic responsibility, and the skills of citizenship while also enhancing community capacity through service. This requires the development of campus-community partnerships that engage faculty, students, and community members in interactive dialogue and action. Certainly, individual faculty can and do set up service-learning activities without any institutional involvement or support. However, as interest in service-learning grows, many institutions are realizing that faculty and students in the community are seen as representatives of the institution and attention to quality, consistency, and reciprocity must be addressed. Even more importantly, institutional leaders are recognizing the potential power of service-learning to address many institutional objectives and are beginning to organize more intentional and well-coordinated programs. As we have argued above, service-learning does not stand alone in isolation from institutional and community context; it is a reflection of the interests and needs of the campus and community working together for mutual benefit.

Service-learning has the potential to create a ripple effect that inspires change and reform in response to new internal and external relationships and collaborative activities. Academic leaders can capitalize on these ripple effects by focusing attention and support on the link between service-learning and key organizational concerns and goals. The link exists because service-learning requires broad institutional involvement as well as collaborative values that are illustrated by the design and conduct of service-learning. Table 2.1 offers some examples of ways that service-learning can contribute to other critical goals of the academic organization and the community.

Table 2.1

The Role of Service-Learning in Meeting Institutional Intentions

Institutional Intention	Role of Service-Learning
Improve town/gown relationships.	Service-learning provides an opportunity for the institution to give back to the community by engaging students in activities that directly benefit the community. Because service-learning is tied to the academic curriculum, the service activities directly link the community not just to students, but also to faculty, increasing familiarity and trust.
Realize the civic mission of the institution.	In addition to their academic missions, many colleges and universities seek to prepare students to become active and productive members of a civil society. Service-learning provides the opportunity for students to apply their academic learning to address an authentic social need in the local and broader community and inspire lifelong commitment to service.
Build learning communities and encourage interaction among the disciplines.	Many colleges seek to foster collaboration among faculty members and students across departments. Through its focus on complex social issues that require the application of expertise from many disciplines, service-learning can be an authentic, academically based vehicle to build learning communities that promote interdisciplinary work and link teaching to research.
Improve instruction.	There is a growing emphasis on the delivery of instruction and ways to improve student learning. As a constructivist and experiential approach to teaching, service-learning helps students to explore more deeply the dimensions of academic content by providing them the opportunity to apply the course content to an authentic community setting.
Fulfill service and outreach mission of the institution.	Along with research and teaching, most institutions also see service as a part of their mission. At some institutions (e.g., faith-based institutions) the service mission of the institution is especially well supported and emphasized. Service-learning can provide an academically based approach to fulfill

	the service mission of the institution and promotes integration of the research, teaching, and service missions of the institution.
Ensure completion of programmatic requirements and acquisition of learning attributes.	A growing number of campuses are facilitating capstone experiences for their seniors. These experiences usually engage students in a series of connected courses through which they develop multiple perspectives that students apply to a community-based research project. Service-learning provides a means to connect the interdisciplinary community-based research project to the series of courses students take.

Key Factors in Service-Learning Institutionalization

The literature is helpful in understanding how academic organizations react to innovations such as service-learning. In his book, *Why Innovation Fails: Institutionalization and Termination of Innovation in Higher Education*, Arthur Levine (1980) investigated organizational responses to innovations in higher education. According to Levine, organizational members, as groups and individuals, assess innovations for their apparent fit with existing organizational norms and myths. Depending on the organizational response, innovations will be diffused across the organization, marginalized and encapsulated, resocialized or revised so as to diminish their impact, or terminated. Most educational innovations fail because they are implemented as separate programs, are poorly supported politically and/or financially, are not prominent on the campus or seen as close to core issues, or are overly compartmentalized. Educational innovations succeed when integrating mechanisms are put in place that allow the members of the institution to see how innovative programs and ideas fit together with existing activities in ways that seem profitable and compatible. As Levine suggests, cross-cutting, universally adaptable initiatives that are seen as complementing existing norms and concerns stand a better chance of transforming the institution and becoming institutionalized. This reinforces the argument that an effective approach to institutionalizing service-learning is for academic leaders to highlight and promote the connections between service-learning and key organizational challenges, as illustrated in Table 2.1. Where little attention is given to the link between service-learning and other campus concerns and priorities, service-learning is often spoken of as an extra activity, an add-on, or a luxury for those who have the time or special funding. Those conditions do not promote sustainability or institutionalization.

According to Michael Kramer (2000), an *institutionalized* educational practice is one that is "routine, widespread, legitimized, expected, supported, permanent, and resilient" (p. 6). Making service-learning a practice that possesses these characteristics requires careful, strategic planning. The institutionalization of service-learning does not happen automatically, nor does it happen overnight. According to the findings of a recent UC Berkeley study of service-learning institutionalization, none of the 43 institutions participating in the study showed a statistically significant increase in their level of institutionalization over a three-year period (Furco, 2002a). The researchers concluded that the full institutionalization of service-learning on a college campus requires a five- to seven-year concerted effort.

To ensure the sustainability of a high quality service-learning initiative, a number of critical organizational factors that impact the institutionalization of service-learning require attention from the earliest stages of implementation. Most of these factors require the support and oversight of the chief academic officer in partnership with other academic administrators and faculty leaders. Recently, a body of literature has emerged that has helped identify the dimensions on which the institutionalization of service-learning rests. Work conducted by Bell, Furco, Ammon, Muller, and Sorgen (2000); Furco (2002a); Gray et al. (1998); Holland (2000, 1999a, 1997); Holland and Gelmon (1998); Kramer (2000), and others has identified a set of common, cross-cutting components that facilitate a campus's service-learning institutionalization effort. The components can be categorized into five broad, interdependent overarching dimensions, each of which helps service-learning take hold in ways that maximize impact on overall institutional objectives (see Table 2.2).

The components within each dimension are the activities, factors, and structures that have been found to be essential for the advancement and sustainability of service-learning in higher education (Bell et al., 2000; Furco, 2002a; Gray et al., 1998; Holland, 1997, 2000). Even

Table 2.2

Dimensions of Service-Learning Institutionalization

Dimension	Components
Mission and philosophy	• Establishing campus-wide definition for service-learning • Completing a campus-wide strategic plan for advancing service-learning • Aligning service-learning with the institution's mission • Aligning service-learning with other education reform and civic engagement efforts
Faculty support for and involvement in service-learning	• Enhancing faculty knowledge and awareness of service-learning through faculty development • Cultivating faculty interest in service-learning and providing opportunities for faculty to tie service-learning to their scholarly work • Creating adequate infrastructure to support faculty in managing the logistics of service-learning • Providing faculty with incentives and rewards to engage in service-learning • Encouraging influential faculty members to assume leadership roles in advancing service-learning on the campus and partnerships in the community
Institutional support for service-learning	• Establishing a coordinating agency that facilitates the advancement of service-learning and community partnerships • Establishing a policy-making entity for service-learning which establishes standards of quality and criteria for evaluation • Supporting an appropriate number of staff members to work on advancing and institutionalizing service-learning • Providing adequate funding resources for service-learning activities using both internal and external resources • Ensuring that campus leaders support and understand the goals and purposes of service-learning

continued on page 32

	• Ensuring that departments support and encourage faculty who engage in service-learning • Establishing an ongoing monitoring system that tracks service-learning activities, participation, and partnerships • Implementing an assessment plan for measuring impacts and identifying areas for improvement
Student support and involvement in service-learning	• Establishing coordinated mechanisms that in foster students' awareness of campus service-learning opportunities • Establishing formal incentives and rewards that encourage students to participate in service-learning • Welcoming and encouraging student representatives to participate fully in official activities designed to advance service-learning on campus • Maximizing opportunities for students to participate in service-learning
Community participation and partnerships	• Building awareness among community partners of the full range of service-learning opportunities and possibilities • Cultivating mutual understanding of needs and purposes between the campus and the community partners • Welcoming and encouraging community agency representatives to participate fully in official activities designed to advance service-learning on campus • Assessing and monitoring impacts of service-learning on partners

though individual campuses adopt service-learning to serve different institutional and academic purposes, the institutionalization components are common across institutional type (e.g. two-year community college, four-year public, four-year private), type of community (e.g., urban, suburban, rural), and institutional intention for service-learning implementation. The balance needed among these components will vary from campus to campus depending on the campus's history of community engagement, its current and envisioned levels of service-learning institutionalization, and the overarching intentions of the service-learning initiative (Bell et al., 2000; Holland, 1997).

For example, at the University of Pennsylvania, service-learning is used as a strategy to advance the broader campus effort to improve town/gown relationships and strengthen the campus's partnerships with West Philadelphia. The campus created a Center for Community Partnerships as the unit to facilitate the service-learning initiative and appointed a faculty member to serve as academic administrator (associate vice president) and director of the center. In contrast, at Saint Joseph's College, a faith-based liberal arts college in Maine, service-learning is a strategy to advance the campus's Catholic service mission. The college partners with local food pantries, agencies that serve senior citizens, and local middle schools to provide much-needed service. At Saint Joseph's College, service-learning is facilitated through the college's campus ministry program and is led by a service-learning faculty liaison. Thus, we see that the larger institutional goals and purposes that service-learning serves will determine how the overall mission and philosophy of service-learning is defined, the types of faculty and institutional support that will be garnered, the nature and extent of student involvement and participation, and the kinds of community partnerships that will be formed.

Institutionalization and the Academic Administrator: Avoiding Pitfalls

Because many of the key factors relevant to the institutionalization of service-learning are centered on the academic structures and purposes of the institution, the chief academic officer has a critical role in leading the campus toward a consensus on the level of commitment to service-learning and civic engagement, as well as articulating the role of service-learning in advancing progress on specific core goals and objectives of the institution. In essence, the primary role of the chief academic officer in institutionalizing service-learning is to help shepherd service-learning's transition "from the margins to the mainstream" of the academy (Pickeral & Peters, 1996, p. 2) through rhetoric and action that affirms the value of service-learning as an institutional strategy and as a hallmark of campus-community relationships. Without the chief academic officer's support of service-learning as a core academic activity, a campus's effort to institutionalize service-learning is sure to face many challenges. Absent executive leadership, continuation of service-learning will depend on the efforts of faculty advocates. Diffusion and institutionalization of service-learning are unlikely to occur without a strong and explicit partnership and shared vision between academic administrators and faculty.

Because the institutionalization of service-learning requires a sustained, carefully planned effort that develops over a five- to seven-year period, a period that often outlasts the tenure of a chief academic officer, assurances need to be put in place that allow the institutionalization effort to continue smoothly as the campus leadership changes. The presence of a formal strategic plan for the advancement and institutionalization of service-learning has been found to be an essential element for maintaining the institutionalization momentum through transitional periods, such as those that occur during staff and administration turnover (Bell et al., 2000).

According to the findings of the UC Berkeley service-learning institutionalization study, institutional buy-in and support for service-learning was the second-strongest predictor (after faculty buy-in and support) for institutionalizing service-learning at the participating colleges and universities. As Bell et al. (2000) report, faculty buy-in and support for service-learning are influenced by the overall support and buy-in service-learning receives from leaders of the institution. Institutions with leaders that demonstrate value for service-learning programs are more likely to create the conditions that promote faculty buy-in, support, and active participation.

In addition to identifying the conditions that promote the institutionalization of service-learning, the emerging literature on service-learning has also shed light on some of the reasons why service-learning fails on some campuses. The chief academic officer and other key administrators, such as deans and chairs, play a critical role in avoiding the pitfalls and barriers to advancing service-learning initiatives. Many of the pitfalls reflect Levine's (1980) insights on why educational innovations fail. Isolating service-learning as a distinct and separate program, for example, is likely to give rise to several common pitfalls that undermine institutionalization.

Pitfalls include a lack of faculty buy-in or acceptance of service-learning as a legitimate, academic pursuit (Ward, 1998); the misalignment and misappropriation of service-learning structures and activities (Gray et al., 1998; Zlotkowski, 2000); the nature and extent of individual involvement in the initiative (Bell et al., 2000); and inadequate support for the initiative (Gray, Ondaatje, Fricker, & Geschwind, 2000). These are major obstacles and deserve further explanation to highlight the key types of academic decisions and actions that can hinder or facilitate institutionalization.

Service-Learning as a Separate Program

Perhaps one of the most serious pitfalls in the institutionalization of service-learning is the establishment of service-learning as an independent, separate program. In this scenario, the service-learning "program" receives much support and legitimization from some administrators and faculty members, has adequate funding and staffing for a period of time, builds strong partnerships with the community, and engages students and faculty in interesting and vibrant service-learning activities. However, this "program" operates on its own and is not integrated with other important initiatives and goals of the campus. To institutionalize service-learning effectively, service-learning must be viewed not as a discrete "program" but as a means to accomplish other important goals of the campus. As is suggested in Table 2.2, academic leaders and faculty must articulate their primary goals for their campus, develop consensus, and then explore the ways in which service-learning can be used to help meet the objectives of those goals. The ultimate goal is to institutionalize service-learning to achieve overarching institutional intentions.

The Degree of Faculty Acceptance

Without a faculty's acceptance of service-learning as an educationally valid pedagogy, service-learning cannot be institutionalized in higher education. Research has found that while most faculty who eagerly embrace service-learning do so for largely intrinsic reasons, others are motivated by forces such as relevance to their discipline, evidence that service-learning has positive impacts on students and/or the community, or the availability of support and other forms of recognition, incentives and rewards (Holland, 1999a). Because faculty buy-in and support for service-learning is the strongest predictor for institutionalizing service-learning in higher education (Bell et al., 2000), institutional incentive and reward mechanisms (promotion and tenure policies as well as other methods of reward and recognition) that genuinely encourage faculty involvement in service-learning must be established.

Connections between service-learning and the quality of teaching and research responsibilities must also be demonstrated and rewarded. Without these incentives and promotion policies in place, faculty are less likely to participate in service-learning, because the reward policies set the standards by which faculty work is judged (Ward, 1998). Indeed, faculty participation in service-learning is high at institutions (Portland State University, California State University-Monterey Bay, Indiana University-Purdue University Indianapolis) that have established tenure and promotion guidelines that explicitly encourage faculty members to participate in service-learning.

Structural Alignment in the Organization

Service-learning cannot be institutionalized if its structures and activities are misaligned and misappropriated. For example, in their national study of service-learning implementation, Gray et al. (1998) found that the advancement of service-learning fared better when a campus had a coordinating entity (e.g., a center) that facilitated service-learning activities for the campus. The findings of this study, as well as compelling arguments made by Zlotkowski (2000), suggest that such centers are most effective in garnering academic legitimacy, faculty participation, and sustained institutional support and interest when they are housed in academic affairs rather than in student affairs. Although this is not necessarily true in every case, the current and fairly widespread trend of moving existing service-learning centers in student affairs to academic units seems to support the perspective of Zlotkowski, Gray, and others who see the academic arena as the organizational alignment most strongly associated with institutionalization. Misappropriating service-learning as merely another *service* program rather than seeing it as a vehicle to accomplish a broad range of educational goals on the campus can hinder an institution's ability to institutionalize service-learning.

The Symbolism of Individuals Leading Service-Learning

A related issue of alignment in institutionalizing service-learning has to do with individual involvement in the initiative. Sometimes, to get the initiative off the ground, campuses will assign the responsibility of managing or overseeing the service-learning initiative to a unit or to an individual who has expressed interest in playing a leadership role. However, if this unit or individual is perceived by campus faculty to be an inappropriate entity to oversee the initiative (e.g., the individual is not well respected on the campus, or the unit is notorious for not following through on programs), then the nature of the individual involvement might actually hinder the advancement of service-learning on the campus (Bell et al., 2000). In other cases, service-learning may be too closely aligned with particular departments or units on campus, giving the impression that service-learning is not a campus-wide effort, but rather is one that targets or is restricted to particular departments or units. Clearly, how and where support for service-learning is established sends serious signals to both proponents and skeptics of service-learning.

The Role of a Supportive Infrastructure

There is no question that a powerful tool for expansion and institutionalization is the creation of infrastructure that acknowledges the complexity and labor-intensive nature of service-learning work for faculty (and for community partners as well). However, the creation of a center, the selection of individuals to lead the center, and the placement in the organization can all send signals that can be misunderstood. Poorly considered decisions about center design, staffing, and positioning can have dramatic effects on expanding faculty and community interest, or the center can be interpreted as a "closed shop" where only certain people and partners are welcome. The chief academic officer's voice must be heard as influencing and affirming these choices, as well as in the creation of appropriate new or revised policies that support service-learning, and in the coaching of other academic administrators (deans and chairs) to ensure their understanding of the role of service-learning in the larger institutional academic agenda.

Sources of Financial Support

A final major pitfall to institutionalizing service-learning has to do with the nature and amount of funding that is provided to support the long-term growth and sustainability of service-learning. While external grants can help get campus activities started in implementing important and key service-learning activities, they provide no security for long-term funding. Programs that rely too heavily on soft money might have a more difficult time developing long-range plans for service-learning because the uncertainty of funding makes it impossible to develop long-range plans and implement a long-term vision for service-learning (Bell et al., 2000). So long as the administration expects the center or service-learning advocates to support activities from external funds, skeptics among the faculty (and community partners who are questioning the institution's sincerity and commitment) can assume the administration is not sufficiently committed to service-learning to invest base funding resources. As in Levine's (1980) analysis, the message is that the innovation is temporary. Allocating and applying an adequate amount of funds for basic or partial support of service-learning not only signals that the administration supports the initiative, but also helps place the initiative on a more promising track toward service-learning institutionalization.

Conclusion

Institutional experiences demonstrate that leadership for service-learning and civic engagement must come from both core faculty and top academic administrators. Academic administrators set the tone by what they say, what initiatives they talk about, and what choices they make in funding, staffing, and promoting. What appears on the agenda of the deans' or chairs' meetings highlights issues assumed to be of importance to top administrators. The rhetorical and symbolic import of these messages is sometimes as important as practical actions on resource allocations or organizational placement.

The heart of institutionalization may be summarized in a few words: intentionality, coherence, and commitment. Choices about the support for and positioning of service-learning should be conspicuously intentional. The agenda for service-learning as a learning strategy must also be linked to a coherent institution-wide agenda in which service-learning is seen as vital to the achievement of multiple institutional objectives. And, the academic leadership of the college or university must be clear with internal and external audiences about the level of institutional commitment to interactions between the campus and community, such as service-learning.

Service-learning also requires reciprocal and sustained interactions with the community and tying these interactions to the academic fabric of the institution. The investments an institution makes, and the decisions of academic leaders to support community partnerships, are closely watched by both campus and community citizens who may hold some historical doubts about whether the institution is really ready to commit to service-learning for the long haul. Encouraging faculty and students to step into the complexity of community scholarship is not risk-free, but as with all things risky and challenging, service-learning offers the hope of rewards for advancements in institutional relationships, instructional quality, student outcomes, and other institutional goals outlined as examples of the impact of service-learning in Tables 2.1 and 2.2.

Attention to intentionality, coherence, and commitment by academic administration can guide the organization to realize its vision for service-learning. In essence, it is the chief academic officer, dean, or department chair who clarifies the logic of the web of relationships among various curricula, programs, initiatives, and reforms that define academic environment and culture. The chief academic officer especially must guide the articulation of a vision for that environment and culture, within which service-learning may be found to be a useful strategy. The universality of service-learning can contribute to the achievement of an academic plan that unites campus and community in common cause through activities that are well supported, well organized, integrative, and sustainable.

3 | Service-Learning as Fulcrum of Educational Reform

Edward Zlotkowski
John Saltmarsh

This chapter presents service-learning as one of the most important comprehensive responses to an array of issues facing contemporary American higher education. Today's graduates need to have developed habits of both civic engagement and active learning, and at many institutions that will not happen unless academic leaders take seriously the widespread gap between rhetoric and reality. The chapter concludes with examples of the many institutional objectives service-learning has helped academic leaders achieve.

Contemporary Concerns

In a 1997 essay titled "Naming Pragmatic Liberal Education," Bruce Kimball, an educational historian at the University of Rochester, reports that he has found seven areas of interest widespread in contemporary higher education:

1) Multiculturalism

2) General education

3) The common good and citizenship

4) K–16 continuities

5) Teaching as inquiry

6) Values and service

7) Assessment

Together, he concludes, these foci can be seen as laying the foundation of a new educational gestalt that has "conceptual and historical roots or find[s] a principled rationale in pragmatism" (p. 97). Not surprisingly, Kimball's (1997) thesis has not gone unchallenged, especially by those who teach at elite and/or research-oriented institutions. Nonetheless, it is becoming increasingly apparent that both the demands on and the nature of much higher education programming are slowly but significantly beginning to change.

No single strategy can be said to embody or address all of the above areas of concern. Interdisciplinary and intercultural programs; learning communities; problem-based, collaborative, and computer-assisted learning; new articulation agreements between institutions on different educational levels—each of these constitutes an important response to the challenges higher education faces at the start of the 21st century. However, with the exception of multicultural programs, no single strategy has generated more interest and enthusiasm than has service-learning—the deliberate linking of service activities with academic study. Certainly no other strategy has given rise to more ambitious and comprehensive attempts to re-imagine and reconfigure the academic enterprise in response to contemporary social and educational demands.

Civic Engagement and Active Learning

The reasons for this are complex, but perhaps they can best be summarized under two headings: civic engagement and active learning. In addressing issues of civic engagement, service-learning facilitates an awareness of diversity and emphasizes systems thinking and values clarification as well as service to the local community. By grounding itself in a pedagogy of active learning, it promotes theory-practice connections, enhances student motivation and retention, utilizes cross-disciplinary perspectives, and develops workplace skills. Hence, insofar as educators have sought strategies to deal with any or all of the concerns in either group, they have found service-learning to be an effective, in many ways protean resource. Indeed, presidents and academic leaders who embrace service-learning invariably do so not because they find the concept itself exciting but because they have discovered in it a highly efficient, serviceable tool.

This is not surprising; both civic engagement and active learning have long been central to the goals of American higher education. Ever since the founding of Harvard in the early 17th century, American colleges and universities have, in the words of Frank Newman (2000), "held a privileged position because they have focused on the needs of society rather than self-gains" (p. 2). Hence, almost any institutional mission statement one cares to examine is likely to identify a commitment to public service or leadership as a core value.

Similarly, a commitment to developing students who can think critically, demonstrate initiative, and exhibit a capacity for lifelong learning has long been a central concern of the American progressive/pragmatic approach to education. Of course, one thinks immediately of John Dewey with his insistence on learning grounded in real world experience, but one can see Dewey's concern with active knowledge production also embodied in Emerson's "new American scholar" and other important documents of a distinctly American tradition (West, 1989).

Rhetoric and Reality

Recently, however, the academy's commitment to both civic engagement and active learning has become suspect. While no school would openly repudiate the public good encoded in its mission statement, many have de facto done just that. As the late Ernest Boyer remarked towards the end of his life:

> . . . from what I have seen, there is no question that the paradigm of faculty rewards is moving toward greater recognition of teaching. I could document that for several hours because we have the evidence in our office. I also have this sense in my bones that service is going to reemerge with greater vitality than we have seen it in the last 100 years, simply because the university must be engaged if it hopes to survive. The social imperative for service has become so urgent that the university cannot afford to ignore it. I must say that I am worried that right now the university is viewed as a private benefit, not a public good. Unless we recast the university as a publicly engaged institution I think our future is at stake. (1996a, p. 138)

Both private and public institutions can be seen as part of this problem, since by and large both have opted for the development of marketable (though not necessarily vocational) skills as their primary raison d'etre. As Boyer noted in another late piece,

> Increasingly, the campus is being viewed as a place where students get credentialed and faculty get tenured, while the overall work of the academy does not seem particularly relevant to the nation's most pressing civic, social, economic, and moral problems. (1996b, p. 14)

The consequences of such a one-sided turn to private benefits include ever greater inequality of opportunity, ever greater reliance on private donors with their personal/proprietary agendas, less public support for nonmarketable interests, and a general cheapening of the very meaning of higher education. Nor are traditional liberal arts colleges and elite institutions exempt from this indictment. As both Russ Edgerton (1997), former director of the education division of the Pew Charitable Trusts, and Alexander Astin (2000), director of UCLA's Higher Education Research Institute, have pointed out, embracing market-driven mechanisms has hindered rather than facilitated many areas of needed reform, allowing the country's top-tier institutions to insulate themselves from both the needs of local communities and responsibility for students with less than stellar records.

A similar, if perhaps less immediately obvious, failure has occurred with regard to effective teaching. Lee Shulman, president of the Carnegie Foundation for the Advancement of Teaching and professor of education at Stanford University, has described what he only half-facetiously calls an "'epidemiology of mislearning,' or the 'taxonomy of pedago-pathology'" (1999, p. 12). According to Shulman, much of the contemporary academy suffers from three well developed pathologies:

> . . . we forget, we don't understand that we misunderstand, and we are unable to use what we learned. I have dubbed these conditions *amnesia, fantasia,* and *inertia.*

Amnesia is one of the most frequent pathologies of learning—perhaps the most frequent. Students ordinarily and regularly forget what they have learned in their classes. Indeed, at times they forget that they even attended some classes. . . .

Fantasia is the name we have given to what otherwise might have been called illusory understanding or persistent misconceptions. . . . It is that state in which students are absolutely confident that they understand something, but they don't. . . .

What about **inertia**? . . . inert ideas are those that simply lie there, doing nothing. They are not forgotten; nor are they in some intrinsic sense wrong. They are simply not in a form that lends them to any useful purpose beyond being remembered. (pp. 12-13)

Furthermore, even when faculty recognize the pervasiveness of these pedago-pathologies and resolve to do something about them (i.e., responsibility for more than formal learning doesn't lie just with students), the measures they adopt are often insufficient to get at the core of the problem. For the more we know about effective education and the better we understand the learning process, the more we suspect that traditional, exclusively campus- and classroom-based instructional methods are not themselves capable of providing the needed pedagogical strategies. This, in fact, is one of the most important observations made by John Abbott, director of the Education 2000 Trust, in a March 1996 interview:

. . . today, people worldwide need a whole series of new competencies—the ability to conceptualize and solve problems that entails *abstraction* (the manipulation of thoughts and patterns), *systems thinking* (interrelated thinking), *experimentation*, and *collaboration* . . . I doubt such abilities can be taught solely in the classroom, or be developed solely by teachers. Higher order thinking and problem-solving skills grow out of direct experience, not simply teaching; they

45

require more than a classroom activity. They develop through active involvement and real-life experiences in workplaces and the community. (Marchese, 1996, pp. 3-4)

If Abbott is correct—and the thrust of his remarks is echoed in numerous other studies (e.g., American Association for Higher Education, American College Personnel Association, & National Association of Student Personnel Administrators, 1998; Ewell, 1997; Romer & Educational Commission of the States, 1996)—attempts to better prepare students to become intentional or lifelong learners (Francis, Mulder, & Stark, 1995)will not succeed simply by rearranging the curriculum, by introducing new classroom exercises, or even by expanding available technological resources. What is needed, above all, is that students literally get out of the classroom and begin learning to learn in unstructured, real-world situations.

Interestingly enough, it is not just cutting-edge research on learning that argues for such a move. The changing profile of today's college students also points in this direction. Schroeder (1993), for example, has cautioned that

As faculty, we have generally espoused the common belief that students learn and develop through exposure—that the *content* is all-important. We have been accustomed to a traditional learning process where one who knows (the teacher) presents ideas to one who does not (the student). Many of us prospered under the traditional lecture system, where the focus was on coverage of material through teaching by telling. This approach may work for us but it may not work for the majority of today's students. Students are changing dramatically, and we need to respond to those changes. (p. 22)

Schroeder goes on to discuss the results of a study he helped lead that showed that "approximately 60 percent of entering students prefer [a] sensing mode of perceiving compared to 40 percent who prefer [an] intuitive mode" (p. 22). The sensing mode correlates with learning grounded in real-world experience, while the intuitive favors learning through concepts, ideas, and abstractions. In contrast to a clear majority of students, "over 75 percent of faculty prefer the intuitive learning pattern" (p. 25). Given the fact that the student population is more and more composed of adult learners, it is also important to note that "approximately 75 percent of the general [American] population has been estimated to prefer the sensing learning pattern" (p. 24). In light of findings like these, the failure of so many institutions to move beyond boilerplate rhetoric to effective civic engagement and active learning should give academic leaders serious pause.

Institutional Examples

And yet, at many institutions, faculty from a wide range of disciplines are demonstrating a genuine—if also cautious and tentative—interest in service-learning. According to the results of the 2002 Campus Compact annual member survey, service-learning is gradually taking root across much of American higher education. Not only did membership in the Compact grow by over 60% between 1998 and 2001, but by 2001, 87% of Compact members indicated they offered service-learning courses—up eight percentage points from 2000. Indeed, institutions offered on average 27 such courses.

To be sure, much of this reported increase in interest will be short-lived if colleges and universities fail to support it through faculty development opportunities and reward structures that recognize excellence in this area. However, as was noted at the beginning of this essay, academic leaders who provide this needed support will find that they can simultaneously address many of the issues Kimball and others have identified as central to contemporary higher education. At this point, a few illustrations may be in order.

At one urban comprehensive university in the northwest, the president and CAO used service-learning to challenge the faculty to create a demonstrably more effective and coherent curriculum. This resulted in the design of new interdisciplinary first-year and capstone experiences, many of which are organized around community-based work. Since the school has a largely commuter student body, service-learning was also used to develop a stronger sense of institutional identification among members of the student body. Organizing the community-based work into team projects provided students with a noncampus-based vehicle for working together and forming social as well as academic bonds.

At another urban comprehensive, this one in the Midwest, service-learning was used as the primary vehicle not only for connecting the university's teaching mission more closely to its mission statement, but also for connecting the work of its many issue-based institutes to courses in the undergraduate curriculum. Thanks to this strategy, the institution has achieved a new level of coherence that has, in turn, allowed it to see itself in a new, more confident and more successful light.

The CAO at a university in the South had still a different agenda. Recognizing that his institution was not in a position to achieve national or even regional recognition by chasing a traditional research profile, he explicitly embraced Boyer's expanded concept of scholarship and challenged his faculty to choose and achieve demonstrated excellence in an area of their own choosing. Service-learning was one important strategy faculty could use to demonstrate success in the scholarship of application or the scholarship of teaching.

At a university in California where the population is unusually diverse—even by California's standards—the CAO saw in service-learning a unique bridge to the area's multicultural communities. By recasting the institution as an engaged neighbor rather than as an island set apart, he was able to utilize new community connections to create new teaching and research opportunities, attract and retain a more diverse student population, and provide new avenues for student leadership. A very similar agenda has informed the service-learning work of community colleges in Florida, Arizona, and Hawaii.

Service-learning's role at a small midwestern liberal arts college suggests a more internal focus. Since the college already boasted strong internship and practicum programs, the CAO saw in service-learning another way to ensure that all the institution's students would be exposed to the dialectic between theory and practice. Indeed, even those students who were already availing themselves of off-campus educational opportunities could use service-learning projects both to expand their experiential base and to sharpen their experiential learning skills. Indeed, at another institution with an already well-developed experiential education profile, the CAO saw in service-learning a way to establish, from the first year on, a foundation for many of the skills, habits, and concepts student would need when undertaking hands-on work in their majors.

Finally, we can cite a historically black liberal arts college that has used community-based work as an organizing principle in redesigning its general education core. What the CAO recognized in this case is that the benefits of maintaining a general education point of reference throughout all four years could be both strengthened and multiplied if that point of reference were anchored in ongoing community-based work. Such an anchor would guarantee that students continued to contextualize academic theory, recognize interdisciplinary connections, clarify values, and develop strong workplace skills throughout the entire course of their undergraduate careers.

What these examples indicate is consistent with the recommendations put forth by the American Association of State Colleges and Universities (2002) in their report on public engagement; namely, that academic leaders should "approach involvement systematically—aligning institutional and intra-institutional efforts as well as institutional and community efforts" (p. 15). When this occurs, service-learning can serve as the vehicle for bringing together a multitude of institutional priorities, whether they relate to general education reform, curricular coherence, the development of workplace skills and attitudes, multiculturalism, or teaching excellence and deep learning. At the same time, it can also strengthen programs associated with admissions and financial aid, retention, student culture and responsible behavior, and alumni relations. Leadership groups at all levels of the institution will find it a useful framework for integrating policies, incentive structures, and professional/personal creativity.

4 | Roles and Responsibilities of Academic Administrators: Supporting the Scholarship of Civic Engagement

Amy Driscoll
Lorilee R. Sandmann

Both intellectual and administrative leadership are critical for motivating and preparing an institution for civic engagement. Academic administrators are urged to facilitate campus practices that encourage and reward faculty scholarship of engagement.

In 1994, when Ernest Boyer elegantly urged higher education to respond to the challenges confronting society, many saw the timing as critical. Some would say that Boyer's call for civic engagement is even more critical today in view of national challenges and increasing global issues. Fortunately, we have listened and responded to the call on a growing number of campuses.

What does it mean to be an engaged university? Graham Spanier (1999) of Pennsylvania State University articulated "putting knowledge and expertise to work on problems its community faces" (p. 1) as fundamental to the definition. The Knight Higher Education Collaborative (2000) discusses the exemplary campuses as those in which "the interests of community and the academy are purposefully entwined" (p. 2). In an effort to mobilize more campuses, the Collaborative advised in compelling language:

Institutions ignore a changing environment at their peril. Like dinosaurs, they risk becoming exhibits in a kind of cultural Jurassic park: places of great interest and curiosity, increasingly irrelevant in a work that has passed them by. Higher education cannot afford to let this happen. (p. 2)

At the heart of most campus commitments to civic engagement are faculty roles and contributions. Holland (1997) identified faculty involvement as a key organizational factor in determining institutional commitment to community service. To ensure and sustain such involvement, academic administrators have begun to consider new roles and variations of their typical responsibilities for providing leadership to achieving a civic engagement agenda. Academic administrators play significant leadership roles in campus policies for promotion and tenure, in the prioritization of faculty workloads, in allocation of resources, and in the promotion of supportive norms and culture for civic engagement. This chapter explores those roles and accompanying responsibilities of academic administrators to stimulate and sustain institutional motivation necessary to commit a campus to civic engagement, to expand conceptualization of scholarship, to revise related reward systems, and to provide a campus context of knowledge and support for faculty scholarship of engagement.

Preparing the Campus Context

There is a critical process of preparation that must take place for a campus to fully embrace and embed an engagement ethos. Our experience in working with campuses across the country has shown that this process includes stimulating an institution's motivation to pursue a civic engagement agenda, pursuing a campus study and learning process, and identifying and supporting existing cases of faculty involvement.

Stimulating Institutional Motivation

Although there are significant extrinsic forces pushing the civic engagement agenda for higher education (Ehrlich, 2000), campuses are also being forced to demonstrate their uniqueness as they respond to calls for accountability and for demonstration of public value. For many institutions, civic engagement provides a way for universities to make sense of their missions or to strengthen their raison d'etre. In many of the cases of highly engaged campuses, the chief academic officer and other academic administrators clearly articulated and led efforts to define campus missions in terms of civic engagement. Some academic leaders probed and highlighted the relationship between civic engagement activities such as service-learning and increased student retention, achievement, and satisfaction with their educational experiences (Austin, Sax, & Avalos, 1999).

Much of the leadership is insistent that higher education goes beyond a proclamation of the importance of civic engagement. On their campuses and in national forums, they advocate the kind of response articulated in the Knight Higher Education Collaborative (2000) publication, "Disputed Territories." The response sought is one of institutions taking seriously their commitment to civic engagement "by changing . . . curriculum and approaches to learning, [or] . . . criteria for awarding tenure" (Knight Higher Education Collaborative, 2000, p. 1) as examples of seriousness. When campuses develop specific learning outcomes such as "promoting responsible, ethical, and committed citizens" (California State University-Monterey Bay, 1994) and design curriculum, pedagogy, and assessment to achieve those outcomes, they are seriously pursuing a civic engagement agenda. Such moves demand strong administrative leadership and faculty support to motivate an institution with all of its constituencies and conflicting priorities to commit to civic engagement.

In order to sustain civic engagement in higher education, to make it integral to the life of campuses, and to keep it from being a set of marginal activities, universities must consider and value changing faculty roles. A related recommendation for administrators is to prepare the campus context for the scholarship of engagement.

A *Study and Learning Process*

Depending on the level of campus readiness, there is an important preparation phase before an institution can embrace an agenda of civic engagement. As a starting point, Ramaley (2000) has urged campuses to respond to questions such as, "What expectations do we have of ourselves as scholars and administrators?" Driscoll and Lynton (1999) recommended that an institution begin the process of envisioning new faculty roles and rewards with a period of intensive study, inquiry, discussion, and reflection. The study process is essential for the creation of a shared knowledge base among both faculty and administration. Many campuses have invested both financial resources and time into this process by bringing in consultants, by sending representatives to conferences and forums about civic engagement, by developing a library of readings and examples of civic engagement, and by sponsoring campus events. Fortunately for newly interested campuses, there are excellent resources for this study and exploration process:

- American Association for Higher Education/Campus Compact Service-Learning Consulting Corps: The Consulting Corps is a collaborative arrangement that provides expert consultation to campuses. The consultants are experienced faculty and administrators who have developed significant expertise in civic engagement and can assist campuses or departments to initiate or expand the implementation of a civic engagement agenda.

- The Clearinghouse for the Scholarship of Engagement: The Clearinghouse provides resources in the form of books and other publications as well as consultation to individual campuses and to regional/state/national conferences. The Clearinghouse also supports the National Review Board for the Scholarship of Engagement.

There are a wide variety of forums about civic engagement at the state, regional, and national level, insightful models of engaged campuses, and a growing literature base to inform most aspects of civic engagement. Ramaley (2000) describes the importance of learning new language as a process for expanding thinking beyond traditional models. The resulting shared knowledge base is critical to the work that follows. Campus constituencies will need to develop common language and concepts, a philosophical stance, and agreement on purposes to be effective.

Achieving an institutional "fit" with engagement. Those of us who provide consultation to campuses or conduct conference workshops about civic engagement agree that each campus must come to its own definition, a contextually driven set of purposes and approaches, and an appropriate process for assessing civic engagement. Lynton (1995) urged that institutional responses to the civic engagement movement, and specifically to service-learning, must be institutionally distinctive. He encouraged not only every institution but also every unit within an institution to deliberate and decide the degree to which engagement is integral and appropriate to the mission of the unit or institution. Lynton believed that if civic engagement is to be sustained, all constituencies must accept that the form and degree of expression of engagement will be highly variable across and within institutions. For such distinction in campus engagement, academic administrators can provide vision and leadership to the discussions and developments that must occur.

The importance of the institutional fit cannot be overestimated. The match between institutional history, identity, and value system and how the campus embraces community will determine how successfully civic engagement is integrated into the life and work of the campus. It will also have a significant impact on how well the scholarship of engagement is accepted and valued among the constituencies.

Setting an inquiry-based agenda. While engaging in the study and exploration of civic engagement, campuses are advised to establish an inquiry-based agenda. As a starting point, universities are urged to review mission and goals, to identify existing examples of civic engagement, to articulate the campus strengths and challenges, and to examine the reason for interest in civic engagement. Academic administrators are critical to the convening and intellectual guidance of such self-assessment forums. They set a tone for the discussions that follow and communicate the importance of the processes. The reflections that emerge will provide a contextually sound foundation for the decisions and institutional fit.

Institutional connections as a resource. The work of establishing a shared knowledge base can also connect the campus with a network of colleagues, programs, and institutions already engaged in civic scholarship. For both administrators and faculty, those networks are a source of support, insight, and inspiration for the preparation phase, but they also contribute to sustainability. Major conferences in higher education intentionally initiate and sustain those informal networks and have begun to establish disciplinary communities as another level of support for individual faculty. Within the campus context of support is another resource for academic administrators—those faculty who are already committed to civic engagement.

Identification of and Support for Existing Faculty Cases

Those faculty who are already committed to civic engagement in their teaching and research pursuits provide another source of support. It has been an informative experience for campuses to look within and identify those faculty and programs that have been engaged with community for some time. Some of those faculty have found and connected with like-minded individuals, individuals who have experienced similar disconnects between their professional lives and their personal motivations and belief systems (Cooper, 2002; Palmer, 1996). With encouragement and support from academic administrators, those faculty networks can provide stimulation for campus interest and motivation for civic engagement.

Some of those faculty have worked quietly and without any formal support, certainly without reward or recognition. Once in the open, those faculty or entire programs often become a source of both insight and inspiration for their peers. Academic administrators need to seek out those faculty and programs and learn from their successes and mistakes.

In the realm of campus change, those individuals are referred to as early adopters, and they often provide a jumpstart for campus movement. Hollander (2001) encouraged administrators to celebrate and reward their work. She also identifies those already committed faculty as sources for broader definitions of scholarship and as experimenters to "devise credible and effective ways to document the scholarship of engagement." Administrators are wise to create advisory roles for already committed faculty as a strategy in their campus preparation work.

Ramaley (2000) strongly counseled administrators to "take care of the needs of those already committed faculty, and to make sure that they do not exhaust themselves in conducting pilot work or initial programs" (p. 4). She described the early adopters as catalysts to involve faculty who are curious or cautious or even resistant. Her recommendations clearly urge the investment of concrete financial resources and an infrastructure to support the beginning work.

In addition to the work of preparing the campus for civic engagement, there is much to prepare before acceptance and recognition for the resulting new forms of scholarship that accompany engagement. As early as possible, it will be essential to assure faculty that their work will be valued and seen as integral to their academic roles. Thus, another form of preparation, that of preparing for the scholarship of civic engagement, is a next step for the campus leadership.

Preparing for the Scholarship of Civic Engagement

Often the work of preparing the campus leads to review and revision of promotion and tenure guidelines. Sometimes institutional guidelines can actually accommodate alternative forms of scholarship. It is the interpretation and application of those guidelines that demand both intellectual and visionary leadership from academic administrators.

Once again, the process of reviewing and revising guidelines must be distinctive to the campus and individual units. Thus, the focus of this part of the chapter is on preparation for evaluating and documenting the scholarship of civic engagement. Such preparation has been the focus of national efforts for the last ten years, so there are resources, models and experiential insights from and for campuses, academic administrators, and individual faculty, as reflected in the chapters of this volume.

Preparing for the Evaluation of the Scholarship of Engagement

There is often the perception that campuses have completed the work of supporting the scholarship of engagement when the ink dries on the revised promotion and tenure paperwork. An early experiment at Portland State University followed several years of "town meetings" in which faculty from across campus discussed, provided input, and raised issues with the proposed revisions of the university's promotion and tenure guidelines. Once the new policy was approved, a group of deans and department chairs was brought together to review and evaluate a fictitious case of a faculty seeking tenure. The differences among the evaluative decisions and the rationales for them were stunning. The results should have been expected, even though many thought that the new guidelines would provide all the necessary support and guidance for the new evaluation processes. It was apparent that faculty and administrators brought to the new institutional criteria their own long-held and well-understood definitions, models, and qualities of traditional scholarship. Those were the lenses through which colleagues viewed new guidelines, criteria, and the notion of scholarship in general.

Confusion for new faculty. Among junior faculty there is an uneasiness and insecurity about pursuing the scholarship of engagement, and they are often without colleagues with whom they can discuss their work. With that isolation comes the fear that colleagues will not know how to judge their scholarship. It is not uncommon for administrators, department chairs, or deans to advise new faculty to wait until after they have been granted tenure before pursuing a civic engagement agenda. There's a spirit of "being safe" about early scholarship—staying within the box of traditional scholarship—to protect academic position. With these kinds of messages, one can hardly blame a new scholar for deciding that pioneering work is too risky after all the labor, poverty, and preparation of completing a doctorate and securing a good position. There is further risk that civic engagement will be narrowly defined as the work of tenured and very experienced faculty. Administrators will need to be vigilant in their watch over the campus culture to prevent such a narrow definition.

Establishing a new knowledge base. For those campuses with a civic engagement agenda and the reward system to support faculty roles in that agenda, another significant resource is essential. That resource is a strong knowledge base, a base of deep understanding of the scholarship of engagement, familiarity with examples of the scholarship, skills in raising appropriate questions about faculty scholarship, and values and commitment to the diverse forms in which the scholarship of engagement may be documented. The knowledge resource will direct faculty documentation work and guide the contents of a scholarly portfolio.

More importantly, the knowledge resource will inform the review and evaluation processes and inspire the work of review committees. Academic administrators provide the leadership for establishing those knowledge resources through their strategies of prioritization, fund allocation, establishing infrastructure, and modeling its importance in their own scholarly pursuits.

Need for evaluation training. At another campus, California State University-Monterey Bay, the institution began its history with an alternative promotion and tenure system that fit the campus mission and values. Nevertheless, when the first round of reviews was completed, it was clear that reviewers (typically full professors who arrived at the new campus with well-developed notions about scholarship) struggled with the new forms of scholarship and how to evaluate faculty work within those forms. Some of those same faculty had designed the new guidelines, but once in the reviewer/evaluator role, tradition took over and disequilibrium raised havoc with their decisions.

At the California campus, much like the experience at Portland State University, it was immediately clear that there was a need to prepare both administrators and faculty who would review and evaluate portfolios. The next academic year began with a campus-wide training required of all who would participate on a review committee. The major pedagogy of the day-long preparation was a simulation of a review process. Informed by the work of William Plater, executive vice chancellor and dean of the faculties at Indiana University-Purdue University Indianapolis, four campus colleagues and two external consultants role-played reviewers for two fictitious faculty cases. The cases were written to intentionally highlight the issues and questions associated with new forms of scholarship.

Since that first training, the campus has reviewed and revised its promotion and tenure guidelines, and an important new section describes the requirement for all reviewers to annually attend a preparation workshop. That requirement represents a significant commitment to new forms of scholarship for the campus but also to faculty colleagues to assure them that their work will be understood, evaluated with a different lens, and valued as scholarship. With or without such a requirement, campus leadership must communicate the importance of the scholarship of civic engagement.

A final issue for faculty is the availability of colleagues outside of campus who are able to review their community scholarship. A common pattern on many campuses is the solicitation of feedback and critique from external reviewers in the tenure and promotion review process. The National Review Board for the Scholarship of Engagement was designed as a logical response to the issues of informed and expert review.

National Review Board for the Scholarship of Engagement
Faculty across the country frequently expressed the need for respected peer reviewers who are experienced in university-community partnerships and who could offer informed judgment about the quality of a program of engaged scholarship. They were concerned that their institu-

tional peers lacked understanding of differing forms of scholarship. In response to a growing critical need for a national pool of peer reviewers who could provide credible, standardized assessment for the scholarship of engagement, a National Review Board for the Scholarship of Engagement was established in 2000. The purpose of the board is to review and to evaluate the scholarship of engagement of faculty who are preparing for annual review, promotion, and tenure decisions. The board is composed of leaders in areas such as community or civic engagement, institutionalization of service-learning, and professional service (for example, cooperative extension), and includes individuals from a wide range of disciplines in a variety of higher education institutions. The National Review Board is supported by the Clearinghouse for the Scholarship of Engagement, codirected by this chapter's authors.

The process of submission to the Review Board begins with a request from an institution, through an academic administrator such as a department chair. Based on availability and background, reviewers are identified and notified of the institution's request well in advance of the submission to ensure the timely and informed review of faculty materials. Administrators are assured of a timely, comprehensive, and expert review for their campus processes. Guidelines for preview letters, dossier development, and criteria for review are available from the Clearinghouse, and they are on the web at http://www.scholarshipofengagement.org.

Criteria for evaluation. The criteria used by the National Review Board to assess and to evaluate the Scholarship of Engagement were drawn from the criteria presented in *Scholarship Assessed* (Glassick, Huber, & Maeroff, 1997) and adapted for a unique fit with the scholarship of engagement (see Figure 4.1). The criteria help in guiding the work of the National Review Board for the Scholarship of Engagement in the external review process. The board is mindful of the variation in institutional contexts, the breadth of faculty work, and individual promotion and tenure guidelines. Such variation demands the leadership of academic administrators and their faculty networks in the presentation of such criteria to campuses.

4.1

Criteria Used to Assess and Evaluate the Scholarship of Engagement

Goals/Questions

Does the scholar state the basic purposes of the work clearly?

Does the scholar define objectives that are realistic and achievable?

Does the scholar identify intellectual and significant questions in the field?

Is there an academic fit with the scholar's role, departmental/university mission?

Context of theory, literature, best practices

Does the scholar show an understanding of existing scholarship in the field?

Does the scholar bring the necessary skills to the work?

Does the scholar bring together the resources necessary to move the project forward?

Is the work intellectually compelling?

Methods

Does the scholar use methods appropriate to the goals or questions?

Does the scholar effectively apply the methods selected?

Does the scholar modify procedures in response to changing circumstances?

Does the scholar describe rationale for selection of methods in relation to context and issue?

Results

Does the scholar achieve the goals?

Does the scholar's work add consequentially to the field (significance)?

Does the scholar's work open additional areas for further exploration?

Does the scholar's work achieve impact or change? Are those outcomes evaluated?

Communication/Dissemination

Does the scholar use a suitable style and effective organization to present the work?

Does the scholar use appropriate forums for communicating work to the intended audience?

Does the scholar communicate/disseminate to multiple audiences?

Does the scholar present information with clarity and integrity?

Reflective Critique

Does the scholar critically evaluate the work?

Does the scholar bring an appropriate breadth of evidence to the critique?

Does the scholar use evaluation to improve the quality of future work?

Does the scholar synthesize information across previous criteria?

Does the scholar learn and describe future directions?

At first glance, the evaluation criteria may look simple and straightforward, but they are rigorous and demanding. Faculty find that the criteria are not easily met by merely engaging in community work and partnerships. The criteria truly ensure the scholarly aspects of engagement and can serve as significant guides for multiple levels of the scholarship of engagement: at the initial level of decision, when faculty make a commitment to civic engagement; at the planning and implementation level; at the documentation level; and at the review/evaluation level.

Academic administrators have a role in periodically elevating the institution's evaluation criteria for examination to assess whether revisions are necessary. This implies a responsibility to keep the knowledge resource current and to ensure that criteria are uniformly, and not selectively, applied.

Preparation for review and evaluation of the scholarship of civic engagement will provide strong support for those faculty who pursue such engagement, but there is also much to be learned about how to document the scholarship. Again, we urge campus preparation with the leadership of a key academic administrator or an administrative team.

Preparing for Documenting Scholarship of Engagement

From its earliest definitions as scholarship, engagement presented new questions and new issues to the notion of scholarship in higher education. Once defined for a campus and woven into guidelines for faculty promotion and tenure, the challenge is for faculty to document this scholarship in ways that are acceptable and rewarded. The National Project for the Documentation of Professional Service and Outreach, funded by the W. K. Kellogg Foundation, addressed this need in a sequence of projects spanning a six-year period. In the first project, 16 faculty and four administrators from multiple campuses engaged in the process of documentation to formulate guidelines, examples, and a framework for documentation. The faculty represented a wide range of disciplines and the campuses represented varied institutional settings. The insights of both faculty and administrators and samples of the faculty work are captured in *Making Outreach Visible: A Guide to Documenting Professional Service and Outreach* (Driscoll & Lynton, 1999).

It was clear to the project participants that, regardless of its focus, the best documentation is that which most effectively communicates and makes visible the evidence of the scholarship. They found that it took careful planning and description to provide scholarly evidence of engagement. Their work respected the traditional criteria for scholarship while broadening the definition of documentation and evidence. While encouraging diversity of documentation within common criteria and guidelines, the results of the project offer a format and a framework.

The initial project participants proposed a documentation framework with three major components: *purpose, process,* and *outcomes* (see Figure 4.2).

Figure 4.2
Framework for Documenting the Scholarship of Engagement

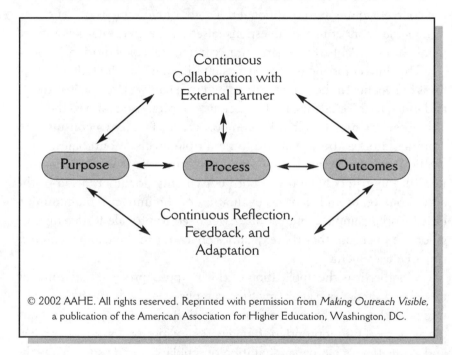

© 2002 AAHE. All rights reserved. Reprinted with permission from *Making Outreach Visible*, a publication of the American Association for Higher Education, Washington, DC.

The *purpose* section of the dossier provides a foundation for the scholarship of engagement. Here, a faculty member is encouraged to consult with administrators and to refer to the university, school, or department mission and priorities that support the engagement work. The needs and priorities of the situation or external partners are described along with those of the school or college as a rationale for engaging in the work. The purpose also assists in the establishment of the faculty member's situation, its specific characteristics, and its impact on his or her professional development, again in consultation with the appropriate academic administrator.

The *process* component is a record of the methodology and the rationale for design used by faculty in their engagement work. To achieve specific and desirable goals for an engagement effort, faculty design and deliver a product using appropriate methods. Adaptations made in the process of collaboration with the community or partners are provided as evidence of reflective scholarship. Reflection and adaptation is a constant need in community-based work because such contexts have few of the controls common to traditional research. Other dimensions of reflection include pondering new questions raised by the civic engagement and highlighting insights that emerge from community collaboration.

The third component, *outcomes*, is multifaceted and includes descriptions of benefits to the community or external partners, to the institution and units, to the students, to the discipline or profession, and to the individual faculty member. It will be important for faculty to consult with administrators as they evaluate the multiple levels of outcomes, especially those that impact the unit or institution as a whole. Ramaley (2000) and others have urged both convincing documentation of the actual outcomes and rigorous evaluation of the impact of community-based work. Campus administrators will need to provide leadership and guidance to ensure that those qualities characterize the campus scholarship of engagement.

Whether it is the application of this purpose, process, and outcome model or a similar one emerging from campus-specific discussions, academic administrators have a key role in initiating and supporting faculty discussions about appropriate frameworks for the presentation, review, and evaluation of a broader definition of scholarship, and specifically the scholarship of engagement. Additionally, it has been found that part of the discussion needs to include specific guidelines, such as the ones to be described below, to inform faculty members as well as their mentoring and evaluation committees.

Guidelines for documentation. To assist in the documentation of professional service, guidelines emerged from the initial Kellogg project previously described. The guidelines can assist faculty and administrators in campus preparation and individual dossier preparation. The guidelines include the importance of documenting the scholarship of engagement as an ongoing process rather than as a summary of outcomes. Faculty and administrators are urged to clarify the intellectual questions that guide engagement in general and for specific faculty work. In both the work and the documentation, it will be important to distinguish the varied roles of all involved. Finally, it is recommended that faculty demonstrate how the outreach activity provides a platform for future scholarship, and then discuss future prospects with administrators for planning purposes.

In addition to those guidelines, two issues are worthy of note when advising faculty who are developing comprehensive dossiers. The first issue is length of documentation. Because engagement work is contextual, collaborative, and developmental, it tends to be highly descriptive in nature. To be read and considered thoughtfully, documentation needs to be skillfully and succinctly presented. As academic administrators typically review a large number of promotion cases, there must be serious communication about the length of dossiers.

A second issue is the importance of policies, procedures, and format or structure. The academic administrator plays a leading role in establishing, holding discussions about, or clarifying institutional expectations or norms about scholarship. Those discussions will need to include a periodic examination of existing policies, procedures, and structures to determine whether they enhance or inhibit a broader conceptualization of scholarship and related review and evaluation practices. If modifications to existing practices are needed and agreed upon, providing widespread and consistent communication is a role of the academic administrator as well. Revisions may mean disseminating guidelines as the "official" institutional rule. Additionally, it could mean highlighting successful cases exemplifying the change.

Insights about the scholarship of engagement. One of the major insights gleaned from the initial Kellogg-funded project for the documentation of professional service and outreach was the importance of collegial support and collaboration in the documentation process. One of the participants, Cheryl Rosaen, professor of teacher education at Michigan State University, describes it well, "The documentation process is not one that should be tackled alone" (1999, p. 30). Others were also clear that the project would not have yielded the insightful guidelines or the high quality portfolios without the intense collaboration of the participants. Another faculty, Patricia Schechter, professor of history at Portland State University, spoke for her colleagues:

> The opportunity to delve deeply into the political and philosophical implications of our work, to revise and refine our documentations in a genuine community of scholars will serve as a model of inquiry and reflection in my career. (1999, p. 30)

Academic administrators are encouraged to provide that same kind of support through discussion groups, mentoring for junior faculty, portfolio preparation workshops, and ongoing documentation groups. One of the side effects of such collaboration and focus on scholarship is the increased quality of the engagement. Many faculty members have acknowledged that their documentation efforts have led to revisions, or to serious queries about existing approaches to engagement. Clearly the process of describing and collecting evidence of their civic engagement work prompts faculty to reflect and assess that work, often leading to refinements in communication, collaboration, and even goals and outcomes. In addition to assisting individual faculty members, such collaboration enhances the quality of an institution's civic engagement projects by fostering an ongoing consideration of process and outcomes, an expanded conceptualization of scholarship to include the impact the work has on sponsoring communities, and an enlarged community of engaged scholars.

Other insights have come from the work of the National Review Board for the Scholarship of Engagement. The most successful cases reviewed thus far are those that present an integrated form of scholarship, scholarship that is an integration of teaching, research, and service. "I, my colleagues, and discipline never came to fully know and understand my work because it needed to be reported as either teaching, research or service. It had to fit in only one of the 'boxes'," lamented David D. Cooper (personal communication, 2002), professor of American thought and language at Michigan State University. The scholarship of engagement gave Dr. Cooper a way to express and to document the integrative nature of his community writing projects. In essence, civic engagement is a scholarly agenda that incorporates community issues and can be integrative across teaching, research, and service.

Within this view of integrated scholarship lies the richness and the promise of the work and its community results and benefits for the faculty member, profession, and higher education. By understanding the integrative quality of the scholarship of engagement, academic administrators can assist faculty in thinking about their work in such ways and in setting scholarly agendas that purposefully and intentionally integrate teaching, research, and service.

Summary

The roles and responsibilities of academic administrators are critical to the success of civic engagement on individual campuses. During the early preparation phase, their leadership must be directed to fostering an institutional culture in which faculty and administrators are motivated to participate, in which there is a solid knowledge base and shared understandings of the engagement, and in which existing cases of engagement are identified, supported, and celebrated. Later, the preparation must focus on the scholarship of civic engagement so that faculty and administrators have clear guidance for both documentation and evaluation of the scholarship. During all of the preparation, academic administrators will be in leadership roles as well as visionary and educator roles. Their responsibilities will include convening discussion and study groups; guiding campus learning; communicating and disseminating information, changes, and clarifications; and modeling both inquiry and openness for change. With their strategic roles and responsibilities, academic administrators can lead their institutions to exciting and effective civic engagement agendas and exemplary models of related scholarship.

5 | Service-Learning and the Problem of Depth

Jim Ostrow

This chapter makes a case for service-learning as part of a broader argument for depth of student contact with academic subject matter. The importance of the principle of depth is examined as a matter of underlying philosophy as well as a strategy in promoting service-learning to faculty.

It is a truism that convincing faculty of the pedagogical value of service-learning lies at the heart of its advocacy by any academic administrator. Yet how one does so, or the framework for doing so, makes a difference not only for quantitative success—that is, how many faculty are convinced—but also for the academic import of service-learning programming on any campus. Of course, lying behind this sort of a strategic decision are one's own beliefs as an educator working within an administrative role. Where does service-learning fall within a philosophy of education, insofar as that philosophy informs one's vision and priorities for an institution?

A priority of mine is the problem of depth in student contact with academic subject matter, and service-learning is promoted as a pedagogical support for depth. There are clearly more overtly social or societal benefits of service-learning that are compelling for many faculty—for instance, increasing student awareness of social issues, developing dispositions of good citizenship or social activism, or making academic activity a real base for positive change in the local and global community. These justifications for service-learning all support the case for a socially engaged campus. When I speak to faculty, I articulate these reasons for service-learning as part of an argument for academic depth. Here, I will discuss both the philosophical and strategic reasons for this approach. I first provide a synopsis of the problem of depth in contemporary education, followed by a discussion of how service-learning serves as one important response to this problem as well as how articulating the value of service-learning in this way makes sense in communication with faculty.

The Deep and the Superficial

In an anonymous college course evaluation, a student expresses dissatisfaction with "the fact that we had to analyze every little thing . . . I never look too deep into things." Allow me, for the sake of argument, to dispute the second part of the remark, that is, that the student "never looks too deep into things." There are surely many things that are engaging for the student (e.g., playing soccer or watching reality TV; dancing, drinking, or instant messaging on the Internet; reading mysteries or playing piano; being involved with someone romantically or caring for an ailing relative), yet academic subject matter may never rise above being a barely tolerable nuisance. Study it and be done with it! Some of these other nonacademic things may hold depth for the student—in the double sense of inviting student concentration as well as having an enduring influence on the student's anticipations, expectations, tastes, and dispositions. There are many things that must capture this student's and all of our students' imaginations, and they are surely influential in the development of character. Course subject matter is often not one of them. Why not?

What is academic subject matter for the student cited above? In John Dewey's terms, it is merely "something to be learned":

> When subject matter is not used in carrying forward impulses and habits to significant results, it is just something to be learned. . . . Conditions more unfavorable to an alert and concentrated response would be hard to devise. (1916, p. 169)

It is Dewey, interpreted often as the founder of learning centered education, who argues against too much of a direct focus on learning activity, thus showing that this is precisely what can compromise the degree to which subject matter *matters* to students. Learning is, of course, the issue of the day, and it seems almost unthinkable to take it as anything less than the most significant of results in the educational process. Subject matter is routinely translated for the classroom into potential evidence of learning, and the teacher's pedagogical experience often proceeds against the backdrop of the success or failure of students to "get it."

In this context, the key problem revealed by Dewey is that subject matter is never significant in itself as something to be learned. Mathematics, literature, engineering, philosophy, sociology, political science, management, biology, and education matter to members of disciplines as ways of engaging the world, as ways of doing things with their bodies and minds. They matter as opportunities for discovery and practice. Academics must learn things in order to progress within their fields, but they do not embrace their fields in order to learn them. They do so to act and learn within them. In a certain sense, the professor is the practices and insights of what he or she teaches. This is not to deny the less spiritual side of discipline-specific, professional academia, where promotions, grants, big-name contacts, or upper-tier publications may lock up the imagination. But this concession aside, subject matter for the teacher is often a richly engaging, character-shaping field of opportunity for perception and action.

Our students often experience subject matter less as a field of possibilities for discovery and action than as potential evidence of its own acquisition—as learning material. This is reinforced especially well by the standardized testing movement in primary and secondary education, designed to make teachers, schools, and their students accountable for learning what is supposed to be learned. The essence of these tests from the student's standpoint is that the tests are simply receptacles for what they know; once dumped there, this knowledge ceases to have value. Students have little more to do with the subject matter they had to "learn"; they will wait until next time, when they have to gorge themselves with something else to "receive and leave behind" (Dewey, 1916, p. 134). Academic subject matter becomes the knowledge that "was" acquired in a course, the primary or sole value of which is that it is now over and done with. Under this bulimic approach to student performance, education can function as effectively to eliminate knowledge as it can to generate it within the culture, and knowledge elimination can occur precisely through the legislature-driven processes that render schools accountable to others for their "success."

The standardized, test-driven classroom represents the logical extension of a view of subject matter that is pervasive and taken for granted throughout all levels of schooling. When Dewey (1964) writes, "It is only too common to hear students (in name) say in reference to some subject that they 'have *had* it'" (p. 425), he rejects a contortion of subject matter occurring under the name of education—the transmutation of subject matter as the active impetus of an encounter between persons and their environments into transmitted information and procedures. This is to simply alert educators to what they should know within their own fields of expertise: Subject matter captures one's imagination deeply not as a collection of recorded knowledge but as an open field of possibility to know and do more. When we ask our students to engage subject matter in the former sense, we compel them, notwithstanding our admonitions against grade consciousness, to value subject matter as mere content to receive and leave behind.

Whitehead (1929) argues that scientists know in order to inquire, not the reverse. Dewey (1916) contends that we need to think of human growth in relation to educational practice as being rather than having an end (p. 50). Discarding this idea as more romantic than real, educators at all levels focus on the problem of contemporary students' readiness for what they need to, in the end, get. But here the question becomes what do we mean by students "getting it"? Students may see subject matter as an exigent text—a closed matter once learned—or as an only partially defined field of opportunities for perceiving, acting within, and changing their environment. When they see subject matter in the latter way, its import lasts—it endures as an impulse to inquiry and as a perspective for understanding. The alternative is subject matter forgotten directly following the course, because it has been discarded through the vehicles of the test and course grade; it has been learned, the student has taken it and doesn't need to take it anymore.

Beyond Performance Measurement: Activating Imagination

Hence, when Dewey stresses the importance of teachers engaging the needs, capacities, and interests of students, he is not advising pandering or lack of discipline. He is stressing the importance of the value of subject matter as something deeper, or potentially deeper, than what could be recorded in any text. Dewey is not advocating an absence of structure in education, or a turn away from content toward process. He is in fact highly critical of the progressive movement in education that largely under his name advocated the principle teach the child, not the subject. Dewey (1938) sees the progressive movement in education as committing precisely the same error as traditional education: treating content and process as separate pedagogical problems.

When the value of student activity is conceived outside the cell of individual "proof" and within the realm of exploration and discovery, subject matter becomes a path for seeing the world anew, as well as for perceiving and formulating solutions to real problems. The counter-argument is that such a move is realistic only subsequent to students learning the basic principles. Additionally, expecting students to be motivated and able to conduct the actual, inventive work of a discipline ignores the reality of why most of them—certainly most nonmajors—take courses. Hence, covering established wisdom in the discipline must be the main pedagogical task. Textbooks and examinations tailored to this purpose are thus employed.

The above argument presumes that a discipline as a performed phenomenon is fundamentally different from a discipline as a taught phenomenon. But with this presumption we lose sight of the value of established wisdom and its transferability. It is only insofar as available principles or techniques are convertible into the operative, embodied dispositions of an inquiring mind that they exist as part of a discipline. We cannot pretend all students will be practicing scholars in a field; yet why not teach the field instead of a pedagogically induced fabrication, a mock version of the real thing?

Exploration, discovery, and understanding do not happen blindly. They necessitate capacity, ability, and knowledge. In the various academic fields, we need to acquire methodological and analytical skill, and we need to know the works and ideas of others. But this does not mean there is a linear, temporal relationship between acquired skill and wisdom, on one hand, and inquiry on the other. When we make the one have to precede the other, we depreciate the value of subject matter in the sense of reducing the chance for an appreciation of subject matter in itself. It is only by teaching subject matter *in itself,* or as it has value and significance for the practitioner, that it can matter to the student as an opportunity for exercising the imagination, which is "the only thing that makes any activity more than mechanical" (Dewey, 1916, p. 236). We need to introduce and foster skill in the classroom within the context of activating the imagination through exploration and discovery. In this way, subject matter has the best chance of developing into habits of mind (Dewey, 1929)—or as a perspective continually yielding new understanding, new possibilities for involvement in the world.

Service-Learning for Depth in a Fluid World

My purpose above has been to lay the primary educational context within which my interest in and advocacy for service-learning is situated. It may seem odd that I have not yet focused on issues more typically considered in discussions of service-learning—such as advancing habits of social responsibility and citizenship, or rendering higher education relevant to local and global social problems. There is no doubt that the social-developmental and direct societal benefits of service-learning are fundamental to understanding its significance in higher education— indeed, for rendering higher education relevant to the advancement of fairness, justice, and citizenship in a democracy, as suggested by Battistoni (2002); Eyler and Giles (1999); Jacoby and Associates (1996); Kenny, Simon, Kiley-Brabeck, and Lerner (2001); Zlotkowski (1998); and others in this volume. My intention is to strengthen rather than diminish the importance of these issues in higher education by establishing their inseparability from the problem of academic depth. I also believe coupling these social-developmental and societal issues with the problem of depth has strategic benefits for the promotion of service-learning to faculty.

Service-learning can be central to achieving greater academic depth by extending the relevance of subject matter beyond the classroom and expectations of performance within it. The key term here is "relevance." I do not mean to denigrate the classroom as a learning environment, but subject matter must *matter* as more than satisfying conditions specific to the classroom if it is to engage concentration and endure in a person's perspective. Dewey (1916) argues against the reduction of subject matter to a "record of knowledge, independent of its place as an outcome of inquiry and a resource in further inquiry" (p. 187). This means the value of subject matter must stretch beyond the walls of the classroom and beyond the perceived temporal confines of a course. The very existence of the classroom and its various learning requirements and measurements must, to a certain degree, become transparent in students' experience. An analogy is found in hi-fi audio. The degree to which music is heard purely as music has an inverse relationship to the degree to which the stereo equipment, and even the walls around the equipment, are visible in experience. Similarly, the degree to which subject matter exists in its original form as a field of inquiry and discovery is related inversely to the opacity of the classroom apparatus and the measurements students receive within it. Learning with depth is founded in principle, then, on its extension beyond the classroom.

Community service-learning projects are perfect vehicles for such an extension, rendering the educational apparatus transparent in favor of the discovering processes inherent in academic subjects. It is true that establishing the value and relevance of subject matter beyond the classroom is possible through other types of pedagogical methods as well. The difference with service-learning is the possibility of developing an active concern for the social problems of the day, as well as an enduring, habitual sense of effecting positive change in the world, within the context of exercising an academic imagination. This distinction, it seems to me, gets to the heart of what academic leaders can advocate for their institutions—service-learning as an opportunity to perpetuate the value of academic subject matter for understanding and for improving the human environment.

In 1927, Dewey wrote that many Americans suffer from the social pathology of a "riotous glorification of things 'as they are,'" arising out of a fear of facing with creative reason a whirlwind-changing world, a pathology that "works powerfully against effective inquiry into social institutions and conditions" (p. 170). A test- or grade-driven, take-it-in, prove-you-know-it, and-move-on-to-something-else approach to subject matter is a key education building block for this pathology. When knowledge is framed as something one receives, holds, and then releases, the message to students is that all knowledge is preexisting. The world needing to be known is as it is, and no more. We thereby train a populace that could not be more ill-equipped for an active responsiveness to a fluid, constantly changing world.

Projects involving students in direct service to others or the improvement of communities, combined with rigorous processes of reflection, can be effective in generating students' sense of the power of disciplinary and interdisciplinary ideas and methods. Through this process, they can combat the pervasive, if unwitting, presupposition in contemporary education of a static, unchanging world. Eyler and Giles's (1999) study of the educative outcomes of service-learning is a good resource for making the argument for depth of contact with subject matter through service-learning. The authors make the crucial distinction between education understood as "acquiring factual information and demonstrating it on final exams [and the] deeper understanding and application" (p. 63) that occurs through service-learning. There are no grounds for claiming that service-learning has any advantage over didactic instruction in learning as measured by test results or course grades, but there is plenty of evidence to suggest that students are more richly involved in subject matter as an active process of discovery through service-learning.

> [Students] had a deeper, more complex understanding of issues and felt more confident using what they were learning. Service made the subject matter come to life and put them inside the subject matter rather than outside, as abstract, disinterested observers. (Eyler & Giles, 1999, p. 70)

Another important point made by Eyler and Giles is the lasting power of subject matter, realized through the service-learning student's disposition to understand and solve real problems:

> The student who is trying to solve a real problem with real consequences sees the need to look up one more case, to understand just how a similar policy failed elsewhere, to learn a new technique for dealing with a child's reading problem. Genuine problems provide the most powerful need to know and are thus motivating for many students. (p. 91)

These dispositions are not acquired through service alone, but through academically charged reflection induced through instructor intervention. Take the following example of anger and frustration expressed by one of my past sociology students serving dinner in a local church food program:

> I heard one of the children say, "Mom, where are we going to sleep tonight?" The mother's voice was quiet, but as I walked I strained to hear her response, "We'll find somewhere, we always do." I clenched my grip around the apple carton. I became so angry, I felt like throwing the box on the floor . . . I wanted to invite all of these people back to [the college] and give them a place to stay. I wanted to do so much but in reality all I could do was pass out apples, and try to get to know and understand them. I was starting to understand.

While not in itself informed by sociological investigation and analysis, this written grasp of an emotionally intense moment provides the platform for investigating the meaning of this situation and employing the tools of sociology toward social change. The student's insight into the limits of volunteerism as a response to the problem of homelessness is perfect grounds for seeking to comprehend homelessness and its causes. It is also grounds for inquiry into the experience of homelessness and existing social attitudes. The student now perceives homeless individuals as being underserved, disadvantaged, as opposed to being necessarily lazy, or in some other way flawed in their character. What, then, leads to the latter opinions of the homeless, and what do these views mean for homeless persons in their everyday lives? There is, in short, more for the student to do than pass out apples: Sociology provides the vehicle for broader and deeper understanding, inquiries that might lead to solutions.

Service-Learning as Service to a Vocation

This last idea may be generalized to virtually any discipline. Through service-learning, students can discover the social value of academic subject matter. Service-learning enables faculty to teach their subjects as true fields of exploration and discovery, simultaneously demonstrating to students the power of academic subject matter to improve the human condition. The 19-volume American Association for Higher Education series on service-learning in the disciplines (Zlotkowski, 1997-2002) is a good resource for making this case to faculty, with each book devoted to a discipline-specific argument for service-learning course assignments. It is no strategic accident that this point is central to my advocacy of service-learning with faculty. Perhaps the single most important thing an academic leader can do when promoting academic initiatives is to recognize faculty work as a socially significant vocation. This can take many public or individually supportive forms, of course. It is faculty, above all, who will appreciate that what they teach merits a depth worthy of holding students' attention and having lasting value in their habits of mind. I promote service-learning as realization of this possibility for depth.

I advocate for service-learning as service to a vocation. But this also means I support it in synchrony with other initiatives that also establish the importance of the academic vocation within a framework of achieving depth of contact with subject matter. An example is the Reflection on Teaching Project, which I created based upon ideas in Pat Hutching's *From Idea to Prototype: The Peer Review of Teaching* (1995). This project involves teams of faculty in reflective exercises and colloquia designed to explore teaching from the standpoint of being a scholar immersed within an academic field. A central idea in the project is an explicit rejection of a recent tendency of the student-centered movement in higher education to focus on teaching strategies or techniques, including service-learning, in isolation from attending to the ever-changing *content* of what is taught. In other words, the focus of the project is the engagement of students in a world opened up by particular academic fields, and how it is precisely this inherent possibility that constitutes the scholarly nature of teaching.

Two other examples of parallel academic initiatives are 1) the Connected Learning Symposium, an annual, weeklong series of presentations by students of projects that engage them directly in the practice of exploration and discovery in an academic field, and 2) an electronic student portfolio designed around creative, project-focused work. I have tried to build service-learning programming in direct connection with these and other initiatives—all intended as supports for depth in the academic environment. Service-learning extends the meaning and import of all of these other initiatives into the realm of positive social change, the latter being what is arguably an essential ingredient of any academic subject.

Service-learning is an excellent vehicle for helping students to experience learning a subject as "wholehearted, purposeful activity in a social environment" (Kilpatrick, 1918, p. 330). John Stuart Mill (1962) argues that constant and ongoing civic involvement is a prerequisite for politically informed citizenship: "A political act, to be done only once in a few years, and for which nothing in the daily habits of the citizen has prepared him, leaves his intellect and his moral predispositions very much as it found them" (p. 69).

Mill's argument is also about the intellectual development of the mind, or the ability and inclination to think imaginatively about both what is and can be. I have argued that this means we must counter the forces of superficiality in education and seek depth of engagement in the academic fields we are charged to teach. In making this argument, I celebrate the importance of a teaching vocation through advocacy for an academic environment supportive of habits of exploration, analysis, and the application of insight to positive social change. Service-learning is then understood as both service to a vocation and service to education, directed toward creating a populace committed to a better world.

Note

Some passages in this chapter are borrowed (with written permission) from the following: Ostrow, J. (2000). The value of subject matter: The problem of depth in education. *Perspectives*, *30*(1).

Part II: Case Studies

6 | Bates College: Liberal Education, Community Partnerships, and Civic Engagement

Donald W. Harward

Bates College has developed an understanding of how its mission as a liberal arts college and its pedagogy of engaged learning make it a partner with its community in carrying out activities of mutual benefit to education and civic enhancement. Service-learning, action research, a community development organization known as LA Excels, and the Center for Community Partnerships provide concrete examples of how a college can become involved in its community and help itself.

I would like to begin with a brief story—a description of an event that took place at the end of a recent spring term. In late May, 12 students from Professor David Kolb's philosophy class, *Architecture, Tradition, and Innovation*, made three presentations to a joint session of the Lewiston and Auburn City Councils, the Maine communities that are the home for Bates College, an independent liberal arts college enrolling 1,700 undergraduates. As will be explained later, these communities provide an extraordinary setting for learning. Professor Kolb responded to the suggestion of the mayor of Auburn that his course consider an emergent proposal for an arts center. Rather than consider a hypothetical project, Professor Kolb agreed that the research expectation for the students be the development of alternative conceptualizations and computer-aided design (CAD) renditions for renovations to the Great Falls School in Auburn, slated by LA Excels (a college and local community-wide collaboration) to be converted to a community arts education and performance center. The project at the time was in the development phase, and it represents a particularly visible example of grassroots support for a major collaborative project between the two cities.

Professor Kolb's students worked in small research teams; they met with all potential users of the space, soliciting program needs and aspirations. They learned a great deal from Graham Gund, of Cambridge, Massachusetts, who was the architect commissioned by the cities to identify sites and to suggest the distribution of multiple projects in the cities. They considered building use, traffic, and how space could be shared among educators, artists, and performers. They completed three alternative conceptual designs that were thoughtful, viable to the site, artful, and responsive to community needs. They so impressed the city councils with their ideas that they generated an enthusiasm for the project that continues to move it forward. They raised points that would have been politically insensitive if raised by a council member; and (not the least consideration) they provided an estimated $60,000 of gratis consultancy work to the cities. At the same time, the process was a rigorous intellectual exercise for the students. As the project develops they will retain a personal interest in it—they have become stakeholders. They have taken on responsibility as members of the community and have added to a positive impression of the value of the college to the community. They are linking their learning to service and to action—a meaningful translation of civic engagement.

Thanks to the good work of so many students and faculty, this story is illustrative and representative of pedagogy and a commitment at Bates.

The Structure of Learning

The aggregation of concepts in the title, "Liberal Education, Community Partnerships and Civic Engagement," is less a description of how disparate topics are bridged and more a progressive unbundling ("unpacking") of elements of a single central concept of learning.

By knowing or understanding through direct engagement, the knower is put in a complex relationship with the known, including having what is known place a claim on the knower. In this respect, the dynamic of learning has been understood as communal. From the relation of knower to known—being both separate and connected—an ethic emerges, marking responsibilities the individual knower has in relation to objects of knowledge.

A parallel structure also underlies educational institutions—"places" of learning. By their nature, they have the responsibility of being both "places apart"—with critical distance from the conventional, the accepted, the popular or civic judgment—and places "fully engaged" with the area and communities that house and support them. Maintaining this tension of responsibilities, this balance, is a key challenge—especially as we explore what civic duty may mean in our contemporary context.

The parallel of individual learning and its ethic—with the obligations of learning institutions to be both places apart from the civic and places engaged with the civic—suggests an opportunity for understanding how our uniquely private residential liberal arts and sciences colleges can weave together the primary elements of teaching, research, and service and simultaneously give meaning to both individual and institutional service.

The particulars of our experience at Bates and the importance of service-learning to an academically intense institution valuing rigor and demanding critical assessment may provide an interesting model of use to others. In particular, I want to share our experience in establishing the Center for Community Partnerships which, by structure and program, emphasizes all "three legs" of our mission. I also want to describe LA Excels, a community and college collaboration specifically addressing the multiple aspects of community development and the ways they connect with the character of learning and the ethic of Bates College.

Finally, I will conclude with a brief outline of how Bates and other institutions committed to liberal education might join energies to accomplish, on a national level, an agenda connecting liberal learning and civic engagement.

Conceptual Distinctions

Twelve or so years ago, we began discussions of how we wanted to understand the quality and intensity of liberal learning at Bates.

To say we began our conversations is misleading. At most liberal arts colleges such conversations are continuous, although they have periods of intensity, and different voices emerge. At the time, our conversation at

Bates prepared us for expanding our attention to interdisciplinary inquiry—itself a difficult and evasive topic. The general drift of the discussion led to a greater appreciation of the arbitrariness of the boundaries drawn by the disciplines, the appropriateness of examining topics that fell among disciplinary approaches, as well as the consideration of issues of interest to our faculty and students that could be examined only by using the lenses of several disciplinary methods or patterns of inquiry.

For Bates, the conversations were liberating. New programs emerged; students led (e.g., environmental studies), or followed (e.g., the neurosciences); faculty vitalized research interests in areas and in ways that reinforced interdisciplinary approaches. Not only was teaching enhanced, but also our faculty members could mark real strengths of professional accomplishment within a liberal arts and sciences context.

In very general terms, our understanding of liberal learning was expanded and deepened. We did not lose our academic focus as a college committed to the liberal arts and, most importantly, the faculty's voice emerged in the discussion as being responsible for shaping these expanded dimensions.

Another thread in the discussion also occurred. Not only was the direction of our programs expanding to address interdisciplinary interests, but the teaching and scholarly qualities of our faculty were moving toward blurring the conventional boundaries that had defined where students learn. That is, engaging and challenging students through teaching and research led to extending the boundaries beyond the classroom, and thereby broadening the concept of a campus. In meaningful ways, old boundaries became porous. *Where* students learned extended to include the community and beyond (including international experiences). And as the "places" for teaching and research expanded, teaching and scholarly activities began to blend with the activities of service. This was important to the direction of these changes being accepted and given credibility within the campus. The categories of research and service became less distinct; certainly the differences between applied research and service-learning dwindled and, as that occurred, the stereotypic notions of rigor, intellectual intensity, and academic value began to shift.

We remained committed to maintaining the core features and skills of liberal learning during this period of transition. Consideration of the expansion of the conceptual geography, the combining of different disciplinary courses of the liberal arts and sciences, and consideration of the extension of its places and contexts led our faculty to discuss a model for liberal learning that was broader and more nuanced than it would have been just ten or 15 years ago. Elements of the liberal-learning model, however, remain at its core. These include acquiring critical skills and gaining access to academic content; nurturing of a disposition to question; looking for patterns and conceptual structures; having students take responsibility for learning, and, once having done so, participating in experiences of discovery and intellectual inquiry.

In our ongoing conversations of a model for liberal learning, we added consideration of the practices and pedagogy of service-learning. Their addition grew directly from what liberal education means. Accordingly, at Bates a more complex and coherent manifestation of a "model" has emerged—one that includes, but is not singularly characterized by, an understanding of knowing that is linked to service. At other institutions, this conversation may be characterized as an understanding of "knowing linked to action" or even "theory linked to practice."

With much credit to Campus Compact, Bates was one of the earliest of hundreds of colleges and universities to have students and faculty link learning and service and establish curricular projects that also serve others and benefit the community.

With the successes of our students and faculty came a more thoughtful reaction and attention to place, and a growing sense of our responsibility to our community. Such a notion became grounded in our understanding of what it means to be a liberal arts and sciences college, of the communal character of learning, and of the ethic that is carried by being connected to, and affected by, what is known and how it is known.

For educational institutions, there has always been a strong sense that we must be "places apart," that intellectual activity must be separate, and thereby independent of place. The primary reason for such an understanding of our mission is the important value for colleges and universities to maintain their responsibility to be contrarian, to contemplate alternatives, and to question authority, that is, to be critical of conventionality, the popular and the accepted civic norms. To do so with integrity requires distance from the community. In our view at Bates, that responsibility must be retained. However, it must be balanced with a second responsibility we have as educational institutions: to be engaged in the communities in which we are located because such engagement is required by the institution's mission to learn. We must be both "places apart" and "places connected." We have concluded that such a duality of responsibility can be sustained and extended by the incorporation of service-learning, research applied to community needs, and collaborative partnerships that link the institution and the community. These are efforts that reach out to the community but are grounded in the legitimate academic and intellectual pursuits of our students and faculty.

At Bates, much of our initial exploration of service-learning has focused on the epistemic basis for understanding the relation of service to intellectual inquiry. We have argued that in the broadest sense of what the ancients called the "moral dimension" of knowing, the outward direction of coming to know must make contact with what is beyond ourselves—and our connectedness to it. Linked to this understanding of learning, and its unbundling, is the recognition that "standing in relation to other" also means putting ourselves in position as object, allowing our own beliefs, priorities, and values to be themselves the objects of critical examination.

Given the communal analysis, we are joined to what we know. We have entered into an association with it, and, in so doing, we recognize the reciprocity of learning—its communal dimension and our complex responsibility to the elements of that association.

When we are linked to what we know, we are changed by it. Without the connections cultivated by learning, we don't see what is other behind a different face, a different gender, a different skin, or a different religion. If ignorance is in large part the lack of imagination, then the lack of practice in recognizing what is other than ourselves, and our connection to it, is its manifestation.

This lesson is particularly poignant in response to the dynamic of a college's or university's response to the community as an object. The college must also be an object to those people who are not a part of the academic community. The community is then the "knower," and we are the "known." As my colleague William Corlett reminds me, this admission of vulnerability allows the other to examine our privileged position—just as we study their lack of many privileges and their resources (including directness and emotional honesty), they claim consideration of our often uncritically examined assets (such as the luxury of reflection, academic resources, instant legitimacy, etc.).

It is indeed a dialectic.

The Bates College Experience

At Bates, we have drawn on our institutional culture as we have created new mechanisms and community partnerships that not only are compatible with academic excellence and liberal learning, but genuinely enhance the qualities of the college.

Most liberal arts and sciences colleges are internally complex, and variations across colleges are extensive[1]. However, it may be useful to describe how we have proceeded at Bates because we can extrapolate from one institution's experience to imagine another's.

At Bates, we employed encouragement (including pilot support funds) from the president and academic leadership—both faculty and deans—and kept watch for those willing to explore and experiment. Our students were eager to be involved, and immediately they reported the positive character of their service-learning experiences.

As we implemented a more complex learning model, we had three goals in mind:

- We wanted to develop and inculcate, within our view of undergraduate learning, "space" for service-learning that would be understood as complementing and enhancing, but not replacing, other important elements of learning.

- We wanted to continue our emphasis on research (which included student engagement with faculty) but expand it to the adoption of zones of applied research, or action research, addressing needs in the community as valued and appropriate undergraduate efforts.

- We sought to establish a community development and civic entrepreneurial emphasis (LA Excels) that included the college as a partner in the process of civic engagement.

To facilitate and reinforce those objectives, we established a significant structural dimension of the college, the Center for Community Partnerships, which is organized within our academic framework. It is sustainable; it has the highest level of administrative attention; and it is endowed sufficiently to maintain its emphases and their appropriate balance. And within the center's structure, we created categories of personnel resources at Bates (Learning Associates) that support the learning model we have put into place and augment (but do not interfere with) direct faculty and student contact.

Service-Learning

While learning at Bates has always been connected to social action, it was a connection essentially expressed after graduation in the choice of careers and in community leadership. Service-learning has brought service and community and social action into the academic learning experiences students have when *at* Bates.

During the 2001 academic year, Bates students spent nearly 60,000 hours in service-learning projects in the Lewiston/Auburn community. More than 24,000 of those hours were given in connection with the public schools; the balance served some 140 local nonprofit and government agencies. In the last six years, nearly one-third of the 170 members of the faculty have incorporated service-learning components into courses. Bates students have been involved in over a thousand community-based projects with diverse public and private agencies. In all of these cases, service-learning experiences have been planned around specific learning and performance goals.

The dean of faculty, Jill Reich, leads our efforts. In conjunction with the dean of the college, James Carignan, she encourages faculty discussions and those willing to experiment with service in their courses. A respected member of the psychology faculty, Georgia Nigro (a Campus Compact Ehrlich Award nominee) spearheaded initiatives of action research with her students, using both funds the college made available and external grants. Professor of political science William Corlett, one of the college's most active scholars, and Rachel Herzig, one of our Learning Associates, designed academic experiences for students and community members in contexts that challenged the conventional structures of power and authority and persistently asked the college to be confident enough to be considered "object" by the community—so that our students could hear the critique of our own values. And we asked Peggy Rotundo, a person who had earlier served as a member of our career services staff and who has a solid record of community involvement (in fact, she served on the local school board and is currently a state legislator) to become our service-learning matchmaker. With colleagues Sue Martin, a former school principal, and Holly Lasagna, experienced in other service-learning programs, they have created meaningful opportunities for learning in the community, exploring with faculty their suggestions, and making the details of the arrangements actually work.

The examples tell the more interesting story. At Bates, students and faculty are:

- Providing court advocacy services for clients of a center for abused women.

- Assisting public school teachers in developing fresh approaches to teaching science.

- Tutoring recent Somali immigrants and establishing an after-school program at a housing complex.

- Working on issues of social justice with a neighborhood organization helping migrant farm workers.

- Conducting an inventory of all historical and cultural archival material relating to Lewiston and Auburn, currently housed in public collections locally and elsewhere in the state, as a preliminary assessment for the feasibility study of a possible local museum center.

- Researching and developing a Geographic Information System (GIS) for use by firefighters and civic and environmental project directors in Lewiston and Auburn, saving over $200,000 in development costs alone to the cities.

- Identifying several models of successful mixed-income housing in cities sharing very similar characteristics with Lewiston and Auburn and using the findings as part of a plan to construct or adapt affordable housing in this area.

- Working on problems of housing, safety, and youth activities with a low-income neighborhood association.

- Conducting the final planning and analysis for the Lake Auburn Bikeway, one component of a larger project to construct a pedestrian and bicycle trail system through Lewiston and Auburn.

- Studying a number of models of community arts centers in communities sharing very similar characteristics to Lewiston and Auburn, as part of the planning effort to establish an arts envelope in the community.

LA Excels

Over the last five years the college has worked not only to form partnerships among students and faculty members through service-learning opportunities locally and internationally, but also to structure commitments of strategic community development at the institutional level. While we were instrumental in initiating Campus Compact in Maine, Bates took the additional step of bringing together the many elements of our two cities, helping citizens set aspirational goals as a single community, and then assisting in securing resources that will enable the community to achieve its own future.

Auburn and Lewiston, Maine, are twin cities bordered by the Androscoggin River. Both cities, incorporated in the late 1700s, grew with the investments of the Franklin Holding Company in the early 1800s—investments that created textile mills, support industries, and city infrastructure. During the period of 1830–1850, the cities quadrupled in size, with different cultures and socioeconomic structures. In the late 1800s, rail transportation to Quebec realized the mass immigration of French-Canadian culture to Lewiston.

For over a century, these historical factors placed the two cities in competition, with the river dividing them. Layered on this history of separate cities has been the economic history of northern New England. Lewiston and Auburn, over the last 50 years, have experienced firsthand the demise of the textile and shoe industries—their former dominant economic engines.

Empty mills, high unemployment, a work force inadequately trained for technical or service industry growth, deteriorating downtowns, low educational-level attainment, an outflow of youth, and an influx of vulnerable and transient populations (the combined L/A population is the second largest population center in the state, approximately 50,000) all combined to lower civic aspiration and confidence.

LA Excels was formed to build upon the planning and accomplishments of the existing organizations that had a longstanding interest in addressing systemic community needs. However, it added to the planning by bringing an integrated approach—Lewiston and Auburn would work together. Hospitals, educational institutions, governments, businesses, and the arts would plan and coordinate together, connecting economic and other forms of development. By encouraging the community to take itself to the highest attainable level and by identifying resources that could accomplish projects that no single element of the community alone could accomplish, LA Excels added real value to both cities.

In addition to what has been achieved from the work of city government and federal programs, over $4 million has been realized from private foundations to support educational aspirations, including a new Leadership Institute, which offers opportunities to over 50 local citizens and involves scores of middle-school teachers and students annually. Plans for major physical projects are now underway with private investment, including new medical buildings, a hotel, a performing arts center, the arts education facility (that Professor Kolb's class worked on) and a convention center. Those are projects that will eventually require $120 million or more of investments.

Those participating in LA Excels are committed to civic entrepreneurship to achieve community gains through selective transformative changes based on a common vision. With the college's help, the organization became registered as an independent 501(C)(3). It has a full-time staff (Ms. Rebecca Conrad serves as its executive director) and multiple volunteers and student assistants. It is housed on the Bates campus, and the college lends professional assistance. But it is essentially a community development and action process that is independent of the college. Bates is one partner among others.

There are basically two competing approaches for colleges to use as they consider what their "responsibility to place" can mean. One productive route is to address the needs of the area immediately adjacent to the campus. This has focus and direct benefits. However, it reinforces a model of being an "enclave," a "place apart," but one attendant to its edges. For many institutions in large cities, especially smaller colleges, this may be the only viable approach because of limited resources and the necessity of focus.

The other approach is more diffuse. It may mean becoming a true partner with the community and surrendering power to an inclusive process—a process that will be influenced but not controlled by the institution. Moreover, it is a process that is likely to be extended in duration because it relies on establishing trust. Strategically, this collaborative or partnership model has significant long-term advantages, but it is a consuming and messy process. It requires that what is to be seen as in the best interest of the greater community be seen, ultimately, as in the best interest of the academic institution and vice versa. At Bates and Lewiston/Auburn, we have elected this second approach and are confident regarding its benefits.

Eight-foot fences once marked "Bates College property." It was unclear whether we were keeping the students in or keeping the community out. But the metaphor of an island or the realities of fences are not part of Bates's present or its future.

The goal of LA Excels was that of civic entrepreneurship, moving beyond what can be accomplished by individual groups or agents (educational, business, social, or political), and working in collaboration to succeed beyond what any specific organization or single dimension of the community could accomplish.

The special qualities of the approach, and the opportunities it engenders, have led the Governor of Maine to cite LA Excels as "the most extensive community development project in the history of the state" (J. E. Baldacci, personal communication, 2000). The U.S. Department of Housing and Urban Development has assessed it as "among the most integrated community development projects" (A. W. Carriere, personal communication, 2000) they have considered. Such observations are actually challenges, suggesting the potential and the promise of every one of our colleges (especially private liberal arts and sciences colleges) to work with our communities, to bring what we are and *do as academic institutions* to the table for our benefit as well as for the community's benefit, and to do so with the confidence that allows the community to examine the college. The context for learning can thus be truly communal.

Remaining "a place apart," Bates is now also "a place connected" with multiple, deep, and persisting linkages to the Lewiston/Auburn community. And we are aware that we are rooted within a community that reciprocally has responsibilities to the college and that must value what Bates brings and what it offers in order to achieve its potential as a community.

The Center for Community Partnerships

Recently, Bates College created the Center for Community Partnerships, thus consolidating the key existing components of the college's academic and service missions, activities involving community collaboration, service-learning, and applied research in a community context. Through the center we will now provide opportunities for enhancing the ongoing, and mutually beneficial, engagement of Bates and the area community. The center is intentionally structured within the overall academic mission of the college, and it has direct access to a Trustee Committee of the Board as well as a Community Partnership Advisory Board populated primarily by community citizens. The center's organization reflects the triumvirate of the elements of our academic mission: teaching, research, and service. The center adds by coordinating all service-learning opportunities and by providing funding for those opportunities.

Research and scholarship, sponsored through the center, provide a focus for work applied to needs of the community that may extend beyond conventional disciplinary boundaries. Applied research, internships, practical and service-learning projects are supported (often from foundation funds administered by the dean of faculty) for both faculty members and students. Where possible, applied research projects are directly connected to the community agenda—the projects being selected from a specific set of identified research needs that can best support established initiatives in the community.

The applied research projects, student internships, and other practical experiences require a great deal of faculty time and effort to be devoted to problem formulation and the selection of appropriate methods of investigation. Faculty and staff work with students and the external agencies to develop implementation, analysis, dissemination of results, and presentation of recommendations. In these ways, the center provides meaningful assistance. By so doing, the college is adding social value to the community from its strengths as an academic entity.

We are about to appoint the first director of the center, following a national search. Administratively, staffing for the center brings together all of the dispersed resources that have been, heretofore, expended for service-learning, internships, applied and action research, student practica, student thesis support, volunteer projects, and civic responsibility programs at the college.

One outreach vehicle of the center will be seminars for students and for external agents, which focus on applied research and provide essential training to students on the methods and techniques of designing and implementing applied research projects and the methodologies of assessment and evaluation used in that research. The seminars address the key issues involved in connecting ideas learned in the classroom to action in the field, in dealing with logistics, and in assessing and disseminating results in a variety of venues.

We have also gathered within the Center for Community Partnerships a new professional category of staff—a set of professionals to augment student and faculty applied research, service, and selected student thesis work. We are one of a very few colleges requiring a thesis or culminating portfolio (at Bates the requirement has been in place since 1917). We view the thesis as a core element of undergraduate education. To enrich this special experience of close student and faculty interaction and to make possible the link of such inquiry to applied contexts, we have added the category of Learning Associates. Usually practitioners of particular methodologies, typical Learning Associates might include a practicing Ph.D. researcher in a nearby medical laboratory who involves our students as part of his research team in neuroscience. These colleagues provide expertise in particular areas of need and interest. While remaining under faculty direction, Learning Associates add value to the student senior thesis, service experience, or applied research. Whether residing on campus, contributing expertise through intermittent visits to Bates, or participating from a distance via electronic networks, some Learning Associates assist students to acquire key research skills and experiences. They provide access to interpretive, creative, practical, applied, or analytical skills, and they help students apply them to their research projects. Community-based organizers and service providers claim academic "legitimacy" through their roles as Learning Associates. Other Learning Associates ensure that the work of our students in the community is fully and effectively integrated into the mission of the particular agency or organization that is our partner in that work. They create structures and processes for carefully monitoring the student's service-learning or practical experiences; they assist with logistics; they implement recommendations and follow-up activities at the client organization after the student's work has been completed; and they will do other work as our experience with them grows.

We have only just begun to develop benchmarks for the work of Learning Associates as the nature and extent of their tasks and the compatibility of the contractual arrangements are worked out. However, we have most successfully used Learning Associates this past year in the humanities, in environmental studies, in economics, and in the natural sciences. With the assistance of the Mellon Foundation and the Christian A. Johnson Foundation, we are also preparing to gauge the effectiveness of having Learning Associates be prospective liberal arts and sciences college faculty. We would consider hiring graduate students who have completed all of their doctoral work except dissertations. These Learning Associates would be with us for at least a year, *not* teaching but assisting with student theses, exploring service-learning and applied research options with students, emphasizing contributions of methodology, completing their own projects, and seeing the reality of opportunities in a liberal arts context. The gains for them would include becoming experienced in areas of predictable future directions for undergraduate teaching and learning. As a liberal arts and sciences college, we would be encouraging the most able and talented people to be future faculty at our institutions.

Institute for Liberal Education and Civic Engagement

Colleges with experiences comparable to that of Bates might join together with each other and national associations such as Campus Compact to form a national Institute for Liberal and Civic Engagement. Such an institute would not duplicate efforts, because it would be focused on the special missions of residential liberal arts and sciences colleges. It would function as a research institute, examining ways to measure civic engagement and social capital in our college communities. It could help us to develop tools for assessing meaningful results of civic entrepreneurship, and it could serve as an intellectual resource for scholars and practitioners at our colleges. As liberal arts and sciences colleges enable students to study abroad, an institute could reinforce international dimensions of service and engagement by linking our institutions with nongovernmental organizations and with universities abroad. It could guide liberal arts colleges in assessing research models that work in our contexts.

97

An institute could pursue an agenda that seeks to better understand the nature of community responsibility for our educational institutions, why it is in the self-interest of our colleges to be engaged in our communities through service, and what our communities see and value in the relationship. It could develop case studies and benchmarks for successful civic engagement efforts, and it could commission studies in related areas such as understanding the possible relation of service to the *residential* experiences of our students or providing insight into beneficial approaches to the challenges of campus living and the social phenomena our students experience. As a shared enterprise among liberal arts colleges, it could help create meaningful relationships as we learn from each other.

Conclusion

At Bates, our conversations regarding the extent and vitality of liberal learning have led us to include service-learning, applied research, and community partnerships through engagement. We have done so while remaining committed to our academic mission and culture. The result has provided the college with the "grammar" of what we uniquely do and offer. But more broadly, we are convinced that service and community engagement (as inherent in our understanding of ourselves) will amplify rather than distract from our providing the contexts for our students' intellectual, as well as civic, liberation. And this is the core of what liberal arts colleges are about.

Note

This chapter is based on a speech delivered during a Campus Compact/Association of American Colleges and Universities event at Oberlin College, June 4, 2002.

Endnote

[1]David Maurrasse (2001) points to many issues that influence the viability and sustainability of any linkage of educational institutions to service in the community. They include the vacillating community and college power dynamic; the problems and vagaries of communication; the difficulty of assuring continuity and sustainability of efforts once they are begun; the failure to establish broad and deep commitments to campus

and community collaboration through ongoing structures; and the challenge to institutions to offer incentives, professional recognition, and support for the service efforts of faculty and students.

7 | DePaul University: Strategic Planning and Service-Learning

Richard J. Meister
Charles R. Strain

A university that is "urban by design" and committed by its Vincentian mission to serve the poor and the disadvantaged, DePaul University engaged in a strategic planning process that postulated community-based service-learning as the means for bringing engagement with society from the margins of the university into the very core of its educational mission. In building its service-learning program, DePaul developed the distinctive concept of a Ladder of Social Engagement. On the basis of preliminary efforts, the university sought and received an endowment gift from a dedicated trustee. The negotiations over the endowment and the subsequent challenge to match the gift have forced the university to elaborate systematically its underlying strategic plan for community-based service-learning.

Beginning Anew

This New American College would organize cross-disciplinary institutes around pressing social issues. Undergraduates at the college would participate in field projects, relating ideas to real life. Classrooms and laboratories would be extended to include health clinics, youth centers, schools, and government offices. Faculty members would build partnerships with practitioners who would, in turn, come to campus as lecturers and student advisers.

The New American College, as a connected institution, would be committed to improving, in a very intentional way, the human condition. As clusters of such colleges formed, a new model of excellence in higher education would emerge, one that would enrich the campus, renew communities, and give new dignity and status to the scholarship of service. (Boyer, 1994, p. A48)

First proclaimed in 1994, Ernest Boyer's call to create the New American College reverberates in faculty workshops, in national and international conferences, and in the minds of deans, chief academic officers, and university planners who seek to redirect American higher education. Boyer grounded his argument in the histories and traditions of a few select liberal arts colleges and the land grant universities that emerged in tandem with major social reform movements of the 19th century. He deplored the transformation of higher education from a "public good to a private benefit" (Boyer, 1994, p. A48).

DePaul University, like a number of other institutions, was and is propelled by the force of Boyer's vision. A large urban Catholic university of more than 23,000 students in 2002, DePaul came into being with the surge of immigrants at the end of the 19th century and since has retained its original commitment to first-generation college students. Founded by the Congregation of the Mission (Vincentians), a religious order dedicated to serving the poor, DePaul University by necessity has had to blaze it own path in integrating what is means to be a university and what it means to be urban and Vincentian.

In 1996, Richard Meister, DePaul University's executive vice president for academic affairs, launched a university-wide discussion by playing upon the title of Boyer's article:

I believe that DePaul can be the New American University: a model of a university that serves the 'public good'. . . In this university, teaching and learning are primary; scholarship is broadly defined; interdisciplinary work is encouraged; and service to the larger society is part of the mission. . . . Faculty, staff, and students are representative of the larger society. The definition of faculty is also broadened; faculty members are both mentors and academic leaders of

this university, with the responsibility of learning being
shared with staff and students. (Meister, 1996, p. 3)

Meister, an urban historian, joined DePaul University as dean of the
college of liberal arts and sciences in 1981. Influenced by the events of
the 1960s and Catholic social action movements, he was attracted to
DePaul by its mission and location. Beginning in the mid-eighties, he
became one of the key individuals in leading DePaul University to reflect
on, articulate, and manifest what it means to be Catholic, urban, and
Vincentian. In 1993 he was appointed executive vice president for academic affairs.

Meister's twist on Boyer's argument came just as the university was
preparing for a comprehensive visit by the North Central Association in
early 1997. The university had experienced eight years of planned enrollment growth from 12,500 to 17,000 students. The 1988 ten-year Strategic Plan led to the creation of a large residential campus in Chicago's
Lincoln Park, the offering of professional programs at four suburban facilities, and an innovative collaboration with the City of Chicago to create
a mixed-use facility to anchor the revitalization of the South Loop.

An Urban University

As the university prepared for its re-accreditation visit, DePaul's executive leadership was mapping plans to take the university well beyond its
then current level of accomplishment by distinguishing it still further as a
Catholic university with an urban and Vincentian mission. There was, of
course, a history to this new planning phase. DePaul had always been an
urban university in the sense of its location and in the fact that its traditional constituency came from the urban core. During the 1980s DePaul,
in the words of Richard Yanikoski, had become "urban by design" (1986,
p. 5). Yanikoski discussed a variety of ways through which DePaul was
promoting its urban focus. First, it was increasing the number of courses
with an explicitly urban subject matter. Second, a still greater number of
courses had begun to use Chicago and its institutions as "a living laboratory." Third, at the pedagogical level more students were encouraged to
undertake applied research projects. For example, Yanikoski praised the
"police lieutenant, [a DePaul student who] developed a physical fitness

plan that was put into effect at his station" (p. 7) a student whose assessment manual for future Catholic lay ministers was adopted by the Joliet
diocese, and the student who created "a handbook for judicial aides in
the Illinois Appellate Court" (p. 7). Fourth, he noted that some programs, in an effort to mine the knowledge and talents available outside of
the university walls, had developed reciprocal relationships with key
urban institutions. The associations between the School of Music and
members of the Chicago Symphony Orchestra and the Lyric Opera were
only the most obvious examples. Finally, Yanikoski cited a wide range of
projects, ranging from the Mental Health Clinic to the Theatre School's
"Playworks" series for Chicago's children, which are integral to the education of DePaul students and provide a service to the larger community.
The Small Business Institute, established in the early 1970s, Yanikoski
argued, illustrated this same synergy between traditional research and
engagement with the larger Chicago community. It brought traditional
students together with aspiring entrepreneurs in seminars designed to
teach both how to start small businesses (Yanikoski, 1986).

A Vincentian University

Vincent de Paul, a 17th century French priest, was known for his service
to the poor and the marginalized. His spiritual legacy continues to ani-
mate the efforts of faculty and staff. This influence is referred to as the
university's "Vincentian mission." It is a mission that is shared with only
two other universities in the United States, St. John's in New York and
Niagara. The mission has served as a unifying force within the university.
It unites faculty and staff who inhabit different sides of a religious/secular
border; it creates a shared commitment across ideological lines of difference. Just as DePaul could build upon several decades of scattered efforts
by faculty connecting students with the city, some DePaul faculty had
engaged their students in service long before the term "service-learning"
was coined. For example, within the College of Liberal Arts and Sciences
the newly established Urban Studies major offered experiential learning
courses, and the Department of Religious Studies developed a course,
"God, Justice, and Social Action," that placed students in agencies that
served those in need.

Throughout DePaul's history new layers of meaning have been added to the Vincentian mission. In opening the Academic Planning Retreat in July 2002, Meister phrased the mission in these terms:

> DePaul University's core strength is its mission. This mission, the zeal to make society more humane and just, flows from its Catholic, Vincentian and urban character. It is manifested by its commitment to expand access to higher education and to engage society. And this manifestation distinguishes DePaul University from other institutions of higher education and drives its current success in enhancing quality and insuring its financial vitality. Since its founding in 1898 as St. Vincent's College through today, DePaul University continues to serve new, as well as traditional, student constituencies and to develop the capacity of individuals, communities and institutions to meet the needs of a global society in this Information Age. (Meister, 2002)

During the late 1980s, as the DePaul University community implemented a strategic plan that called for repositioning the university as a national Catholic university and a premier urban university through enrollment growth, it also developed programs that more actively manifested its Vincentian and urban character. This resulted in the establishment of a number of centers and institutes, including the Monsignor John Egan Urban Center in 1994. This center is named for a Chicago priest whose life and work was dedicated to social justice and epitomized DePaul's Catholic, Vincentian, and urban mission. Through the support of the Chicago Community Trust and the MacArthur Foundation, the Egan Center became a catalyst for developing programs and partnerships with Chicago communities and agencies and also operated a large conference center designed to serve community groups. Elizabeth Hollander, former commissioner for planning for the City of Chicago under Mayor Harold Washington, was the first executive director of the Egan Center.

In February 1997, Elizabeth Hollander, who was soon to leave DePaul to become executive director of Campus Compact, convened a group of about 30 faculty and staff to explore ways in which service might be integrated more closely into the life of the university. Interestingly enough, this was a self-empowered committee; it was not called into being by the senior leadership. It genuinely represented a grassroots coalition determined to build upon past accomplishments. Quickly the discussion focused on service-learning as an extension of the Vincentian mission into the heart of the classroom.

The group worked through the spring and then asked the faculty council to devote its one-day June planning retreat to exploring issues related to service-learning. The retreat was held in June 1997 and included over 135 faculty, staff, and students. The issues raised by skeptical faculty at the retreat were precisely those that the committee had been struggling with for five months and that were prominent themes in the national research on the impact of service-learning.

- Are you just giving credit for experience? In other words, "where is the learning in service-learning?" (Eyler & Giles, 1999).

- Are you helping or hurting the communities that you serve?

- Is service-learning simply a way of sugarcoating social injustice?

- Alternatively, is service-learning held hostage to the ideological proclivities of one faculty group or another?

Having already raised these same issues itself, the committee structured the retreat to address them. Faculty who had been teaching what, in effect, were service-learning courses described their courses and their impact on students. Workshops were held to address the most pressing issues and also to talk about possibilities of service-learning in various disciplines. But a panel of students and alumni who described their experiences with service-learning was the high point of the day. The most important comments by the students and alumni were those that pointed to how service to the community had motivated them to serious academic investigations of the roots of the problems that they dealt with. They emphasized that service-learning required them to draw on the knowledge gained in other courses, thus integrating what the faculty were teaching and what they were learning. This is an ideal that faculty seek but seldom experience. The alumni went on to discuss how these experiences had redirected their career aspirations, leading them to positions in public service organizations.

Strategic Planning and Service-Learning

Throughout the 1996-1997 academic year, the university's executive team—Fr. John Minogue, C.M., who had become president in 1993, Kenneth McHugh, the executive vice president for operations, who had served as vice president for business and finance during the eighties, and Meister—were leading the discussion within the DePaul community on the university's future. As a result the Academic Affairs Planning Retreat (July 1997) and the President's Planning Retreat (August 1997) focused on the articulation and adoption of three *academic* goals that were to form the heart of a new strategic planning process in anticipation of DePaul's 1998 Centennial year.

> Goal 1: To provide all full-time students a holistic education that will foster extraordinary learning opportunities through a highly diverse faculty, staff, and student body (Meister, 1997, p. 1)

> Goal 2: To be a nationally and internationally recognized provider of the highest quality professional education for the adult, part-time student in greater Chicago (Meister, 1997, p. 2)

> Goal 3: To research, develop, deliver, and transfer innovative, educationally related programs and services that will have significant social impact and will give concrete expression to the university's Vincentian mission (Meister, 1997, p. 3)

What is distinctive about this set of goals is that for the first time engagement with society was articulated as part of the *academic* mission of the university.

Though the Vincentian mission was now part of the university's academic mission, it was not at all clear how Goal 3 would be connected to Goals 1 and 2, that is, the goals that focus on the traditional degree-granting programs of the university. The underlying truth was that DePaul's previous engagements with the larger urban society had remained marginal to the regular academic business of the university and involved few faculty and students. This needed to change if Goal 3 was to take off.

Riding the crest of its successful June retreat, the committee working on service-learning was able to argue at a President's Retreat that community-based service-learning should be included as one of 12 initiatives that would support the three goals precisely because it could function as a linchpin joining Goal 3 to Goals 1 and 2. Service-learning pedagogies were one way in which service to the community could be brought in from the margins.

Having gained consensus on the broad outline of the university's strategic plan, the executive team asked Charles Strain, professor of religious studies, to direct the process of implementing the plan. Strain's charge was to establish and coordinate the work of the committees in establishing goals, measurements, costs, and timelines for each of the 12 initiatives. The final draft of the strategic plan was discussed and finalized during the planning retreats held in summer 1998. Vision 2006, an integrated plan, linked the three academic goals and 12 initiatives to financial planning, facility planning, and enrollment planning. Enrollment growth was the driver of the strategic plan that had repositioned DePaul University between 1988 and 1998. It is no accident that the two largest Catholic universities in the United States are urban and Vincentian. Providing access to education, especially for first-generation students, has been for more than 100 years the educational mission of the Vincentians, that is, the educational manifestation of the commitment of service to the poor. Vision 2006 called for DePaul University to continue that mission through increasing enrollments to 24,000 students. Thus, the two major manifestations of DePaul University as a Vincentian university are its commitment to access to degree programs and its commitment to engaging the larger community.

It was not hard to reach the consensus that DePaul University needed an office or infrastructure to develop partnerships with community organizations, to offer workshops for faculty, to find placements appropriate to the individual courses, and to handle the logistics of placing students and supervising them on site. The committee looked at the organizational structures and best practices of pioneer programs in service-learning across the country. It began to build on existing relationships and partnerships with community organizations that had been established by some of the DePaul centers and institutes and by University Ministry in its many service programs.

The Office of Community-based Service-Learning (CbSL) opened in November 1998 with Laurie Worrall, an associate director in DePaul's Egan Urban Center and chair of the service-learning committee, assuming the role as the first director of the office; Tom Drexler, who headed the DePaul Community Service Association for University Ministry, became associate director. To support this initiative that linked Goals 1 and 2 with Goal 3, the university made a sizable commitment to sustaining CbSL, and the Vincentian community at DePaul made available two floors in their campus residence to provide office and classroom space for the program.

Designing the office as a support structure was actually one of the easier challenges of the planning process. DePaul is on the quarter system with the typical course lasting for ten weeks plus examination week. The distinctive challenge of a compressed academic calendar forced the planning task force to think deeply about how to organize service-learning at DePaul. The task force was well aware that short-term service involvements could, in fact, have deleterious effects on students. Without adequate time to process students' reactions to their service involvement, faculty could well end up reinforcing negative stereotypes. Likewise, faculty with strong connections to community organizations worried that DePaul moving in and out of communities would provide the people that would be served only with lessons in abandonment. DePaul's own version of the Hippocratic Oath—"First, do no harm"—became a mantra in the committee's deliberations.

So the planning group decided very early to work deliberately with a limited number of partner organizations developing a variety of continuing and layered relationships. While a given course, offered on a two-year cycle, might place students in an organization for only one quarter out of six, the office would do its utmost to ensure a DePaul presence each quarter. The committee decided early on—and the office has been working diligently to make this work—that it would combine "low-end" with "high-end" service placements. Undergraduates might in some cases offer limited skills and, in fact, learn more from the experience than they contributed, but the office would strive to provide a partner organization also with faculty and students who possessed higher levels of skills. For example, students in DePaul's College of Computer Science, Telecommunications and Information Systems have worked on software design projects for community organizations. Similarly, marketing majors have developed marketing plans for community organizations. Students in DePaul's Master of Public Services Program have worked in classes with community organizations to develop multiple strategic plans that the organizations could mine for ideas in shaping their own grassroots planning process. Consciously pairing these kinds of high-end service-learning projects with undergraduates doing tutoring projects would create a "balance of payments," as it were, so that DePaul was not exploiting community organizations to enhance the learning of relatively untrained undergraduates.

The most ambitious of DePaul's attempts to provide a high-end benefit to its community partners is the work of the Center for Community Technology Support (CCTS). DePaul has a number of government grants supporting "digital divide" projects in conjunction with local community organizations and schools. There are also, as mentioned above, a number of service-learning courses within the School of Computer Science, Telecommunications and Information Systems that provide assistance in software design and development. Yet who will perfect the software after the course is completed, and who will provide maintenance and updating after the grant funding has been exhausted? Those are the gaps we hope CCTS will fill. DePaul wants to assure its community partners that it will stick with them beyond the brief life of a ten-week course or the limited duration of a grant-funded project.

If the planning task force was forced by the constraints of DePaul's own academic calendar to think more creatively about the nature of its community partnerships, it also had to be equally deliberate in thinking about the impact of a ten-week experience on its students. Those faculty members who had led short-term immersion courses knew just how quickly those seemingly transformative experiences could evaporate. However, one thing leapt out of the comments of the alumni and students at the June 1997 retreat. They had pieced together their own developmental "majors" in community service, combining traditional course work inside and outside of their conventional major with service-learning courses, service opportunities through University Ministry, self-designed internships and even study-abroad opportunities involving service-learning. The fact that some of these alumni had moved rather easily into careers in community service was a testimony to their ingenuity. So the planning task force asked itself how DePaul could become much more intentional about creating linked opportunities so that there might be developmental paths weaving through curricular and cocurricular learning opportunities. At each level the student would take on greater responsibilities for social engagement. The task force began to call such developmental opportunities "Ladders of Social Engagement." Putting such ladders into place might obviate the tendency of short-term, single-shot experiences with service to evaporate; it also might counter the tendency for service-learning classes to be isolated experiences in traditional curricula. One version of the ladder looks like this:

Freshman Year

- Participation in a "service enhanced" section of an Explore Chicago course (Explore Chicago is offered as part of the First Year Program; the "service enhanced" section introduces the student to the practice of service-learning.)

- Join faculty-student team for Vincentian Service Day

Sophomore Year

- Begin Community Service minor with "Perspectives on Community-Service" course

Junior Year

- Continue Community Service minor

- Student Coordinator located in Steans Center

- Summer internship in community-based organization

Senior Year

- Community Coordinator/peer supervisor located in community-based organization

- Internship course to complete Community Service minor

Several aspects of the above schema are noteworthy. First, it builds upon possibilities for creative interchange between noncredit service opportunities and service-learning opportunities. This has led to extensive collaboration between University Ministry that coordinates service opportunities and the Office of CbSL, the ladder includes service-learning opportunities that run the gamut from courses that entail a minor involvement with service ("service enhanced" courses) to full-fledged service-learning courses (minimally 25 hours of service per quarter) to longer term internships (100+ hours). In every case, the program emphasizes the importance of the in-class reflective component to achieving the cognitive and affective goals that service-learning courses typically set. Third, because 79% of DePaul students work part time or full time to support their college education, the office created "learn and earn" opportunities, including student coordinator and paid internship opportunities. Fourth, as the above schema indicates, the Ladder of Social Engagement concept led Strain, Worrall, and key department chairs within a year after the inauguration of the program to develop an interdisciplinary community service minor, joining courses in the theory, ethics, and group dynamics of community-based organizations and movements with cumulatively demanding experiences of social engagement. And finally, the executive vice president for academic affairs had to find the funding to support this ambitious expansion of service-learning and had to encourage the collaboration and cooperation of many academic and student support units within the university.

While struggling to implement the ladder, Meister, Strain, and Worrall realized that students needed to be involved before they entered DePaul. So, working with Enrollment Management, the Office of CbSL developed a community-service scholarship program. This program deliberately focused on above-average high school students who had strong backgrounds in service and a significant potential for leadership but who might not qualify for an academic merit scholarship. As part of their commitment in return for the scholarship, these students will enroll in the community service minor and fulfill a service requirement each quarter. In fall 2002, 22 community service scholars took their first steps up the rungs of the ladder.

While some of the special challenges in developing a service-learning program were evident in the planning process, the solutions were not always so evident. The evolution of the Ladder of Social Engagement both in theory and in practice extended well beyond the initial planning stage. Many of the program directions that are sketched here emerged only after the Office of CbSL had been well established. Besides grappling with challenges, the office also took advantage of opportunities. For example, the core curriculum for undergraduates included a junior year experiential learning requirement that could be filled by service-learning as well as study abroad or traditional internships. This enlarged the initial base of interested students. But there were opportunities that the planning process had not anticipated, like the strong interest among students in DePaul's adult college in participating in service-learning courses. Meeting the challenges and grouping the opportunities, the office grew at a phenomenal pace. In 1998-1999 it supported 15 courses placing just over 300 students. In 2001-2002 it supported 74 courses placing almost 1,200 students. The office has worked with 161 community-based organizations during this period.

Assessing the strengths and weaknesses of the program while simultaneously building it has presented special challenges. The Office of CbSL has been aided through a close collaboration with faculty and graduate students from the psychology department in the development and testing of survey instruments and analysis of the data. To make sure that all aspects of the program are evaluated, students, faculty and community supervisors provide feedback on the achievements of each course and the performance of the office. Careful analysis of quantitative and qualitative responses from community leaders has shaped the evolution of our partnerships (Ferrari & Worrall, 2000).

Focusing on the learning in service-learning, the office measures the contribution of each service-learning course to five of the ten university learning goals. The contributions of the ladder to student development are tested by comparing the persistence, GPA, and graduation rates of students who have taken 1) no service-learning courses, 2) one course, 3) several courses or 4) the complete community service minor. Community service scholars all take the Cooperative Institutional Research Program survey on entering DePaul to provide baseline data. As these students move up the ladder and into the world of work, the office will track their responses to a DePaul graduating student survey and alumni survey in order to discover what changes have occurred during college life and whether these changes persist over time. Following the university's guidelines for assessment of all academic programs, the office examines each year actual student performance across selected courses in achieving a particular learning goal.

Roles of the Executive Vice President for Academic Affairs and the Associate Vice President for Academic Affairs in Strategic Planning

In 1997, Strain took on responsibility for implementing the strategic planning process. Throughout the process he worked with Meister, who identified the funding to support the initiatives, set fiscal constraints, approved drafts of plans, and repeatedly articulated the vision that underlay the three goals. The overall plan, Vision 2006, became finalized in 1998. Meister, in short, was the gyroscope keeping the entire process on course. Strain worked directly with the 12 task forces and their faculty and staff membership. He constituted a feedback loop between Meister and these task forces but also a goad to keep them working on schedule and within the constraints set by Meister. This collaboration was very successful. From 1997 through 1999, the university created forums and workshops for faculty and staff to discuss, react to, and advise on Vision 2006 and its implementation. The board of trustees endorsed enthusiastically Vision 2006 based on the work of the task forces and the university's early success in meeting financial and enrollment goals. The CbSL initiative was the first of the planning initiatives to be completed and accepted by the senior leadership. In particular, this initiative resonated very positively with the members of the board of trustees.

In fall 1999, a vacancy in Academic Affairs led Meister to appoint Strain as associate vice president for academic affairs. Strain had been working with the newly formed Office of CbSL in weekly staff meetings to get the fledgling program off the ground. As a result, Meister included the supervision of the Steans Center in Strain's areas of responsibility. In 2002, Strain assumed direct administrative and financial responsibility for many of the civic/social engagement projects, such as the Egan Urban

Center, the Center for Centers (physical space shared by the three largest centers), and the Council of Centers and Institutes.

Endowing Social Engagement

Over a number of years, Meister had built an especially strong relationship with a Chicago banker and philanthropist, Harrison Steans, who came to chair the board's academic affairs committee. Steans's contact with DePaul University began in the late eighties through his request for support for the I Have a Dream Program that his family sponsored. Meister, then dean of the College of Liberal Arts and Sciences (CLA&S), assisted in arranging for the program to have the use of classrooms and recreation facilities for its summer program. This led Harrison Steans to become a member of the CLA&S advisory council and then a very active member of the board of trustees. As a Presbyterian and a believer in stewardship, Steans found that DePaul University's Vincentian mission complemented his values. His family's continuing commitment to civic engagement, including the sponsorship of a charter school in an inner city neighborhood, was and is substantial. As the planning on service-learning was proceeding, Meister discussed with Harrison Steans a possible endowment gift. In late fall 1999, Meister, Strain, and Worrall made a formal presentation to the Steans family to endow the Office of CbSL.

Modeling good stewardship, Steans provided significant initial program support and made quite evident that he wished to test the management of the office to see whether it would accomplish its initial goals for program development before he would commit to an endowment gift. Steans pushed still further by insisting that the university articulate not only how the office would evolve over five years but also how any endowment would be leveraged to have an impact on the university as a whole and particularly on its commitment to Goal 3 and civic engagement. Finally, Steans insisted that the university would need to demonstrate alumni support for the concept of service-learning.

Over the next year and one-half, the working relationship that Meister and Strain had built during the strategic planning process carried over into the elaboration of a plan for the five-year growth of the Office of CbSL and for establishing its leadership role in the university's overall commitment to social engagement. Meister, Strain, Worrall, and key development staff built the case for an endowment based on:

115

- Substantiation of faculty and student involvement in numbers that significantly exceeded initial expectations.

- A five-year plan for growth in numbers of faculty, students, and courses involved and in the variety and scope of the programming.

- An articulation of the concept of a Ladder of Social Engagement and examples of students who had successfully climbed it.

- A plan for leveraging endowment support to broaden its impact beyond the programs of the Office of CbSL.

This last point was the most difficult to develop and, to his credit, Harrison Steans applied consistent pressure by insisting that this part of the plan be fully elaborated.

In part, the pressure was a challenge to match a $5 million endowment of a newly named Irwin W. Steans Center for Community-based Service-Learning (named for Harrison Steans' father) with an equal amount of fundraising. In response, the university argued that no *single* center, however crucial to the linking of Goals 1 and 2 with Goal 3, could have the transformative impact desired by both the university and the donor. Instead, change would need to come from *multiple* centers and programs within the university, each with its own community partnerships and programs for engaging faculty and students. Most of the challenge gifts, the endowment plan argued, should go to support the work of these centers of engagement. To qualify as meeting what we called the "Steans Challenge," the funded program would need to do three things: 1) provide a direct benefit to a community or community organization, 2) engage faculty and students in a learning process connected with a community partnership, and 3) loosely coordinate its efforts with the Steans Center. It was obvious that tight control of efforts to engage society would not work in DePaul's fairly decentralized culture. It would quash the entrepreneurial spirit that DePaul cultivates. It was also clear that the Steans Center had its hands full in meeting the growth targets outlined in the endowment proposal. To funnel all of DePaul's efforts to link faculty and students with community partners through a single center would only limit involvement and restrain creative energy. Again, Steans and his family demonstrated great flexibility in both their understanding of the DePaul culture and their willingness to work with the university in supporting its commitment to Goal 3. In May 2001 the final terms were agreed upon and the university office became the Irwin W. Steans Center for Community-based Service-Learning.

Working with the Steans family forced Meister and Strain in conjunction with Worrall and Steans Center staff to think strategically about the concept of the Ladder of Social Engagement. The endowment itself has allowed the Steans Center to pilot programs and to experiment with building the ladder. Responding to the Challenge, DePaul has paid particular attention to finding internal and external funding for the initial and culminating rungs of the ladder.

In December 2002, a gift from the McCormick Tribune Foundation endowed an internship program within community-based organizations that secures the uppermost rungs of the ladder. The Steans Center has also focused attention upon the pathways that will lead students to the ladder. The Community Service Scholarship, inaugurated in fall 2002, is one such pathway that obligates the student recipients. The Steans Center has also established its presence in the first year program through "service enhanced" courses that give students and faculty a preliminary taste of service-learning pedagogy. Finally, DePaul will link, as other institutions have, students eligible for federal work-study support to communities through the Steans Center, and it will develop the programming to ensure that critical thinking develops in tandem with service-learning.

Would DePaul have moved in these directions without the endowment? Certainly the concept of building a Ladder of Social Engagement predated negotiations with the Steans family. Just as surely, there would be numerous missing rungs to the ladder and not only because of a lack of sufficient financial resources. The combined process of reaching an agreement on the goals of the endowment and of the subsequent challenge forced the key planners to develop a systematic and strategic approach to building the ladder and to civic engagement. Simultaneously, DePaul learned how helpful a close collaboration with a sympathetic prospective donor can be in articulating the connection between a gift in support of a specific program and the larger strategic goals of the university. Without the endowment, community-based service-learning would have spread throughout the university. There was a strong cadre of supportive faculty from the start. However, it is doubtful that what has become the Steans Center for Community-based Service-Learning would have had the catalytic effect that it has had in stimulating other centers and institutes to rethink their commitments to social engagement apart from the endowment and the Steans Challenge. DePaul had made a significant advance in understanding how Goal 3 could be integrated into the life of the university and how a gift to one office could have ripple effects throughout the institution.

Joining the Global and the Local

The planning process that led to the endowment of the Steans Center spurred further thought about how efforts to promote service-learning could work in tandem with other learning experiences. A good example of this is the Fund for the Improvement of Post-Secondary Education (FIPSE) grant supported project, "Bringing It Home: Linking Foreign and Domestic Study through Language Immersion and Service-Learning."

Generation after generation of college students have had the experience of taking one or two years of a language in college but never achieving even a modest fluency in conversation. Those who have achieved such fluency in almost all cases attribute their success to a study-abroad immersion experience. Because many of DePaul's students struggle to afford a college education, semester- or quarter-length study-abroad programs are out of reach for a good proportion of our student body. Additional financial aid is only marginally helpful, since study abroad for a quarter often means quitting the job that is keeping one in college. Consequently, short-term (two to three weeks) study-abroad programs have become very popular at DePaul. However, the impact of such trips in terms of language acquisition is negligible.

Staff from the Steans Center and the Study Abroad office, with faculty from Latin American and Latino Studies programs and instructors in Spanish, asked how coordinated efforts might overcome the weaknesses of the separate programs. Several preexisting conditions made this effort possible:

• The Steans Center had already developed important connections with community organizations in several Latino communities in Chicago.

- The Study Abroad program has two short-term experiences in Latin America, one in Sonora, Mexico and one in El Salvador, that focused on issues of global justice and injustice.

- The Latin American and Latino Studies program had already integrated service-learning into its core courses.

What if we could link service-learning with Spanish language classes, a short-term immersion experience in a Latin American country and an intensive internship experience in a Latino community? Would a conscious combining of global and local learning experiences aid in language acquisition? A short excerpt from the Steans Center's FIPSE proposal neatly summarizes the goals of the project:

> This pilot program focuses on Spanish language acquisition in order to test our hypothesis that integrating community work, short-term study abroad experiences, community internships and domestic home-stays into these courses will, in fact, provide a practical motivation for students to acquire a language. Our proposal builds upon a foundation of intermediate level Spanish language courses . . . Integrated into this year-long sequence of language courses will be a short-term study abroad experience in El Salvador or Nogales, Sonora, Mexico and an opportunity for an internship at a community organization in an Hispanic community where students will be required to utilize their emerging language skills. (Worrall, 2001, p. 6)

The FIPSE project illustrates a synthesizing of the service-learning strategic initiative with our international initiative by weaving it into the fabric of the institution. The Junior Year Experiential Learning requirement and the language requirement in the CLA& S embed all three programs—service-learning, study abroad, and language study—in the institution; they each have a structured foundation on which to build. Yet each, acting alone, while offering students important learning opportunities, can fall short of its learning goals. We have already discussed the shortcomings of quarter-length service-learning courses, but a one-year language requirement or a short-term study-abroad experience also must grapple with obvious shortcomings. Weaving the programs together creates interdependencies as it strengthens each program individually. To be truly successful, service-learning needs to be more than an important option or a discrete requirement within multiple curricula; it needs to become a resource that all sorts of programs will seek out to achieve their individual learning goals.

Planning for Social Engagement: Lessons Learned

In her chapter in the very instructive text, *Colleges and Universities as Citizens*, Barbara Holland (1999b) provides a useful chart that measures the extent of a university's engagement with society along a spectrum from "low relevance" to "full integration" (p. 60). Holland looks at such factors as promotion and tenure practices, faculty and student involvement, and support structures for social engagement. DePaul, in most of Holland's categories, is at level three, "high relevance," one step below the goal of full integration. For example, in the category of faculty rewards and expectations, DePaul does have "formal guidelines for documenting and rewarding service" (Holland, 1999b, p. 60), including service to the community. But the university cannot honestly claim, "community-based research and teaching are key criteria for hiring and evaluation" (Holland, 1999b, p. 60). At DePaul, as elsewhere, engagement with the community, whether in areas of teaching, research, or service, is acknowledged and rewarded but as supplementary to other evaluative measures. First make it over the bar in traditional fashion, our university seems to say, and then boost your ratings through forms of engagement.

One way of describing the difference between these two levels is the distinction between service-learning or other forms of social engagement that are embedded in the institution and ones that are woven into its very fabric. Workshops in service-learning draw enthusiastic faculty from across the university. Service-learning courses are sprouting in majors as well as in the core curriculum. But DePaul will know that a weaving process has truly taken hold when faculty at the very outset of planning, say, a new MBA concentration come to the Steans Center asking, "We know we need a community engagement piece in this concentration. Can you help us develop it?"

The arena in which DePaul is furthest from achieving full integration is in community involvement in the planning for social engagement. On the journey toward reciprocal partnerships with community organizations, the university almost invariably is the one to say, "I'll drive." Holland (1999b) describes full integration in this aspect of engagement as community involvement "in defining, conducting, and evaluating community research and service" (p. 60). While we have a long way to go, there are glimmerings of such mutuality in some of the planning of the Steans Center (e.g., community partners played a role in reviewing and evaluating drafts for our community service minor) and in projects of faculty involved in action research. Most importantly, the Steans Center and several other centers engaged with communities provide forums in which faculty, staff, and students can practice the arts of reciprocity.

DePaul had developed numerous programs to engage society before the 1997 round of strategic planning. These programs had successfully partnered with community organizations, but they had not been successful in involving faculty and students by connecting with traditional degree granting programs. *Persistence* is the first lesson that we have learned from our planning process. The goal of truly becoming "urban by design" was one that Meister adopted by empowering faculty to establish or to become involved with a variety of centers and institutes, from the moment he first arrived at DePaul as dean of the CLA&S in 1981. In the early eighties he made possible the establishment of the Institute for Business Ethics, the Center for the Study of Values, and the Chicago Area Studies Center, as well as created the environment for increasing the number of minority and Vincentian faculty. He believed that such faculty would contribute directly to the university's mission. By the late eighties, through his dean's discretionary funds, he established a scholarship fund to encourage students to take courses that would allow them to do what later came to be called "service-learning," as well as support faculty and centers to become engaged with society. In each case his hope was to find a new expression of the university's Catholic, Vincentian, and urban mission that would not only catch fire but also spread. Perhaps this significant number of relatively isolated and marginally successful efforts laid the necessary foundation for the ones that not only provided important services to communities but also had a lasting impact on the university itself.

As we said before, the planning for community-based service-learning was *organic* in the sense that it grew *in both* a bottom-up and a top-down fashion. It was, in fact, the coalescence of forces in *both* directions that propelled the service-learning initiative forward and led to its successful completion.

A third factor that led to the significant expansion of DePaul's efforts at engagement beyond initial plans was the presence of an *external spur* in the form of both the opportunity for an endowment gift and the challenge that came with it. The potential to accomplish something beyond what the university could reasonably expect to do, given limited internal resources, led a planning team to elaborate concepts, like the Ladder of Social Engagement, and to actualize them in ways that broke loose of the constraints of more pragmatic planning.

An external spur can conceivably take many forms: a challenge gift to the institution from a group of committed alumni, a joint project with a local community organization to pursue grant funding, even the promise of a mentoring program for student interns from alumni and community leaders in the not-for-profit sector. In other words, whatever can be pointed to as enlarging the possibilities for action beyond the predictable constraints of the university's process of resource allocation can become an external spur.

A fourth factor in our planning was the effort to *embed* forms of social engagement in the more traditional programs of the institutions: creating an office of community-based service-learning; building the program by taking advantage of a junior year experiential learning requirement; developing and gaining college approval for a community service minor; inventing a community service scholarship program. All of these efforts ensured a continuing presence of social engagement beyond the waxing and waning of the enthusiasm of individual faculty members. Persistence in an organic planning process that seeks to embed forms of social engagement within traditional programs and structures and that responds to external challenges and opportunities characterizes what DePaul has done successfully.

What we have done well flows from what we have become as a university over many decades. Ernest Boyer spoke of "clusters" of new American colleges that together would create "a new model of excellence in higher education" (Boyer, 1994, p. A48). Perhaps we should begin to expect that within those clusters will be a healthy diversity. No single form of social engagement fits all, and no university can do all forms well. The variant forms within the new model will spur its evolution, just as the new American college or university will challenge the reigning but limiting assumptions that govern higher education today.

8 | Indiana University-Purdue University Indianapolis: Advancing Civic Engagement Through Service-Learning

Robert G. Bringle
Julie A. Hatcher

This chapter is a case study of the development of service-learning and civic engagement at Indiana University-Purdue University Indianapolis (IUPUI) and specifically focuses on the leadership role of the dean of the faculties (provost). Holland (1997, 1999b, 2000) identifies seven key organizational factors that support the development of service, service-learning, and civic engagement in higher education (i.e., mission, organizational structure, faculty involvement, promotion and tenure, student involvement, community involvement, and publications and university relations). Each of these is explored by describing the strategies used at IUPUI and by identifying implications for chief academic officers to further advance service-learning and civic engagement.

Indiana University-Purdue University Indianapolis (IUPUI) takes its role in the community seriously. Forged in 1969 from a partnership between the two major public institutions in the state, IUPUI is located in the metropolitan center and state capital of Indiana. Comprised of 22 academic units, with heavy representation from professional schools (e.g., engineering, law, medicine, nursing), this commuter campus provides highly diversified certificate and degree programs to over 29,000 full- and part-time students. The strong emphasis on professional training has supported a long tradition of community involvement across teaching, research, and service. During the past ten years, initiatives focused on service-learning have provided opportunities to broaden the civic agenda.

Since 1993, with the formation of the Office of Service-Learning (OSL), the dean of the faculties, who serves as the chief academic officer (CAO), and the equivalent of a provost at many institutions, has made a number of strategic decisions to support service-learning and promote a more engaged campus. The CAO has recruited capable faculty and staff leadership, appointed campus-wide committees to advance the work, designed the organizational structure to sustain campus-community partnerships, and reallocated institutional resources to support civic engagement. This has been critical to the success of service-learning over the past decade and the emergence of civic engagement as an area of scholarly work and institutional character. As a result, the campus was recognized by *U.S. News & World Report* in September 2002 as having an exemplary program in service-learning.

Multiple interventions have been made under the academic leadership at IUPUI to stimulate the engaged campus. Based upon the work of Holland (1997, 1999b, 2000), seven key organizational factors that support the development of service, service-learning, and civic engagement in higher education (i.e., mission, organizational structure, faculty involvement, promotion and tenure, student involvement, community involvement, and publications and university relations) are used to organize the case study of IUPUI. Implications for chief academic officers are identified to advance service-learning and civic engagement on other campuses.

Mission

A serious consideration of mission can provide a basis for institutional development of civic engagement to support service-learning, and a widely understood mission statement can constitute a covenant for the institution to act upon its commitments (Holland, 1999b). The campus Mission, Vision, and Values statement asserts that IUPUI is a campus with a clear mission to "serve as a model for collaboration through *partnerships with the community*" [italics added]. The executive leadership established the OSL in 1993, through the reallocation of campus resources, as a way to act on the campus mission by working with faculty to design service-learning courses and create a culture of service on campus.

Service-learning is defined at IUPUI as a

> course-based, credit bearing educational experience in which students (a) participate in an organized service activity that meets identified community needs, and (b) reflect on the service activity in such a way as to gain further understanding of course content, a broader appreciation of the discipline, and an enhanced sense of personal values and civic responsibility. (Bringle & Hatcher, 1995, p. 112; see Zlotkowski, 1999)

This definition recognizes service-learning as a curricular strategy and contrasts with other approaches that include cocurricular and voluntary community service in the definition of service-learning (e.g., Jacoby & Associates, 1996). Service-learning is valued as an academic enterprise at IUPUI, and the OSL, under the leadership of a faculty director, reports directly to the dean of the faculties.

In fall 2000, the IUPUI Civic Engagement Task Force was formed by the dean of the faculties and the vice chancellor for planning and institutional improvement to prepare for the campus's ten-year accreditation through North Central Association. Civic engagement was selected by academic leadership to be one of two areas of self-study to best represent campus mission for the accreditation review. The Civic Engagement Task Force was asked to examine methods to document civic engagement activities (e.g., reports, web displays of information), evaluate the quality of civic engagement activities, and envision a civic engagement agenda for the campus and its surrounding communities. The task force defined civic engagement as collaborative activity that builds on the resources, skills, expertise, and knowledge of the campus and community to improve the quality of life and to advance the campus mission. Civic engagement includes teaching, research, and service in and with the community (see Figure 8.1).

Figure 8.1

Engagement of Faculty Work in the Community

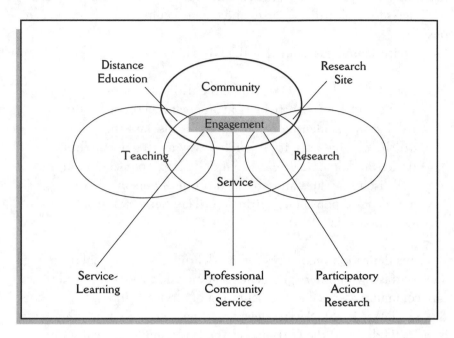

A web-based institutional portfolio documents IUPUI's civic engagement (see www.iport.iupui.edu). A Civic Engagement Inventory captures the many ways that IUPUI faculty, students, and staff are involved in campus-community partnerships, including service-learning, and provides a searchable database for internal and external constituencies. Performance indicators have been identified to document campus progress toward measurable goals for enhancing capacity for civic engagement; enhancing civic activities, partnerships, and patient and client services; and intensifying commitment and accountability to Indianapolis, central Indiana, and the state. Performance indicators have been an integral part of IUPUI's accountability practices. This institutional portfolio enhances the capacity to document the alignment between mission and practice to internal and external constituents, to develop cross-disciplinary programs to address community issues, and to work with the community to set a civic agenda.

The discussion of mission that has occurred as a result of these and other campus initiatives provides an impetus for institutional change in such core areas as the curriculum, faculty roles and rewards, and budget allocations. For example, annual faculty reports and academic unit performance reports now request documentation of service-learning and civic engagement activities. The lasting outcomes of these interventions will still evolve; however, the process has demonstrated that mission can be more than a hollow statement for brochures and that the exploration and development of mission can be a tool for institutional change to support civic engagement and service-learning (Holland, 1999b).

Implications

The following lessons can be learned from IUPUI's experience of focusing on mission:

- A clear mission statement that includes civic engagement is important; but more important is for the CAO to facilitate continued activities (e.g., appointing task force, sponsoring teaching symposium, faculty governance) to develop consensus about ways in which service-learning and civic engagement are congruent with the mission of the campus.

- Campus definitions of civic engagement, professional service, and service-learning should be deliberated, articulated, and used in publicity, campus policies, and forums.

- Academic administrators must ensure that mission, especially as it relates to civic engagement, plays a clear role in annual performance reviews of the campus, academic units, and faculty; internal planning (e.g., committee work, faculty governance, budgeting, promotion and tenure); and external activities (e.g., speeches, publicity, fundraising, developing partnerships) of the campus.

- Professional staff concerned with civic engagement and service-learning should keep the executive leadership, faculty governance, deans and chairs, and community partners regularly informed about how their work is fulfilling this aspect of campus mission.

Organizational Structure

A number of administrative decisions were made by the dean of the faculties over the past decade to create a centralized organizational structure at IUPUI to support service-learning and to advocate for civic engagement. In 1993, the OSL was organized within Academic Affairs to work with faculty on service-learning. In 1994, the Office of Community Service was created in Student Affairs to promote cocurricular community service and campus-wide service events. In 1997, the Office of Neighborhood Resources was established by the dean of the faculties, with a direct reporting line to the chancellor, to promote the sharing of knowledge and resources with communities by strengthening interaction between IUPUI and neighborhoods in close proximity to campus. In 2000, these three offices were integrated to create the Center for Service and Learning (CSL). The CSL places three distinct, yet related, aspects of civic engagement within a centralized unit that can be flexible, responsive, and innovative in addressing community issues. The CSL has a tenured faculty member as director (25% in 1993; 50% FTE currently) reporting to the dean of the faculties because the executive leadership recognizes that faculty leadership is critical to successful growth and development of these initiatives (see Figure 8.2).

The importance of establishing and maintaining the academic integrity of civic engagement was understood by the executive leadership and resulted in the decision to position the CSL under Academic Affairs. Research has found that greater institutionalization is associated with a centralized unit for service-learning that is placed under academic affairs (Bringle & Hatcher, 2000). The CSL has a substantial professional staff (1 FTE in 1993; 9.5 FTE currently), office space in one of the central buildings on campus, and institutional funds to support its core activities. This fiscal arrangement prevents an inordinate reliance on external funds, demonstrates to the campus and the community the level of campus commitment to civic engagement, and provides a secure base to leverage additional external grants for program expansion.

To bridge the gap that can often exist between Academic Affairs and Student Affairs, a unique staff position, Coordinator for Community Service, was created in 1999 as a shared position between the CSL and Student Life and Diversity Programs. The position is jointly funded, and both units provide supervision and input on program development. This professional staff member has primary responsibilities to promote student involvement in cocurricular service and to foster student development through service and service-based scholarship programs. In a short time, this shared position has yielded very positive results in terms of civic par-

Figure 8.2

IUPUI's Centralized Organizational Structure to Support Service-Learning and Civic Engagement

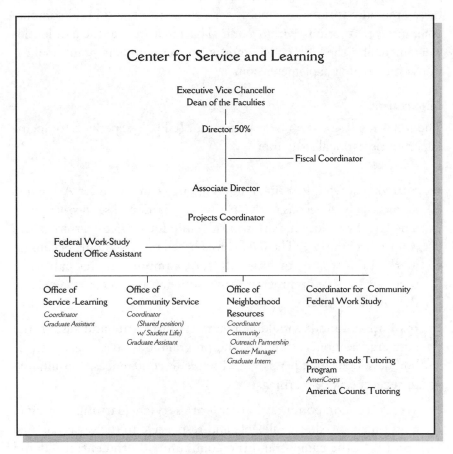

Center for Service and Learning

Executive Vice Chancellor
Dean of the Faculties

Director 50%

Fiscal Coordinator

Associate Director

Projects Coordinator

Federal Work-Study
Student Office Assistant

Office of Service -Learning	Office of Community Service	Office of Neighborhood Resources	Coordinator for Community Federal Work Study
Coordinator	*Coordinator*	*Coordinator*	
Graduate Assistant	*(Shared position) w/ Student Life)*	*Community Outreach Partnership Center Manager*	
	Graduate Assistant	*Graduate Intern*	America Reads Tutoring Program
			AmeriCorps
			America Counts Tutoring

ticipation of students on a commuter campus and serves as a model for collaboration to involve more students in service and service-learning.

The CSL has served an important centralized function in promoting service-learning and civic engagement on campus. However, there have been other decentralized initiatives that have occurred due to an institutional culture that values campus-community partnerships. The dean of the faculties meets regularly with directors of nine centers on campus (e.g., Center for Earth and Environmental Science, Center on Philanthropy, Center for Urban Policy and the Environment, Indiana Business

Research Center) that have civic engagement as a central component of their mission. Additionally, some units (e.g., School of Dentistry, School of Medicine, School of Nursing, Student Life and Diversity Programs) have created positions to support service-learning and build campus-community partnerships within a unit. This replication at the unit level is welcomed, and the CSL collaborates with these units in grant applications and program implementation.

Implications

The following lessons can be learned from IUPUI's experience of focusing on organizational structure:

- Situating service-learning and civic engagement under Academic Affairs is advantageous to the institutionalization of service-learning. The CAO provides important leadership for service-learning as an academic enterprise. The CAO has a broad understanding of campus work and a vision for how different campus entities can work together to develop programs that contribute to a campus culture that values service.

- Institutional funds should be committed to create and sustain the core organizational structures and program initiatives (e.g., curriculum development stipends, travel funds to conferences, consultants) to support service-learning.

- Structural components that support service-learning and civic engagement need to be flexible and responsive to the organizational context of the campus and the community. Both centralized and decentralized initiatives can contribute to campus-community partnership development.

- Both executive leadership and faculty leadership in a centralized unit are critically important to sustaining the institutionalization of service-learning and civic engagement.

- The CAO can develop mechanisms and program initiatives to bridge the gap that often exists between student affairs and academic affairs in service-learning programs.

Faculty Involvement

"Educational programs . . . need champions. Those champions must be found in the faculty if an innovation is to be profound and long lasting. Administrators should not be shy about seeking out faculty champions" (Wood, 1990, p. 53). Recruiting a faculty director for the OSL, and subsequently for the director of the CSL, was an important institutional strategy at IUPUI. The faculty director, in conjunction with the dean of the faculties, has emphasized the importance of scholarly work in all aspects of service-learning. As a result, the CSL has gained national recognition for developing resources, conducting scholarship and research in service-learning, and exploring important issues in civic engagement in higher education. This climate of scholarly work has involved the director and staff in regional and national conferences and projects related to service-learning. Equally important is the active role the director and associate director assume on various campus committees (i.e., Civic Engagement Task Force, Financial Aid and Scholarship Programs, Metropolitan Affairs Committee of Faculty Council, campus-wide Promotion and Tenure Committee, NCA Accreditation Steering Committee, Task Force on Service, University College). Their involvement promotes successful collaboration between the CSL and many other campus initiatives and keeps civic engagement in the midst of faculty discussions.

The success of civic engagement ultimately hinges on involving faculty. Faculty will be interested in developing civic agendas as part of their professional work to the extent that civic engagement adds value to teaching, student learning, scholarly pursuits, and professional contributions. Recruiting faculty to teach service-learning classes is a matter of faculty development and curriculum revision. A wide variety of faculty development workshops have been conducted at IUPUI (Bringle & Hatcher, 1995; Foos & Hatcher, 1999; see http://csl.iupui.edu/faculty-info.html). These workshops are important in developing service-learning classes that are successful for student learning, valuable to community agencies, and satisfying for the instructor, and that adhere to principles of good practice (Howard, 1993). The CSL has no formal control over how service-learning classes are designed and implemented and, therefore, good faculty development activities are the best assurance of quality control. The CSL has a faculty resource library, provides an internal packet of information and *Service-Learning Tip Sheets: A Faculty Resource Guide* (Hatcher, 1999) to interested faculty, and posts information about resources for faculty on the CSL home page (http://csl.iupui.edu/home.html). CSL staff also consult with faculty, review syllabi during course development, facilitate meetings between faculty and community partners, make presentations on service-learning to departmental and faculty meetings, and routinely participate in university symposia (e.g., new faculty orientation, teaching conferences) to support the work of faculty in developing, implementing, and evaluating service-learning courses. Some campuses have developed criteria to designate courses as service-learning courses (e.g., University of Utah, see Zlotkowski, 1999); IUPUI has not done so.

Recruiting faculty for work associated with service-learning and civic engagement is only the starting point. Mature programs need "a different set of interventions . . . to sustain and improve curricular reform" (Bringle, Hatcher, & Games, 1997, p. 46). IUPUI has successfully obtained internal and external resources for faculty (e.g., course development stipends, service-learning assistants, research grants) to further the development, implementation, and evaluation of service-learning courses. The CSL has provided matching funds for faculty to present their work at disciplinary conferences and collaborated with faculty on service-learning research projects. For the first three years, the CAO designated portions of existing curricular development funds specifically for service-learning. The CSL regularly highlights the achievements of faculty both internally and externally through publicity and awards (e.g., Campus Compact's Ehrlich Faculty Award for Service-Learning, Lynton Award for Faculty Professional Service and Academic Outreach).

Collaborating on regional and national projects related to service-learning and civic engagement has been an important intervention to support faculty development on campus. Under the invitation of the dean of the faculties, four faculty members participated in the Kellogg Peer Review of Professional Service project, a national project that resulted in the resource guide *Making Outreach Visible: A Guide to Documenting Professional Service and Outreach* (Driscoll & Lynton, 1999). Three IUPUI faculty members serve on the National Review Board for the Scholarship of Engagement (Driscoll, 2000), which provides a cadre of peers to review and evaluate the scholarship of engagement in faculty dossiers for administrative decisions. Seven faculty have been faculty Fellows in Indiana Campus Compact's program that integrates teaching, research, and service of the engaged scholar and has become a national model for faculty development (Bringle, Games, Foos, Osgood, & Osborne, 2000).

The dean of the faculties has taken additional action steps to further campus discussion of service, service-learning, and civic engagement. These have included asking each dean to designate two faculty to attend a series of campus workshops on documenting professional service, hosting an Indiana University system-wide conference on the Scholarship of Engagement, cohosting with Indiana Campus Compact the National Gathering for Service-Learning Educators, inviting national leaders to campus to consult with faculty and deans, and identifying civic engagement as a topic for the campus-wide Moore Teaching Symposium. Some of these initiatives have required use of special campus funds; others have required no extra funding, simply a redirection of program focus.

Implications

The following lessons can be learned from IUPUI's experience of focusing on faculty involvement:

- Service-learning is the most important way to involve faculty in civic engagement, because service-learning changes the curriculum, involves faculty and students in educationally meaningful service, and contributes to ongoing campus-community partnerships. The CAO and staff need to identify what matters most to faculty on a campus and help faculty help themselves to improve their teaching, student learning, scholarship, and professional service through service-learning and civic engagement.

- The CAO can appoint faculty and staff responsible for service-learning to campus committees to support collaboration across units and to further campus understanding of service-learning and civic engagement. The CAO should be opportunistic in identifying leverage points to develop strong partnerships between service-learning and other campus initiatives and units (e.g., diversity initiatives, general education, first-year experience, assessment of student learning, financial aid, athletics, honors programs, alumni relations).

- Faculty participation in regional and national initiatives will lead to faculty development and advocacy for service-learning on campus.

- Faculty recruitment activities must be complemented with faculty development activities. Centralized units should find ways to support faculty (e.g., grants, travel funds, release time, service-learning assistants) and to collaborate regularly with faculty (e.g., research projects, conference presentations, grant proposals) over time.

- Civic engagement in general, and service-learning in particular, will only be endorsed by chairs, deans, and departments if it helps them meet their academic and scholarly goals (e.g., attracting majors, retention, student learning, faculty scholarship).

Promotion and Tenure

Making changes in the roles and rewards structure (i.e., faculty annual reports, promotion and tenure guidelines) is a challenging, albeit critical, task for the CAO to embark upon in order for service-learning and civic engagement to become campus priorities. Thus, the dean of the faculties initiated a wide range of activities at IUPUI over the past ten years to change the promotion and tenure guidelines and to encourage recognition of a broad range of scholarly activities. Activities focused on professional service, civic engagement, and service-learning have increased the salience of and literacy about an area of faculty work that is not well understood. In 1994, the IUPUI Task Force on Service, jointly appointed by the dean of the faculties and the president of the faculty council, was charged to develop a concept paper on service as a university responsibility. This document was to be used, first, to stimulate discussion among faculty, librarians, and academic administrators and, second, to help make collaborative decisions about recognizing service within the formal advancement structure. The Task Force on Service conducted research on the role and rewards associated with service in each academic unit, gathered information from peer institutions, studied the extant literature on professional service, met twice with the late Ernest Lynton, and submitted the *Task Force on Service Report* to the IUPUI Faculty Council in fall 1996. A subsequent three-year project expanded the campus discussion of the *Task Force on Service Report* to the entire Indiana University system. In 1997-1998, two representatives from each campus of Indiana

University met to discuss the nature of professional service, its documentation, and criteria for its evaluation. In fall 1997, a presentation on the faculty work was made to the chief academic officers of all eight IU campuses. *Service at Indiana University: Defining, Documenting, and Evaluating* (http://csl.iupui.edu/documents/eval.pdf) presents a framework for subsequent discussion and development of the role of service in the mission and practice of each Indiana University campus, provides examples of faculty documentation of professional service, and provides resources for conducting campus-based workshops to continue dialogue and assist faculty in preparing documentation.

As a result of these activities by the dean of the faculties, changes have been made in the faculty annual report format, promotion and tenure guidelines, and unit performance reports. For example, the Faculty Annual Report asks faculty members to indicate if they have implemented service-learning. Promotion and tenure guidelines provide more detail about the types of activities that constitute scholarly service and the types of evidence that can support the evaluation of the work. Unit performance reports ask each school to report on civic engagement activities. Presentations about professional service as scholarly work have been made to the all-university promotion and tenure committee. Each year, members of the all-university promotion and tenure committee receive a modified version of Glassick, Huber, and Maeroff's (1997) criteria for scholarly work and the guidebook *Service at Indiana University: Defining, Documenting, and Evaluating.* These activities must be sustained by the CAO, in part, because the audience changes (e.g., turnover in administrative positions, turnover on committees) and because multiple presentations are necessary to inform and remind key individuals about the manner in which civic engagement can be the basis for scholarly work and how it aligns with institutional mission. Although it is difficult to achieve consensus on promotion and tenure criteria at a highly diverse institution, there is increased latitude among key persons (e.g., deans, chairs, faculty governance, members of promotion and tenure committees) for recognizing civic engagement as scholarly work.

Implications

The following lessons can be learned from IUPUI's experience of focusing on promotion and tenure:

- Faculty promotion and tenure is a central issue to service-learning and civic engagement, and the CAO provides crucial leadership in initiating campus activities that enhance literacy. Promotion and tenure provides a leverage point through which institutional change can occur; however, it takes time and multiple strategies to make changes in the reward structure.

- Centralized units responsible for service-learning must understand and pay attention to the breadth of faculty roles and reward issues on a campus, learn from other campus examples, and advocate for changes in promotion and tenure guidelines and norms that support civic engagement as scholarly work.

- CAOs and centralized units must develop a diverse set of ways of informing the campus community about promotion and tenure issues associated with the civic agenda, including symposia, committee work, workshops, departmental and school meetings, and newsletters.

Student Involvement

Strategies to involve students in service and service-learning must be adapted to align with campus culture. Commuter campuses such as IUPUI face a difficult challenge establishing norms and campus traditions to foster student involvement in the community. Much of this work typically falls under the realm of Student Affairs; however, there are important ways in which the CAO can make resource decisions to support student involvement in service activities. Under the leadership of the dean of the faculties, the CSL has made significant progress towards establishing community service as a distinctive aspect of the educational culture for students at IUPUI through service-learning classes, service-based scholarships, and community-based Federal Work-Study (FWS) programs.

Service-learning classes are offered across schools and levels of the curriculum. Service-learning classes are dual-listed under "Service-Learning" in the schedule of classes, and course descriptions provide information about the nature of the course and the community service that is expected. Service-learning is not a requirement for graduation at IUPUI; to date, only the School of Business requires all students to enroll in a service-learning course (Introduction to Business Learning Communities).

In 1997, the dean of the faculties appointed a committee in University College to explore service-learning for entering students and to make recommendations for a service-based scholarship program (Hatcher, Bringle, & Muthiah, 2002). The Community Service Scholarship program uses $124,000 of campus-based scholarship funds to support students who demonstrate merit in service. Five different scholarships are offered (i.e., Freshman Service Scholars, Community Service Scholars, Community Service Leaders, Service-Learning Assistants, America Reads Team Leaders), and programming has been designed to involve scholars in service-learning, campus-wide service events, conferences, and leadership opportunities. The coordinator for community service works with service scholars and student groups to develop leadership and social advocacy through service.

Consistent with a national trend, employment is central to IUPUI students: Over 80% of IUPUI undergraduates work more than 30 hours per week. The unique combination of conducting community service as employment provides an important way in which students can become engaged in communities. In 1996, the IUPUI chancellor was one of the early leaders to endorse President Clinton's America Reads challenge to involve FWS students to improve reading levels of the nation's elementary school children. IUPUI's America Reads program has some 75 college students providing free tutoring to over 350 children annually. Last year, 17% of FWS funds were devoted to community placements, far exceeding the 7% currently mandated by the federal government. The dean of the faculties has set a campus goal of designating 25% of all FWS positions to community placement sites and ensuring that FWS students are academically successful. A shared position was established in 2001 between the CSL and University College for a coordinator for Community Work-Study to support growth in America Reads, to begin an America Counts Tutoring Program, and to design Hispanic and family literacy programs. These community-based FWS programs are valued as a way to contribute to student academic success and retention towards graduation.

Implications

The following lessons can be learned from IUPUI's experience of focusing on student involvement:

- The CAO must be innovative in identifying campus resources and programs (e.g., student organizations, housing, scholarships, FWS, athletics, first-year experiences) that can become realigned, modified, or expanded to advance civic engagement.

- Service-learning is an important way to involve students in their communities, particularly at a commuter campus where the classroom is so central to student life. However, the CAO and professional staff must develop a diverse set of curricular and cocurricular civic activities for students.

- Professional staff should determine what is most central in the lives of their students (e.g., employment, preprofessional development) and develop programs that start with those motives.

- Bridging Student Affairs and Academic Affairs in systematic ways is important to increasing student participation in service and service-learning.

Community Involvement

Faculty development activities (e.g., workshops, colloquia, newsletters, one-on-one consultation) must attend to the critical role that community partners and reciprocal relationships play in successful service-learning. For example, faculty need to know that community agency personnel may be confused about differences between volunteers and students in a service-learning class. Understanding these differences is enhanced when community persons are involved in the design of the service-learning class and the development of the syllabus. Furthermore, responsibilities associated with orienting service-learning students to a site, providing training and supervision, and evaluating students' behavior and performance need to be clarified. Often, community agency personnel assume co-educator roles either at the site or in the classroom. When a service-learning course is offered repeatedly, faculty often become involved in community sites in additional ways (e.g., professional service, research, volunteers) and community partners become involved in university work beyond the service-learning class.

Designed to extend higher education's participation in communities, a U.S. Department of Housing and Urban Development Community Outreach Partnership Center (COPC) grant supported IUPUI's engagement in the Near Westside neighborhoods of Indianapolis to enhance educational opportunities, economic development, and the neighborhood association. The dean of the faculties serves on the COPC Council, a campus-community committee that oversees COPC activities and envisions future partnership projects. After three years, an evaluation of IUPUI's COPC found reasonable success in the targeted program areas. In addition, however, the study found that a significant campus-community relationship had developed that established the community's confidence that it could access the university and vice versa. The success of establishing a COPC has provided the basis for more civic engagement in these neighborhoods by students, faculty, and staff.

IUPUI has established shared staff positions that have joint responsibilities to both the campus and the community. A staff position in Student Life and Diversity develops collaborations between the campus and four community cultural organizations: Eiteljorg Museum, Urban League, Hispanic Center, and Madame Walker Theater Center. Campus-community committees have been appointed to design programming for each of these partnerships. Additional staff and faculty positions that bridge campus and community are envisioned.

Implications

The following lessons can be learned from IUPUI's experience focusing on community involvement:

- The CAO and professional staff associated with civic engagement should help develop and nurture good community relationships (Bringle & Hatcher, 2002).

- The CAO can select professional staff to communicate with faculty on the importance of reciprocity. High quality service-learning classes should demonstrate reciprocity between the campus and the community in that the service activity is designed and organized to meet both the learning objectives of the course and the needs identified by the community agency.

- A centralized campus unit plays an important role in the early phases of campus-community relationships. A centralized unit can provide clear information on campus units and programs that might partner with community agencies as well as community resources that might be of interest to the campus and instructors.

- The CAO and staff should identify effective means for affirming the value of campus-community partnerships and conducting ongoing assessment of outcomes of civic engagement. Executive leadership, campus staff, and service-learning instructors must regularly gain feedback from community partners about their perceptions of the nature of the campus-community relationship and outcomes of the work from a community agency perspective.

- The CAO must be vigilant for opportunities to use campus-community partnerships to leverage both campus and community resources to address critical issues in the local community.

Publications and University Relations

Appreciation of the unique contributions that the campus makes to the quality of life in communities is important to garnering respect on campus and among community constituencies. A steady stream of internal publicity about all stakeholders (e.g., students, faculty, staff, community agency partners, service recipients) is an important factor in establishing the role of civic engagement in campus culture. As a result of providing recognition, information, and explanation, campus members develop an understanding of the relationship between mission and practice. External publicity is important for the same reasons. Campus identity is established and maintained through the understanding that others have of the value that civic engagement plays in campus life. CAOs can play a key role in developing this appreciation among politicians, community leaders, the corporate community, members of the board of trustees, alumni, members of the media, and the general public. Even more challenging is establishing in diverse audiences the academic integrity of high quality service-learning, professional service, and applied research. Again, CAOs can advocate to internal audiences that value theoretical scholarly activities over applied work (e.g., chairs, deans, promotion and tenure committees) and external audiences that are not always well prepared to understand the academic importance of community work.

IUPUI's web-based Institutional Portfolio (www.iport.iupui.edu) is designed to demonstrate to a wide range of persons (e.g., future students, parents, alumni, legislators) that IUPUI is achieving its mission and has strategies, policies, and procedures in place to continue improving its level of achievement. Thus, the Institutional Portfolio involves more than simply collecting and organizing a presentation of work; it also includes evaluation and progress towards performance indicators, with a view to assuring quality in the three major themes of the campus goals for IUPUI: effective student learning, excellent research and scholarship, and exemplary civic engagement.

Another manner in which IUPUI has publicized its work is through traditional academic outlets. Presentations at academic and disciplinary conferences and consultation with other colleges and universities provide opportunities to reflect on one's work, describe and explain program developments, and exchange information that contributes to continued development. In addition, journal publications, books, manuals, and other resources describe components of the work and conceptually explore and extend that work beyond local accomplishments. For example, as a result of collaboration with Indiana Campus Compact on the Universities as Citizens project, a critical exploration of Boyer's vision of the engaged campus resulted in *Colleges and Universities as Citizens* (Bringle, Games, & Malloy, 1999). This academic work has positioned IUPUI as a collaborator in regional (e.g., Midwest Consortium) and national projects (e.g., National Review Board for Civic Engagement, National Research Advisory Board of Campus Compact, AAHE Consulting Corps) that enhance IUPUI's relationships to other organizations and associations (e.g., Campus Compact, American Association for Higher Education, Community–Higher Education–Service Partnerships project in South Africa).

Implications

The following lessons can be learned from IUPUI's experience with publications and university relations:

- CAOs provide leadership and resources for academic and scholarly work related to civic engagement. Publicity, including academic publications, provides important opportunities for reflection, critical examination, recognition, and increased understanding of civic engagement.

- Multiple audiences warrant using multiple methods for disseminating information on service-learning and civic engagement.

- All stakeholders need to be recognized through formal publicity.

Conclusion

Smith (1998) notes, "There are no market forces reinforcing any institutional interest in accomplishing progress on the civic dimension" (p. 2). This is a significant observation, for if there are no market forces to support civic engagement, then the motives must be found in other realms. Harkavy's (1996) analysis finds the will and energy for civic engagement in how the work can improve research, teaching, and learning; tangible secondary benefits that the institution gains among key stakeholders; and making the morally responsible choice for a campus to contribute to a democratic society.

IUPUI has demonstrated a renewed commitment to a civic agenda since 1993. The decade of work has included different types of interventions and activities, formal and informal discourse on many related topics, and developing and redirecting resources and activities for the campus, the community, and higher education. In approaching this work, IUPUI's CAO has established high aspirations for service-learning and civic engagement to:

- Produce high quality work that reflects good intellectual content.
- Persuade others to be curious about the work's potential.
- Build mutually beneficial campus-community partnership programs.
- Articulate the expanding role of higher education in local communities.

At the heart of this work is the commitment to discuss, envision, and critically examine the implications of Boyer's challenge for campuses to develop and bring dignity to the scholarship of engagement (Bringle, Games, & Malloy, 1999). Ernest L. Boyer (1996b) challenged higher education to connect the rich resources of campuses "to our most pressing social, civic, and ethical problems, to our children, to our schools, to our teachers, to our cities" (pp. 19-20) through the scholarship of engagement. Boyer did not specifically discuss the role of service-learning; however, service-learning has become recognized as a fundamental academic intervention to promote civic engagement and further the public purposes of higher education. We trust that others in higher education, and CAOs in particular, will join Boyer's challenge to bring dignity to civic engagement by taking steps to make it an integral part of the fabric of their campuses and higher education.

9 | Johnson C. Smith University: A New Era of Excellence

Rosalyn J. Jones

Johnson C. Smith University, a small liberal arts university located in northeast North Carolina, has emerged as a leader in the service-learning arena as a result of restructuring the general education program. The revised liberal studies program consists of a core curriculum, complementary studies, and a service component. The president has made faculty development and service-related grant-writing priorities, with a major impact on the sustenance of the university's civic engagement agenda. A Ford/UNCF grant enabled the university to set up a service-learning center, and the center has become a hub for civic engagement.

Civic engagement and education for citizenship are not new to Johnson C. Smith University. Located in Charlotte, North Carolina, with an enrollment of approximately 1,500 students and 89 full-time faculty members, Johnson C. Smith University has been able to create and sustain a mechanism that keeps in touch with the community. The mission of the university is to provide an environment in which students can fulfill their learning, physical, social, cultural, spiritual, and other personal needs while developing a compelling sense of social and civic responsibility for leadership and service in a dynamic, multicultural society. Likewise, the university embraces its responsibility to provide leadership, service, and lifelong learning to the larger community. Its story is similar to other small private liberal arts colleges that have a need to remain connected to the community. Service-learning activities have ushered in a new era of excellence at Johnson C. Smith University. University archives provide tremendous examples of community engagement projects throughout its rich history. As the needs of the community are redefined, however, service-learning is enabling the university to use new voices and new tactics to form new alliances to continue its historical impact on the community.

Tradition of Service

In his commencement address entitled "What Constitutes a Great University," Eugene Armstrong told the Johnson C. Smith University 1936 graduates, "Every university must not remain aloof but concern itself with the solution of the problems in the immediate community and society in general." As early as 1938, the brothers of Alpha Phi Alpha sponsored essay contests on "Education for Citizenship." The brothers of Omega Psi Phi visited churches and schools lecturing on Negro achievement. In 1940, Johnson C. Smith University president Henry McCrorey found that Johnson C. Smith University students responded willingly to the call to assist in adult education in order to reduce the number of illiterates by holding classes in reading, writing, and arithmetic twice a week. For years the university sponsored Sunday school extension classes for the children of the community and offered community language programs in French and German (Parker, 1977). Peace strikes and assemblies took place on the campus during the civil rights movement. Students participated in literacy campaigns, voter registration drives, and protests at bus stations, restaurants, and movie theaters until the laws of segregation came down.

In 1963, the university approved plans to build a $3 million interracial housing project on the north edge of Charlotte. In 1984, Johnson C. Smith University and the Charlotte Housing Authority implemented Project Impact, which provided homes for teens and motivational workshops. In 2003, Johnson C. Smith University is using its Housing and Urban Development community development services to improve 12 neighborhoods in the city's northwest corridor. Throughout the years, the university has been engaged.

A New Era of Service

In 1994, when Jay Leno brought national attention to the new community service program at Johnson C. Smith University on his segment on oxymorons, he cited a newspaper article titled "Johnson C. Smith University wants Volunteering to be Mandatory" (Kelly, 1994). Little did anyone know that the spotlight would remain on that particular program nearly a decade later. Administrators boast today that the service-learning program has carved out a unique niche within the character of this historically black university. It is apparent that the intense planning period for the original service-learning grant is largely responsible for the solid foundation of the existing program. The vision of the president and the concomitant strategic planning by the executive cabinet were the beginning of the renewed interest in civic engagement. The continued support of the Office of the President, the grant-writing efforts of the Office of Development, the leadership of the Office of Academic Affairs, and the cooperation of the Office of Student Affairs have sustained the program. Exemplary program designs and implementation have received local and national accolades. In 1999, a call went out from the North Carolina State Department of Education for a high level of service needed to help close the minority achievement gap; a strong viable service-learning program allowed the university to answer the call in a noteworthy way.

Planning

During the strategic planning process, goals and priorities were set for a five-year period. In the early 1990s the university had as one of its academic goals the revision of the general education program. The vision of the administration was that the general education program should contain components to empower students to become better citizens; in their view, this meant that students needed to be able to have experiences outside the classroom. The development of the service-learning program came about as a direct result of this process.

Johnson C. Smith University's new Liberal Studies Program, a four-year interdisciplinary program that is a radical change in the required curriculum, responds to the changing technologies, emerging need of communities, and evolving ways of designing an environment that will produce a quality of life to benefit all citizens. The program features a

multidisciplinary emphasis on 1) learning how to learn; 2) making connections among historical perspectives, institutions, literacy, literature
and the arts, science and quantitative thought, values and moral reason-
ing, and work and leisure; 3) making self-discoveries; 4) conducting
inquiries into identity; 5) learning about people of other cultures; developing a sense of efficacy and engagement with the underlying concerns of
all humans; and 6) creating community through service. The program
consists of freshman studies, a core curriculum, complementary studies
courses, and a service component. As social problems of our society pro-
liferate and as communities look for new ways to nurture a concerned,
involved citizenry, the university feels that it is important to find the
means of equipping people with the knowledge and experience that will
help them respond as caring citizens who view community service as an
obligation of a liberally educated person.

As early as 1993, countless hours had gone into the structuring of the
new Liberal Studies Program. Teams of faculty met continually to ham-
mer out the content for each new core. The vice president for academic
affairs made faculty development activities in service-learning pedagogy
and methodology a priority. The Liberal Studies director supplied
resources in the form of experts and research material on general education, which led the faculty to Benjamin Barber's ideas about civic engagement. Barber (1991) argued that service in the community service should
be made mandatory. He was opposed to having service as an extracurric-
ular activity or making it a matter of choice. He also viewed civic education to be as important to students as math and science. The faculty
latched on to his words. They discussed his ideas at length. Barber
became somewhat of the "father" of the movement on campus. He literally believed that "volunteering" service should be mandatory. He also
believed that service-learning teaches people how to listen. He felt that it
is about genuine empowerment, the empowerment of citizens, not just
volunteers. Soon the "V" word (volunteering) was banned on campus
and replaced permanently with "community service" and "service-learning."

Similarly, the prophetic words of Ernest Boyer (1990) became a part
of the university discussion and documents:

> All students should participate in community service, to see
> the connection between what they learn and how they live.

There is an urgent need for our students to reach beyond themselves and feel more responsibly engaged. A community service requirement (helps students). . . realize that they are not only autonomous individuals, but also members of a larger community to which they are accountable.

A service program would bring young people into closer contact with neighborhoods and workplaces, and help them understand that to be truly human one must serve. (p. 4)

The president and executive cabinet envisioned a community service requirement for all students, and faculty set out to fashion a program that would satisfy this requirement. This new program dimension would help achieve the goal of educating the entire person. After extensive debate among the faculty, the administration decided that the community service requirement would be phased in with an incoming class of freshmen in the second year after the revised general education program had begun. This service component of the Liberal Studies Program was originally labeled a "nonclassroom experience required for graduation." It was designed specifically to meet the university goals of personal, social, cultural, and spiritual growth, within the mission statement, and for the newly created Liberal Studies Program it would serve to help students develop greater self-esteem and civic mindedness.

It is fortuitous that the Ford Foundation's interest in community service and the university's need for a more coordinated comprehensive community service program converged. Upon the direction of the president, the vice president of development put together a grant-writing team consisting of faculty and staff to write a proposal that would include civic engagement in the general education program. The university submitted the proposal to Ford/UNCF (United Negro College Fund) to implement a service-learning program and it became one of the first Historically Black Colleges and Universities (HBCUs) chosen for funding. The grant afforded the university the time and the resources to plan and to develop a meaningful service-learning program.

There was a clear rationale for the original proposal. Specifically, the problems and conditions which have defined Charlotte's northwest corridor (the community seat of Johnson C. Smith University) include adult illiteracy, teenage pregnancy, drug abuse, lack of elder care, secondary school truancy, low achievement, poverty, lack of significant economic development, high incidence of crime, and the absence of community activities and programs that redirect the energy of "idle" youth.

Upon the direction of the president, the university sent a team to participate in the first Ford/UNCF semiannual conference that was held in Atlanta. The team consisted of the project director, a psychology professor, the associate director of Johnston YMCA, and a freshman at Johnson C. Smith University.

As panelists participating in the workshop, they were able to share their views regarding the need for the development of the program. The psychology professor talked about the need to address economic and social needs within the community surrounding the school. She expressed her views regarding the demographics of HBCUs and stressed that "if the community around the school is strong, the school will be stronger." The associate director of the Johnston YMCA addressed the importance of having other existing agencies, organizations, churches, and schools working with the YMCA because they do not have the financial resources to solve all of their problems. He stressed their need for help in achieving their goals of reaching out to children, strengthening families, and building community.

In his opening remarks at the first Ford/UNCF Community Service Partnership Conference, Edgar Beckham, officer from the Ford Foundation, talked about the reason that Ford was supporting the service-learning initiative. He said, "the foundation is concerned about citizenship in a democracy and how education is training youngsters to be good citizens. Service-learning provides a powerful tool to realize this" (Beckham, 1994). He added that the

> foundation is also concerned about the distorted image of the community service movement, that it is thought to be largely white and middle class. But the impulse towards service is alive and well in communities of color. The foundation wants to fix that image and show that the movement crosses the lines of racial and ethnic divisions. (Beckham, 1994)

In his speech later in the conference, William H. Gray, III, UNCF chairman, said, "HBCUs know their community better than anyone else. The partnership between communities and black colleges is a fundamental linkage that has to occur if there is going to be empowerment and change" (1994).

The conference became the catalyst for program development. Campus engagement in civic life began to take shape as an ethic of the university. The president met with community leaders to discuss strategies for community improvement. Similarly, other university administrators made a concerted effort to coordinate and strengthen existing partnerships with local community organizations and schools. They obtained community needs assessment results from the Northwest Corridor Community Development Corporation and initiated conversations and exchanged letters with the local high school, neighborhood enrichment programs, community agencies, and churches. The university development office worked directly with community organizations to submit grant proposals for community improvement.

Faculty Development

The vice president for academic affairs appointed the service-learning advisory team and worked with the faculty development office to provide workshops and activities to introduce faculty to service-learning theory and best practices.

The work of Dr. Fleta Mask Jackson on service-learning assessment caught the attention of the vice president for academic affairs; subsequently she was invited to describe the "complex process" involved in service-learning to Johnson C. Smith University faculty.

In her essay "Evaluating Service-Learning," Jackson (1993) talks about the impact of service-learning:

> While it is intended to give academic content a basis in reality, its impact goes beyond improving performance on tests and quizzes. It encompasses the content and structure of the courses as directed by the instructor, the interactive dynamics and introspection between students' simulated classroom and out-of-class activities, and the equally profound educational experience gained from agencies and

communities. Ideally, this pedagogy, as a methodical form of consciousness raising, can influence the likelihood that they will engage in a lifetime of advocacy. (p. 129)

Dr. Jackson conducted a two-day faculty workshop with faculty. The first day was spent with the full faculty introducing them to service-learning theory and successful practice. Some of her views were met with resistance from those who believed that research and academic scholarship would suffer under this new pedagogy. The most vocal opponent came from the philosophy department. The second day was spent solely with the service-learning advisory team on development of course syllabi, including assessment and evaluation. After Jackson's visit, "leadership" and "advocacy" became buzz words in the Johnson C. Smith University service-learning program. The team set out to design a program that would develop these skills in the students. They decided that the vertical structure of the new Liberal Studies Program would provide them with the curricular base necessary to do so. The team decided that service activities would be designed to match the maturity level of the student, graduating from freshman to senior years. This steady progression of involvement in community service should prepare students to take meaningful leadership roles in society.

As a result of reading Robert Sigmon's 1994 the essay, "Linking Service with Learning," the service-learning advisory team invited Sigmon to come to the university and conduct a faculty workshop. Of special interest was Sigmon's framing of the four common emphases in the linking of service-learning in private liberal arts higher education:

- SERVICE-learning focuses on the service as primary and learning as secondary.

- Service-LEARNING focuses on learning goals, with service secondary.

- Service-learning acknowledges that each is separate and important, but not linked.

- SERVICE-LEARNING frames the reciprocity issue that all the partners in the experience are servers and served and are teachers and learners. (p. 10)

The faculty's work with Sigmon enabled the team to evolve a fluid definition of what their program emphasis would become. Both the president and the vice president for academic affairs monitored faculty development activities hoping to identify faculty members who were willing to make the commitment to community service activities.

Recruitment of faculty into the service-learning program is a continuous effort. Grant resources have enhanced the recruitment efforts by providing funding for faculty to develop service-learning courses and to attend and participate in regional and national conferences and workshops in order to broaden their understanding and expose them to other program models. Each year, a service-learning curriculum workshop is offered as a component of the pre- and post-school workshops. Faculty members are encouraged to design service-learning courses in their disciplines. They receive stipends for course development.

The president rewards faculty members who write successful grants by providing monetary incentives at an annual grant reward ceremony. This strategy has motivated more faculty to seek out grant-writing opportunities. Grant writing has become a university priority. Deans work closely with the service-learning coordinator to identify faculty who are able to design community impact programs using the service model. The team works closely with the development office to submit quality proposals in response to grant requests. The president makes the final approval of all grants submitted for funding.

The Service-Learning Coordinator

The advisory team played a key role in overall program development. It was responsible for recruiting and hiring the service-learning coordinator and developing the service-learning track of the Liberal Studies Program.

First, the responsibilities of the service-learning coordinator were framed. The coordinator would be expected to 1) establish contact with community agencies, 2) provide faculty and staff with training, and 3) maintain records of student service hours. The coordinator would also work with the Service-Learning Advisory Team to plan and develop the service-learning alternative track.

It was determined that the coordinator must have experience working with community and educational organizations, excellent organizational and administrative skills, and a bachelor's or master's degree. We were also looking for a coordinator who would be a positive role model for students and who would reflect the aspirations the university had for them to become men and women with a compelling sense of civic and social responsibility to the local and world community. After advertising the position locally and nationally, and interviewing several candidates, we found the person that we were looking for. The success of the program has depended largely on having a full-time service-learning coordinator who provides a strong link to the community. The organizational chart of the university was redone to include the position of the service-learning coordinator. The coordinator reports directly to the director of the Liberal Studies Program who reports directly to the vice president for academic affairs. With this organizational change, the service program was given a permanent place in the university.

The original location of the Service-Learning Center was in the student union facility. Administrators felt that it would be more visible and accessible to students. The vice president for academic affairs worked in conjunction with the vice president for student affairs to determine governance of the center. After considerable discussion and examination of governance of service-learning programs at other universities, it was decided that the center should be under the jurisdiction of the vice president for academic affairs. Using the university's organizational structure as a guide, the center was relocated to an academic building. It has remained at that location. Because of its academic link, the location has proven to be an asset to the program's stability and maintenance.

The service-learning coordinator is responsible for supervision of the student-run center. Students are trained to manage the center. They share information with other students regarding the service site menu, facilitate students signing up for service, collect time sheets, and perform other tasks as needed. The center has become a university resource for civic engagement activities.

Because it was built on a strong foundation, the program has been able to maintain its integrity as a quality program when setting up partnerships in the community. The vision of the original crafters of the program has come true in that the service-learning center is a hub of activity on the campus. While the original Liberal Studies Program has been modified to cut down on required hours, the service-learning alternative track remains a strong component of the program. Students take their community service requirements seriously, and service has become an ethic of the university. Assessment results show steady evidence of the positive impact that service is having on the students. The services provided by the center have had a similar major impact on the new era of excellence at the university.

Service-Learning in the Liberal Studies Program

The Service-Learning Advisory Board and the service-learning coordinator developed the alternative service-learning track of the Liberal Studies Program. The planning team contacted programs that had service-learning programs and read selected books, articles, and related literature on community service. They invited colleagues from colleges that had exemplary service-learning programs.

The curriculum module includes core courses (academic preparation), a service and experiential domain (service component), and a domain of integration and evaluation (reflection). Recently, celebration has also been added to the model. Originally, the alternative track of the Liberal Studies Program was conceived in four developmental phases.

- **Phase I. Exploration in Community: Identity**

  In this phase, emphasis is given to providing a series of exploratory service opportunities (clinical observations, short-term projects) that will introduce students to the concept of service-learning.

- **Phase II. Meaning and Growth in Community: Studies in Society**

  In this phase, the student develops skills in organizing and participating with others for action in addressing a community need. The critical element in this phase is working in teams and small groups to achieve stated goals.

- **Phase III. Diversity and Equity: Studies in World Cultures**

  This phase gives students the opportunity to participate in experiences (internships and practica), which nurture self-direction, commitment and responsibility, and perseverance.

- **Phase IV. Commitment and Reflective Practice: Self, Citizens, Planet Earth**

This phase gives students the opportunity to integrate and develop a heightened awareness of the process of self-discovery through service and reflective practice. This phase gives opportunities for the demonstration of leadership in creating a community of learners and responsible citizens.

Two pilot courses of the Freshman Identity core were offered the first year with great success; 60 students participated in the pilot program. They conducted a community needs assessment survey for a community improvement agency, served as tutors and mentors in a local after-school enrichment program, and participated in an oral history project in two nursing homes. Students enrolled in the alternative track of the Liberal Studies Program had higher retention rates when compared to students in the regular liberal studies courses. Similarly, as a result of their civic engagement they exhibited greater attitudinal changes as well as stronger advocacy and leadership skills.

Subsequently, a service-learning component was designed for students who had begun their major courses of study. The curriculum was developed through a faculty development workshop offered twice annually by the Service-Learning Center. Instructors in the area of psychology, health and physical education, and sociology were among the first to offer major-level service-learning courses.

Early Public School Collaboration

The Ford/UNCF Community Service Partnership Project also included a School-College Collaboration involving the local school system. The university was provided with the resources to introduce service-learning theory and practices to selected local schools. The service-learning coordinator and the Ford/UNCF Project director conducted three faculty development workshops for faculty and staff at Eastover Elementary because of their use of the service "Village" concept.

The service-learning coordinator contacted the principal and explained the project; the principal agreed to become a partner. A memorandum of understanding was drawn up between Eastover and Johnson C. Smith University. This agreement was designed to specify the partnership arrangement. Once the details of the agreement were drawn up,

Eastover's principal, Johnson C. Smith University's vice president for academic affairs, and the university's president signed it.

The facilitators used the first workshop to introduce the elementary school teachers to service-learning theory. The education models of Dewey and Kolb were examined and linked to service-learning pedagogy. During the workshop the teachers used the academic preparation, service, reflection, and celebration model to make K-6 lessons come alive.

The other two workshops focused specifically on developing service activities that enhance K-6 curriculum material. They decided to design a project that would have real impact both on their students and on the community. In addition to the Village, they also decided to do an intergenerational project. They decided that the school would "adopt" a nursing home that is in close proximity to the school and design service-learning activities for each grade level. They used concepts discussed in "Young and Old Serving Together" as a source for intergenerational projects guiding principles and best practices (Scannell & Roberts, 1994). At the end of the planning phase, the JCSU/Eastover Service-Learning Project involved all grade levels in two capacities. Four grade levels participated in an outside partnership with the Renaissance Health and Rehabilitation Center. The additional three grades participated in service-learning by providing service to the school through Eastover Village. Projects ranged from first graders serving as pen pals to residents to sixth graders planting flowers for the residents. During the partnership, it became apparent to the workshop facilitators how genuinely interested in service-learning the teachers became once they recognized how useful it could be in making their lessons come alive. As a result, the teachers, the K-6 students, and the nursing home residents became a community of learners.

A High Level of Service

In North Carolina, state tests during the 1998-1999 school year found only 49% of African American students scoring at or above grade level in reading and math tests; 79% of white students scored at or above grade level. Statistics show that African American students have lagged more than 30% behind white students for a long time. The problem has been evident for years, but it became more important with new promotion standards that hold students back who do not pass end-of-grade tests.

Throughout the State of North Carolina in 1999 a call went out to historically black and minority colleges to play a major role in helping to close the achievement gaps in local school systems. The Department of Public Instruction and North Carolina Central University have created a Historically Minority College and University Consortium that collaborates with the community to plan, coordinate, and implement strategies that will narrow the achievement gap in the state of North Carolina. Historically minority colleges were asked to establish an institutional commitment to address the minority achievement gap by participating in the consortium and by encouraging departments within their institutions to develop other activities. Each institution was asked to provide profiles of its programs that address student achievement, conduct focus groups for community input and involvement, and identify models and best practices.

At that time Johnson C. Smith University was already implementing a Learn and Serve America grant program that provided a Saturday Enrichment program for fourth and fifth grade students at Thomasboro Elementary School. An article in the local paper featured an educator who had agreed to come out of retirement to help improve the performance of students at Thomasboro Elementary School, which had been identified as a low-performing school. The article caught the attention of the service-learning coordinator. She was so impressed by the story that she recommended that Johnson C. Smith University use its grant resources to help the new principal meet her goals. As it turns out, the school was in close proximity to the university and the principal was an alumna of the school. Soon thereafter, Thomasboro was invited to become a partner. Fourth and fifth graders who score at either level one or level two are eligible to participate in the program. After the agreement was reached with the principal, a parent interest meeting was held to familiarize parents with the program. Parents who wanted their children to participate signed liability forms and consent forms for release of student scores. The parents were also asked to make a commitment to attend the parent sessions.

The program design is unique in that it places college students as one-on-one tutors for fourth and fifth graders within a structured classroom setting. Student reflections have told us that Johnson C. Smith

University students feel greater self-esteem when they realize they have played a direct role in helping another succeed. Early in the program one student reflected,

> I get a lot out of helping fourth graders because when I was that age I struggled and there was no one around to help me out and I do not want the same thing to happen to them that happened to me. I want the younger generation to feel that there was someone there to help them succeed when they needed help.

Another reflected,

> It was hard for me to get up at 7:30 on a Saturday morning. But now that I think about it, it was truly worth it. I feel good about myself. I think it's because I was doing something good for a little girl. I enjoyed helping her and answering her questions.

Learning Through Service

Empathy is instrumental in motivating people to help others. In this program, providing students with information regarding the seriousness of the task at hand engenders empathy. Johnson C. Smith University students are familiarized with the North Carolina "ABCs of Public Education," the comprehensive plan to improve public schools in North Carolina. This includes accountability and high standards for student achievement. They are made to realize that the students must pass the test in order to move to the next grade level. They are told what the levels mean and which levels are required for passing. This helps them to understand how important it is for them to provide stellar tutoring to their students.

Service-learners are also prepped in advance for each Saturday session. Each week prior to the tutoring session, they are given the worksheets that will be used. They are familiarized with the skills and the materials that will be covered in the session. This enables them to be more effective tutors. Service-learners also receive training in how to be positive role models. Thus, as a result of extensive sharing of information and comprehensive training they become true stakeholders in the service-learning activity. They begin to identify with the students and want to make a difference in their lives. It became apparent only a few weeks into the program that they became disappointed if their student didn't show up and vice versa. Student Bree Chaplin relates: "Vicky seems to enjoy the program also. At the end of every Saturday she says, 'Make sure you're here next time. I will be looking for you'. And I say, 'I'll be back if you'll be back.'" That was the pact they made with one another.

At the end of the first fall semester of the program the other service-learning pairs were saying to each other, "I'll be back if you'll be back." They made a yearlong commitment in order to continue with their students for the entire public school year. The Service-Learning Alternative Track is designed so that the next course in the sequence of required courses is offered as the service course for the project. This sustained period of time was also instrumental in the success of the program both for students and the community. Toward the end of the program students were feeling ever better about themselves and their participation in the program. A resounding theme in the student reflections was how good they felt about themselves after each tutoring session. Student Carletta Richardson says, "All of these tutoring techniques and experiences are helping me become a better person and I'm helping someone else's child better herself." Similarly, D. Kennedy reflects, "Service-learning is indeed a program that is going to help these students better their standardized test grades. This program will also give us a better sense of respect for helping others, and helping to better our own communities."

Results

At the end of the first year of the program 100% of students who participated in the program increased at least one grade level in math, and 78% increased at least one grade level in reading. By the end of the third year, the school increased the number of students scoring at grade level three or four by 14.8%. This year Thomasboro Elementary has been identified as an exemplary school. The achievement gap is closing. The college students exhibited high attitudinal changes and greater self-identity and self-esteem.

Children need to know the power of education and the power of ideas. Too many of them think that power is in guns and violence. These programs have proven that service-learning breaks down the walls as stakeholders begin to listen and respond to each other. When we bring the elementary school students to the college campus, we are opening up a whole new horizon for many of them. When they interact with college students, it is helping them to grow and to know that they have a chance to be a college student some day.

Service-learning enables the university to reach out to the community in a meaningful way and develop projects and linkages that truly make a difference. Careful planning and institutional leadership have reshaped the relationship between the university and the community. The service-learning program has enabled the university to be more responsive to education and civic needs; in the process it has enhanced its civic and social engagement. It has transformed its image and generated more public support for the institution.

Conclusion

At Johnson C. Smith University, a new era of excellence was ushered in with the institutionalization of its service-learning program. It is incumbent upon the chief academic officer to set up the framework and provide the infrastructure to produce a model program. The president has provided the visionary leadership needed for civic engagement projects. Today the entire university is committed to civic and social responsibility. This has come about also as a result of successful grant-writing efforts and the commitment of university resources to providing the infrastructure needed to implement the various programs. The organizational structure of the university was amended to incorporate the position of the service-learning coordinator in the academic affairs division. Grant-funded activities have been sustained by incorporation in the university's budget. The vice president for academic affairs charged the deans of the colleges with faculty recruitment into the service-learning program, and tremendous emphasis has been placed on faculty development and training. Faculty members are given the opportunity to participate in workshops and seminars to increase their knowledge of the service-learning pedagogy. Creation of a service-learning center has provided the university with the needed liaison with the community. Students are recruited as freshmen to participate in the alternative track of the Service-Learning Program. There is a 40-hour community service graduation requirement for all students, managed under the auspices of the service-learning center.

The president is continuously looking for ways to recognize and reward faculty who participate in civic engagement projects. Grant-writing incentives are in place to motivate faculty to pursue grants. The board of trustees is kept abreast of the university's involvement in civic-engagement projects through regular board reports. Program assessment results are provided to the president on a regular basis, and best practices are promoted both on and off the campus. The president has also made a commitment to meeting with community leaders and participating in community sponsored events paving the way for the establishment of partnerships. The university works closely with the public school drawing on using college students, faculty, and staff as resources to help teachers address some of the needs of their students. Johnson C. Smith University stands in a pivotal position to influence the future of the larger society. An engaged university requires strong leadership and the appointment of a committed and dedicated staff that can design and implement programs.

10 LeMoyne-Owen College: Using Institutional Context for Curriculum Change

Barbara S. Frankle

LeMoyne-Owen College is a private, church-related, small liberal arts college in Memphis, Tennessee, that drew from its heritage as a historically black institution and its mission of developing students for service and leadership in the development of a service-learning program. In 1994, the president and the vice president for academic affairs charged (and gave release time and the authority of the Office of Academic Affairs to) the associate dean to lead in the development of a service-learning program. The use of faculty teams, integration of a variety of community activities, use of stakeholder advisory boards, and design of a cost-effective curriculum are all elements of program design which other academic administrators might consider helpful.

Civic Engagement and Institutional Tradition

Private liberal arts colleges have many advantages in integrating service-learning into their fabric. The goal of developing good citizens who can contribute to the commonweal is inherent in the work of many of these institutions, and service-learning is a sound contemporary vehicle for advancing this purpose. Further, the collegiality and independence from state or other controls often makes the process of change less cumbersome than at other higher educational facilities. However, the role of academic affairs not only in effecting change, but also in sustaining effective educational practices necessitates the active leadership of the academic administration in the design, implementation, and assessment of service-

165

learning as much as in any program, particularly since service-learning of necessity crosses the disciplinary boundaries that so often define academic programs.

In providing students with a rich array of opportunities for civic engagement, LeMoyne-Owen College remains true to its heritage as a Historically Black College/University (HBCU), and as a small, liberal arts, private, church-related institution. Primarily a commuter urban campus in Memphis, Tennessee, in the heart of one of the most economically deprived census tracts in the nation, the college is an anchor for the federal l enterprise zone in which it is located. A population of some 800 students comes primarily from Tennessee and the surrounding delta region.

An undergraduate institution focusing on its teaching mission, LeMoyne-Owen grants the baccalaureate degree in 22 major programs. While the largest single major is business, the number of students selecting programs in the arts and sciences is more than double the amount in business. A large portion of the nonbusiness students are seeking teaching certification.

In line with its strong liberal arts emphasis, LeMoyne-Owen has emphasized the importance of a values-laden education preparing students for participation in a democratic society. In accord with the mission of HBCUs across the South, LeMoyne-Owen promotes the development of leaders who will provide uplift for their communities. It also reflects the history of strong involvement with the community; HBCUs traditionally build bridges, not fences, for their neighbors. The HBCU tradition is relevant to most small liberal arts colleges, whose missions often reflect social responsibility and the goal of educating an informed and active democratic citizenry. Similarly, colleges founded on religion typically express missions that incorporate the development of values and service among their constituents.

Harking back to their founding, the HBCUs consider civic involvement an essential role of the college. LeMoyne-Owen is not unique in its origin as a candlelit tent in a Civil War camp where a New England nurse taught basic literacy to a cluster of former slaves. From the very beginning, the institution embodied a strong commitment to the public good, civic equality, and community uplift.

Initiating Institutional Change

Service-learning is then a contemporary approach to a fulfillment of a sacredly held traditional purpose. Even so, it requires institutional commitment and administrative support to reinterpret that heritage into a functioning academic program. As one who has been directly involved with service-learning at LeMoyne-Owen since its 1998 inception, I can attest that careful nurturing led to the current effective operation.

Academic affairs played an active role in the reinterpretation of our service mission that evolved into the current service-learning program. In 1994, as the associate dean with a deep personal involvement in the community and a dedication to the ideal of civic education, I was pleased when the college president asked me to help establish a service-learning program. The vice president for academic affairs readily committed to making the second academic officer her voice in this initiative; she supported the effort by granting me the time and the power of the office to move the program forward. All of us believed that by joining in the national movement for service-learning, we were furthering and updating the traditional service mission of the HBCU, as well as providing an important avenue for the development of student leadership and civic capacities. Thus, there was a clear commitment from the college at the highest management levels to the development of service-learning.

Participation in various networks in my role as associate dean, such as the Association of American Colleges and Universities' (AAC&U) American Commitments program and in conferences such as those of the Association for General Liberal Studies (AGLS) and the American Association for Higher Education (AAHE), all offered some grounding in the latest movements in experiential and civic education. Such administrative opportunities for professional breadth make academic affairs officers important players in movements for educational innovation. Given the background I had developed, I was able to write successful proposals that won support for advancing the initiative. Initial funding from the Council of Independent Colleges (CIC) seeded the program. Subsequent grants from the Ford/UNCF (United Negro College Fund), Community Service Partnership Project (CSPP), and the Learn and Serve America Program of the Corporation for National Service supported significant opportunities for growth.

The granting agencies offered much more than financial support. All three provided important avenues for intellectual enrichment and capacity development. Their networks stimulated practitioners with conferences, newsletters, consultancies, and evaluation services. The collegiality and validation they engendered were vital. Local dilemmas could be resolved through a phone call to a friend at a networking institution who had faced similar issues. Personal contacts with national leaders and recognition at the national level placed us in a viable position at home when local leadership changed. Thus the networking derived from the granting agencies was in many ways as essential as the funding.

Importance of an Appropriate Coordinator

In fact, our launching of the program coincided with the first meeting of the CIC network, which proved to be an important orientation for our newly hired coordinator. An alumna of the college with a law degree who had been working in the legal office of the Memphis Housing Authority and teaching part-time at the college, the new coordinator brought important attributes to the program. Familiar to the faculty, she had their trust, an absolutely essential quality if one is to lead a program of change in academe. Her experience with the housing authority was important, since our main thrust was service to our immediate neighborhood, then dominated by a public housing development. Her legal expertise was extremely useful in establishing a procedures manual and in developing policies for risk management that inevitably accompany the placement of students in external settings.

The coordinator's position is essential to the development of a program. Time is the chief barrier to faculty acceptance, time for faculty to establish and maintain the necessary relationship with outside agencies, to develop the mutually beneficial relationships, to prepare contracts and manuals, to recruit the students, to develop a center, to write grants, and to develop course materials. A coordinator can more efficiently handle many of these tasks. If there is one single lesson our experience has taught us, it is that the coordinator is key to program success.

Gaining Faculty Support Within the Institutional Context: Strategies for Change

But of course even with a coordinator, the program cannot get off the ground without faculty support. Faculty involvement is then an essential component, but encouraging busy and sometimes skeptical academics to participate can take some persuasion. Unless one wants to herd cats, institutions must strategize on how to engage faculty in the process, and that includes identifying the ones who can most help to advance the cause and then creating appropriate mechanisms for their development.

The role of an academic administrator is crucial at this stage, providing the base from which to encourage faculty involvement. Not only was I the associate dean, but I had two and a half decades of service on the faculty, so I was a familiar colleague comfortable with the campus culture. I both knew individuals and had experience with methods that worked at LeMoyne-Owen to impel change. This ability to negotiate and develop mechanisms that could propel us forward proved valuable in winning faculty support.

Experience with the campus was important. The faculty's familiarity with both me and the coordinator offered a comfort level with our suggestions and proposals. Equally, or perhaps more, important was our understanding of campus culture. Knowledge of the loyalties, players, procedures and, of course, politics helped us to negotiate more smoothly the avenues of institutional change.

Understanding of the campus helped us to engage key people and to work within the locus of decision-making. At LeMoyne-Owen, the faculty home is the division (we are small, and departments would be impractical, so we are organized in five academic divisions of approximately 15 faculty each). Here is the dugout where loyalties lie. Therefore, we formed a faculty steering committee with carefully selected representation from each division, targeting some of the most influential members of the units. They ranged from creative junior faculty who had demonstrated interest in civic engagement to noncommittal campus leaders. We even chose one of the most senior but outspokenly skeptical faculty who constantly questioned the program's relevance to his discipline. Fortunately, our hopes that his involvement would lead to conversion were rewarded. He became just as outspoken a supporter, who could point to his own earlier cynicism to answer other naysayers.

Not only did the steering committee represent each division, but the members were asked to report regularly to them on the progress of the initiative, asking for input and concerns. Before any substantial proposal went before the full faculty, then, it had been examined carefully in the home bases. The steering committee was charged with establishing institutional criteria and standards, and it was asked to continually confer with divisional colleagues as the process moved forward. As the representative of academic affairs, I remained a participating member of the steering committee throughout the process.

Acknowledging the centrality of faculty in any curricular development at LeMoyne-Owen, the faculty steering committee was charged with formulating the original classroom criteria and educational goals. It was complemented by an advisory committee of community partners, who came from a wide range of agencies, educational programs, nonprofits, and the local neighborhood association. They worked with the steering committee to help design the kinds of field experiences the students would encounter, and to plan opportunities beneficial to all stakeholders.

Service-Learning and Institutional Development of Student Competencies

Again, working within the context of our institutional culture, we turned to a curricular centerpiece. A few years earlier, the faculty had collegially designated ten competencies the LeMoyne-Owen graduate should attain as a result of an education at LeMoyne-Owen. These competencies were at the heart of academic planning, because their development in students was the major purpose of the academic program. Again, the role of the academic administrator is important in keeping institutional goals at the forefront and in ensuring that processes appropriately mesh. Rather than creating a whole new set of learning anticipations, the college should build upon existing statements of outcomes, and it is the administrator's responsibility to coordinate initiatives to avoid fragmentation. Therefore, with encouragement from me as associate dean, the steering committee identified ways in which service-learning could contribute to the development of each of these competencies in what became an engaging exercise. This experience alone convinced them of the value of the enterprise and helped them recruit the support of their colleagues.

The steering committee, with the help of consultants and resources recommended through our various networks, then helped the director and coordinator to design the vehicles we would provide to deliver service-learning. The result was the proposal for an interdisciplinary service-learning course open to all students and the opportunity for divisions to offer their own service-learning course provided it met the established criteria.

Defining Service-Learning Within the Campus Context

The major goal was to create courses that appropriately balanced and integrated academic reading and reflection with field experience. Criteria were necessary since it was understood that areas and divisions could develop their own courses, and it was essential that there be consistency across campus. The faculty adopted the following seven criteria for service-learning courses.

- Guided reflection must be included in the course.

- Challenges that encourage critical thinking, reading, writing, and speaking will be included.

- Volunteer services that link the college with the community (public responsibility) will be developed.

- Courses will be rooted in an academic discipline.

- Courses will include a historical component of citizenship.

- Students will write a short essay on their expectation at the beginning of the course and a detailed exit paper on their learning experience at the end.

- Students will spend a minimum of 15 and a maximum of 30 hours in the classroom, and a minimum of 30 and a maximum of 45 hours in the agency, for a three-credit-hour course. Reading and assignments should equal an estimated 60 hours.

The college also charged the coordinator with ensuring that any placement in an agency should truly be a learning experience for the students. The agency should agree to structure the community assignment so the student would learn the workings of the agency and the social environment it served, and also would agree to assist in the evaluation of the student.

The proposal from the steering committee went through established curricular change channels—the curriculum committee to the full faculty to the academic dean. Before that occurred, however, we planted seeds for acceptance through faculty development.

Workshops for the full faculty introduced them to the concepts of service-learning before they were asked to act upon it. Unable to offer the ultimate inducement of stipends, we used the next best rewards for faculty participation: food and fun. Refreshments and lunch usually draw a crowd. Further, our creative coordinator used games, contests, audio-visuals, puzzles, and door prizes to keep the workshops lively so faculty actually began to look forward to them. Through the gaiety, however, the faculty recognized that we were examining serious and challenging issues of pedagogy and purpose. The initial session introduced the concept of service-learning, explored definitions, and related them to our institutional mission. Subsequent workshops examined the ways the steering committee had linked service-learning to the graduation competencies and possible curricular benefits.

By the time the proposals reached the faculty, they were fully attuned to the program and enthusiastically gave approval. Since academic affairs had been represented throughout the design phase, the proposal also already had the blessing of the administration. Implementation did not conclude the process, however, as once the program was underway further workshops explored the progress, raised new opportunities, and encouraged greater participation.

Faculty Roles and Rewards

Administrative commitment must translate into a reward system or the institutional involvement will be shallow indeed. Faculty justifiably recognize that they must satisfy the demands of those who decide tenure, promotion, and renewal issues. In fact, many HBCUs, LeMoyne-Owen among them, have long incorporated service into the evaluation process. Faculty annually negotiate a year's plan with division chairs based on three categories: teaching/advising, research, and service. Academic area administrators must here take the lead to ensure that service is indeed fully integrated into the faculty evaluation process, that service-learning is perceived as a part of this service, and that all of the constituencies fully understand the meaning of the terms and their importance to the institution. Careful work with the academic division chairs in the academic council (managers who report directly to academic affairs) and later with the faculty on the evaluation instruments helped us to establish this crucial component as part of the process.

These are the three categories of effort, each with a required minimum of importance: Teaching and advising (65%), research (10%), and service (10%). The remaining 15% can be allotted to the arena the faculty member selects, with the concurrence of the chair. Therefore, up to 25% of the annual evaluation could be for service; but at the very least, 10% must be devoted to it. While those who select the 10% minimum normally fulfill it mainly with campus committee work, those who negotiate for more in fact cite the work they do in the community and in promoting student civic involvement. This inclusion demonstrates clearly that the administration is so fully committed to service that it weighs faculty performance based on the quality of involvement.

The Service-Learning Program

The faculty decided to offer an interdisciplinary course as the major vehicle for service-learning at LeMoyne-Owen. The course combined readings on democracy, social issues, and diversity with assigned field experiences. Offered every semester and in the summers, it regularly enrolls about 15 students.

Luck and serendipity play their role, as well, and a happy concatenation of circumstances provided a new dimension to our program. The college was debating whether service-learning should be required, and if so how, when an offer we could not refuse came our way. An interdisciplinary social science course was a mandatory class for all students in our core curriculum general education program, which is a series of specified courses. The division saw the need to demand oral presentations of their students, but could not resolve how to fit them into an already full curriculum, especially since the classes were then very large.

At this interesting juncture, Junior Achievement arrived on the scene. This national program provides volunteers in K-12 classrooms who give presentations on socioeconomic questions. Their third and fourth grade curricula mirrored the subjects on community our freshman students were confronting at a much higher level in the social science class. Recognizing that students learn a subject best when they have to teach it, the faculty jumped at this chance to have the college students teach the K-12 pupils. The win-win situation benefited everyone. Junior

Achievement undertook training and evaluating the students and arranged the placements, relieving the faculty from that prohibitively time-consuming task. The students not only gained valuable experience in interpreting what they were studying and in oral presentation (which is where we started), but they also had the chance to serve the community and receive external validation.

An assessment of the student portfolios suggests that the Junior Achievement project made a strong impact on students. Journal after journal reveals initial trepidation followed by a rise of confidence and a realization of the genuine rewards of service. Many students reported a new sense of purpose in completing their college careers. Important as this might be to any student, this is especially significant for the minority first-generation college students whom LeMoyne-Owen serves. Thus, happy circumstances provided us with the required component we sought, an efficient and highly effective part of our program. Creative students latched on to service-learning and enthusiastically sought new ways to engage the community. We provided them with a flexible opportunity generated from ideas learned at a CIC network conference. Through the one-plus option, students could add one credit hour to any course in which they were enrolled if they undertook a service project related to the discipline and course content. Both the instructor and the service-learning coordinator had to approve. Fertile minds have led to some interesting projects. Students in a basic design class landscaped areas on campus and in the neighborhood. Students in literature classes offered dramatic readings to schools and senior citizens. Biology students did environmental testing. A history student collaborated with peers from other local colleges to organize a series of public forums on diversity.

Many layers of learning and community benefits derived from one of our most engaging one-plus projects, Images of Peace. In conjunction with the Memphis Jewish Foundation, the college held an exhibit of peace images created by Israeli artists. College art students carried the images beyond our walls, taking them to nearby Cummings Elementary School. After discussing the Israeli designs with the youngsters, the students suggested to them that they draw their own. Responding with a zeal not always present at this inner city school, the children plunged into the paint and brushed images of suns, birds, mothers, happy friends playing games, and even a group of houses labeled "gang free." The next day an excited principal called the Service-Learning Office. "The children went home last night and kept on working. They drew more images with siblings, parents, grandmothers, anyone they could draw into the adventure." This was an all too rare engagement with school activities for these inner city families. Recognizing the power of the occasion, the college hung the children's work in a hall adjacent to the Israeli exhibit for all to enjoy at the opening reception and subsequent showings. Our president held a special party for some starry-eyed youngsters who got to see their images hung beside those of international artists. We all learned messages about brotherhood and creativity from that poignant service-learning project. Along the way, the college learned lessons. Students accepted many forms of service, but by far the most popular was working with children. They balked at a program to teach literacy skills to adults, claiming embarrassment at teaching their elders. They responded enthusiastically to any project to enhance the learning of children, especially African Americans. While many students created individual activities, the college structured some specific projects to include whole classes. The focused effort was more effective at providing a greater impact in the community, and it enabled the coordinator to design a coherent course. The readings, class discussions, and reflection exercises could be more effectively shaped. The major thrust provided tutoring and cultural enhancement programs for children in the neighborhood and at two nearby elementary schools. During the summer, the college offered a summer camp with skills classes, free lunches provided by the city, and crafts and arts activities. Through a service-learning project and a Learn and Serve grant, the college also helped establish a Family Resource Center that serves the two neighborhood schools.

Future Directions

Assessment suggests that the program has been successful at meeting the goals of the program, the greatest of which is increasing the involvement and capacities of the students to become civic leaders. Several indicators attest that service-learning engenders a heightened community awareness and involvement among the student participants. Students who enroll in one service-learning course tend to follow up with more experiences, through additional registration in the interdisciplinary class, the one-plus option, or the leadership seminar. They also tend to enroll in the American Humanics program, which educates students for careers in the nonprofit sector. At least one student per year in the service-learning program has joined the nonprofit sector upon graduation, a career path they did not generally anticipate when they began college. Two have even formed their own community-centered agencies. Assessment review of student journals, particularly among the Junior Achievement participants, reveals testimony of life-altering experiences, leading students to greater confidence in their abilities to contribute, as well as commitments to further engagement with the community. Our participation in a Rand survey demonstrated several indicators of the effectiveness of the program, including increased student participation in political and civic life.

With assessment so positive and the service tradition so deeply engrained in the institutional purpose, the college has committed to sustaining and enhancing the program. In the five-year comprehensive development plan for the entire institution, student leadership development is one of five target areas for focussed development, which should lift an already successful program to a new level. The program is housed in the Center for African and African American studies, and it is charged with developing a leadership program. For two years we have offered an interdisciplinary seminar for invited students that includes lectures from civic leaders and internships in public offices. Also tied to service-learning is the American Humanics certification program. Affiliated with a national effort, it leads to certification for nonprofit management. The college was one of the founders of a Memphis collaborative between nonprofits and higher education that is a national model. The nonprofits offer financial support, host internships, and provide expertise for classroom instruction and institutes. The three colleges and universities provide volunteers and future well-grounded management personnel.

We are also now collaborating with other major neighborhood initiatives. The College Community Development Corporation uses internships in a wide variety of neighborhood-building efforts. We are also closely tied to an exciting initiative to establish a museum and music academy on the site of the old Stax Recording Studio, two blocks from the campus. Celebrating the rich Memphis music heritage, the museum and academy will use student volunteers as docents and counselors.

The LeMoyne-Owen program fits the culture of this college, as any program must if it is to be successful. However, it has qualities transferable to any private liberal arts college. Among the strategies that can be used by similar institutions are the development of an interdivisional (or interdepartmental) team to lead in the planning, the use of already articulated student outcomes to shape the goals of the program, and the use of all faculty meetings to keep everyone informed about and involved in the process. The interdisciplinary seminar and the one-plus curriculum options are also manageable and cost-effective ways of providing options for students.

By broadening our involvement in the neighborhood, drawing civic leaders more integrally into the program, and providing institutes and workshops on leadership, the college then hopes to enrich the service-learning program even more. LeMoyne-Owen thus continues in the tradition of the historically black college of serving the community and educating new generations of leaders.

11 | Miami-Dade Community College: Past, Present, and Future of Service-Learning

Robert J. Exley
Joshua B. Young

The most successful leader of all is one who sees another picture not yet actualized. The leader sees the things which belong in the present picture but which are not yet there . . . Above all, the leader should make co-workers see that it is not his or her purpose which is to be achieved, but a common purpose born of the desires and the activities of the group.

(Mary Parker Follett, as qtd. in Rouche, Baker, & Rose, 1989, p. 1)

This chapter provides an executive summary of the development, implementation, and evolution of the service-learning initiative at Miami-Dade Community College—a large, multicampus, urban community college. Special emphasis is placed on the different leadership roles fulfilled by chief academic officers (both college-wide and campus-specific) and other administrators from the college. The chapter also provides an opportunity to explore how the heritage of one community college exemplifies the community college spirit in general. This shared heritage and value system seem to make service-learning a natural means for achieving the community college mission.

With its dual emphasis on access and excellence, Miami-Dade Community College exemplifies the mission and goals found in community colleges throughout the country. Not only do community colleges accept all students regardless of academic history, they also believe that the college bears the burden of ensuring that these same students meet high standards. In both academic pursuits and the development of human poten-tial, the community colleges, by their very nature, strive to reach out and embrace individuals within the community who might not otherwise venture into the arena of higher education. In so doing, the community college serves as a primary source of higher education, economic devel-opment, sports opportunities, entertainment, and the arts, convening key community groups and leaders to address important issues. This leads to a more likely chance that engagement with the community is perceived as a natural expectation for the community college and its constituent groups.

Just like many others, Miami-Dade has at its very core the desire to serve the total community—especially those individuals from the edges of influence in society—by providing a complete educational experience. It also recognizes that through its own status in the community it inherits unique responsibilities. Within this context, service-learning simply makes good educational sense for Miami-Dade, as well as hundreds of other community colleges, because service-learning can be a means for connecting individuals to community, institutions to community, and individuals to institutions.

History

Miami-Dade Community College, a large, urban community college with six campuses, more than 140,000 students (credit and noncredit), and nearly 700 full-time faculty members, possesses a rich history of service. From its inception, it has actively pursued the goal of serving as the pri-mary point of access to higher education for those often left behind and left out of the more traditional institutions of higher education. Miami-Dade Community College was the first institution of higher education in South Florida to integrate its student population, and it remains a college environment rich in cultural, racial, and ethnic diversity that reflects the diversity of the Miami-Dade County community.

The student body is diverse (84% minority); nearly 70% attend on a part-time basis, and approximately 80% of incoming freshmen must take at least one remedial course. The county includes more than 50 distinct ethnic groups, and the campuses range from the urban Medical Center Campus, specializing in health career education, to the rural Homestead Campus, located in far south Miami-Dade County. Miami-Dade Community College has long been recognized in the community college arena as a source for innovative teaching that places a high priority on student learning. This history of innovation combined with significant commitment to students and community was just the right environment for service-learning to take root and flourish.

Eight short years ago, service-learning was relatively unknown and undeveloped. Even though individual faculty members routinely used community service experiences to enhance their courses, these efforts were not the norm and occurred without attention or a supportive infrastructure. Dramatic change began in 1994 with the establishment of a formal, college-wide service-learning program known as Partners in Action and Learning, funded by the Corporation for National Service. This has evolved into the current Centers for Community Involvement led by a district director, Mr. Josh Young. The Centers for Community Involvement include three full-time campus coordinators (devoted solely to service-learning and civic engagement activities), campus-based faculty coordinators, part-time coordinators, 12 community service Federal Work-Study student assistants, multiple campus student ambassadors, more than 150 community partners, thousands of student participants, hundreds of engaged faculty members, and myriad other community engagement projects beyond service-learning.

The fact that since 1994 more than 200 faculty members have utilized service-learning involving more than 20,000 students in course-related service projects shows its remarkable acceptance. These students have contributed more than 400,000 hours of service to approximately 500 agencies in South Florida. It has been an amazing journey.

This journey began in earnest when a three-member team (one faculty member, Mr. David Johnson; one academic administrator, Dr. Robert Exley; and one student services administrator, Ms. Leslie Roberts) participated in a Campus Compact Service-Learning Institute at Brown University in summer 1994. By design, each member of the team was from a different campus. The selection of members of this team was a joint decision including three campus presidents and the college's vice president for education (college chief academic officer). These college leaders desired that the college connect its civic mission more closely to its academic mission. They provided leadership and encouragement to the team leader (Dr. Robert Exley, director of the Wellness Institute) in his efforts to coordinate this initial experience. An example of the importance of their leadership is that upon learning that he had been identified as the faculty member of this team, Mr. David Johnson (who had no prior experience with service-learning) was skeptical of its value and rigor, yet the fact that his campus president and the college chief academic officer supported it made it easier to engage him in the proposed activity. And the institute proved to be a crucial experience for him and the entire team.

Leaders of the service-learning movement from around the nation facilitated the institute. As they shared their expertise and the Miami-Dade team interacted with representatives from other colleges, the enthusiasm for service-learning blossomed. Upon the team's return to Miami, the action plan developed at the institute served as the catalyst for submitting a three-year grant to the Corporation for National and Community Service designed to help the college build a sustainable service-learning program. This grant was one of only 65 funded by the Corporation for the years 1994-1997. Of particular interest is that it specified that the service-learning effort would be directed from the Medical Center Campus but serve the entire college. For the purpose of directing service-learning, Dr. Exley would continue to report to his campus president but also report to the college vice president of education. Thus, the college chief academic officer and a campus president combined to provide visual support for the initiative. In addition, Mr. David Johnson was assigned to the initiative (60% of his workload) as the faculty coordinator to assist his peers in their work with service-learning. This proved to be an essential decision, as he brought much legitimacy to the effort through his devotion to assuring academic rigor and integrity. Support for this decision came from his campus president, academic dean, and department chair as they reduced his teaching load (funds from the grant provided the resources to employ adjunct faculty members to teach the courses).

At the conclusion of the three-year cycle, the college received a second three-year grant from the Corporation for National and Community Service for the years 1997-2000. This second grant produced the significant enhancement of the service-learning program to include a major commitment to supporting the America Reads Challenge. It is precisely the support from the Corporation for National Service, coupled with significant cash and in-kind college resources, that made it possible to lay a solid foundation for service-learning. As we built this foundation, we dealt with many fundamental issues that must be resolved if a program of service-learning is to be successful and sustainable.

Philosophical and Theoretical Underpinnings

We determined that *who* the builders and architects are is just as important as the work to be done. For example, service-learning has been seen primarily as a teaching strategy from the start. This presumption in our thinking naturally required that we engage faculty members as key leaders in the evolution of the program. Thus, during the initial three years of our service-learning effort we used grant funds to purchase released time for faculty members to serve as leaders and consultants for their peers. The single most important responsibility for these faculty coordinators was to assure the academic rigor of service-learning at the college. These individuals provided critical training and development with the pedagogy, conducted service-learning experiences for faculty members themselves, and developed and reviewed policies and practices. In short, peers-leading-peers made it possible for this to be a faculty-driven initiative with significant administrative support.

Obviously, the work of these key faculty coordinators had to be approved by their academic supervisors. In our case, these supervisors were their department chairs and the respective campus academic deans. The campus academic deans made service-learning a visible priority by inviting the service-learning program leaders (director, faculty coordinator, etc.) to present the project to campus executive groups and by approving the designation of a faculty coordinator on each major campus (in addition to David Johnson's position as the college-wide faculty coordinator for service-learning). They also encouraged the participation of faculty members in ongoing professional development activities about service-learning that were developed and led by the faculty coordinators. They did so in both formal ways (e.g., approval of travel requests to attend service-learning conferences) and informal ways (e.g., consistent verbal support for service-learning via recognition of faculty members' work).

A second group of key builders included our campus directors (three full-time employees, one assigned to each of the three major campuses) whose primary responsibility lay in developing and managing the network of community agency partners. These individuals served as linchpins connecting the college resources to the community needs. They provided daily support for all participants in the effort—students, faculty members, and community agency leaders. The third group of builders included campus and college senior leadership, who provided ongoing guidance, direction, and support for the program. These individuals varied from campus to campus but consistently included the campus and college chief academic officers, chief student services officers, and presidents.

Two key working groups were established to coordinate the work. The first was a management team made up of the campus directors (including Josh Young), faculty coordinators (including David Johnson), and the grant manager (Bob Exley). This team met biweekly and completed all of the day-to-day planning and implementation of the various activities. The second group was a college-wide advisory group that included senior-level leadership and focused on issues of policy to assure that the service-learning efforts were fully integrated into the life of the college.

One key early challenge was to clarify our concept of service-learning. To do so, our faculty coordinators jointly wrote a *Faculty Guide to Service-Learning*, which defines service-learning as " . . . the process of integrating volunteer community service combined with active guided reflection into the curriculum to enhance and enrich student learning of course material." In essence, our aim is for the faculty member to use service as a vehicle for students to reach their academic objectives, in part, through serving our community in a way that integrates course teaching/learning objectives. This operational definition serves as the beginning point for all other thinking.

We consciously focused on three areas as we developed our program. First, service-learning demands sound, academically anchored partnerships. The nature of the partnership between the college and any community agency must be based on a shared commitment to the student's education. Second, service-learning requires that the service assignment be driven by community needs. It is essential for community agencies to identify the needs of their constituents and the service opportunities for students. Third, service-learning must include a faculty-led reflection component that specifically addresses the issues of democracy and civic engagement. To successfully implement service-learning, we found it essential that faculty members develop the skills necessary to teach their students how to harvest the learning available through their service experience. We determined that our responsibility to our faculty members was to provide them with a theory-based rationale for reflective teaching as well as with specific skills training. For many throughout the service-learning movement, including the service-learning management team at Miami-Dade Community College, perhaps the single most important aspect of a service-learning course is the reflection component.

Reflection

Reflection can be thought of as the intentional, systematic processing of the service experience to accomplish rational harmony. Rational harmony is the result of the individual cognitive development of each student. The developmental psychologist William Perry (1970) labels the acquisition of new information either "assimilation" or "accommodation." He states that assimilation occurs when one simply places new information into his or her knowledge base without processing it. The information does not result in any change in the individual's thinking or actions. On the other hand, accommodation requires the operation of consciously processing new information to fit into one's present thinking. This almost always results in individual change. Without this process, we run the risk that the student will not truly learn from the experience. In short, true cognitive development and learning occur only when accommodation takes place, and reflection greatly enhances the probability that this will happen.

In fact, since community service experiences often produce conflicting emotions and cognitive dissonance in our students, faculty members are presented with rich opportunities to foster student learning. Rodgers (1980) writes, "If a person's attitudes toward, reactions to, and feelings about the challenge s/he has experienced are facilitated with support, feedback, and integration, then the probability of achieving accommodation is increased" (pp. 18-19). The key is the support the student receives, which integrates the experience into the course constructs. With the faculty member's help, each student begins to realize the benefits of service-learning as he or she resolves internal conflicts regarding the personal and community issues brought out by the service-learning experience. Furthermore, the student begins to comprehend his or her place in the context of community responsibility. To sum up, service-learning at Miami-Dade Community College requires an active involvement in the learning process from faculty, student, and community members as we connect real-life issues with course theory and context.

Taking Stock: Where Are We Now?

Hard work, leadership, tremendous institutional support, and connecting with the larger national service-learning movement have combined to allow us to exceed even our highest expectations. Service-learning has become an important and permanent part of the college. The program has tangible and widespread support from administration and faculty alike and has successfully transitioned from grant funding to become part of the college budget—no small accomplishment when one considers that this occurred during a time of significant budget cutbacks throughout the state of Florida and the nation.

In addition, the service-learning program has persisted through a major change in institutional leadership. The college today has both a different president and a significantly different organizational design at the executive level than when we started the service-learning effort. Under the current college president, we now have six campuses instead of five, a college provost rather than vice president for education, and multiple college-wide disciplinary schools, whereby one campus coordinates all of the work in a discipline throughout the college. In short, the organizational structure has evolved to the point that the service-learning program is an even tighter fit to the college today than in the beginning. One key development is that the current college provost served as a campus academic dean before and is a major supporter of service-learning. He is personally involved in working with the campus presidents on a routine basis to assure the future of service-learning.

Four full-time directors (one college-wide and the other three campus-based) and a host of part-timers and faculty coordinators continue to build and improve the program. The college has rightfully earned a reputation as a national leader in the field of service-learning. Clearly we have much of which to be proud. Nonetheless, much remains to be done to achieve the level of quality, impact, and sustained institutionalization we desire. As service-learning becomes more widely utilized and accepted—both at Miami-Dade Community College and nationally—we must push ourselves to continue to improve the quality, effectiveness, and impact of this important national movement.

The Challenges of Quality-Building and Sustained Institutionalization

Having overcome the challenges of surviving, of transitioning onto college funds, and of winning administrative and faculty support, we now face new challenges as we work to take our program to the next level. The service-learning program can best be characterized as being in a quality-building stage, and we face three central issues on a continual basis. First, we must constantly strive to maintain a shared definition for our work in service-learning and to consistently expand the fund of knowledge possessed by our faculty as a whole. Second, we must expand our program from a placement/clearinghouse model to one that relies more on strong faculty-community partnerships. And third, we can do even more in the area of professional development for our faculty members to assure that they are fully supported in this shared endeavor.

As we move forward, the role for our chief academic officer becomes even more significant in many ways. For us, the fact that the college provost is personally engaged with the American Association of Community Colleges' work with chief academic officers from institutions with AACC service-learning grants is critical. Through this collaborative work, his personal fund of knowledge grows and he has committed the college to continuous evaluation of the institutionalization of service-learning. The data gathered from this ongoing evaluation is then shared with the other CAOs at an annual summit. In short, by going on the record publicly, he has increased his personal leadership for service-learning within the college. Also, the campus academic deans play a pivotal part when they support the work on their specific campuses through designation of campus faculty coordinators and their support for faculty participation in a multitude of professional development activities on service-learning found on each campus through the college training and development center(s).

Definition of Service-Learning
Many faculty members still do not fully understand service-learning.

Some think of service-learning as community service added to a course rather than seeing it as an academically rigorous, complex pedagogy. We are addressing this in a number of ways: by creating a brief, one-page definition of service-learning that includes expectations and characteristics; by generating a best practices summary to provide examples of exemplary service-learning utilization; by focusing more effort on faculty development; and by bringing new faculty along more slowly and purposefully to allow adequate planning time.

Community Partnerships and Overemphasis on Clearinghouse Model

In the early development of our program, Miami-Dade Community College created a program that is described best as a placement or clearinghouse model. This is a very common approach. However, it results in students' picking their service sites from a massive list of options, and in turn it gives insufficient attention to the importance of faculty-agency relationships. Until recently, we encouraged faculty to focus solely on connecting the service experience with their course learning objectives. The expectation was that the college's Center for Community Involvement would take care of the community partnership side of service-learning. The result: Very few knew much about the agencies their students served, other than that the agency was an approved service-learning site and had been through a training session offered by the college. Although faculty members may have had their favorite agencies, in general, their students went to a host of different agencies each semester, resulting in less than the desired experience for everyone involved.

This clearinghouse model failed to foster ongoing, sustained faculty-agency partnerships, which in turn often led to superficial experiences. Many experiences failed to provide students and faculty with an in-depth understanding of and commitment to the community agency and its needs. In addition, agencies complained that there was insufficient ongoing commitment from the program; in some semesters they received numerous students, in others none at all, and the students who did come were often unprepared, resulting in more work for the agency supervisor and less commitment from the students.

Recently we have made a fundamental shift to a faculty-agency partnership model. In all our interactions with faculty, we are encouraging them to pick one or a limited number of agencies and create an ongoing, sustained partnership. We are encouraging faculty to personally visit their agency partners and to spend time understanding the agency, its needs, and the underlying social causes of the problems it addresses. Our expectation now is that each faculty member will have a limited number of agency partners who can count on the faculty member and his or her students' involvement every semester. This is a true partnership and is already resulting in greatly improved quality and much higher levels of agency satisfaction.

Campus Compact regularly offers Engaged Department Institutes that bring together a departmental team and their community partners to explore and develop service-learning partnerships. We have sent faculty to one of these institutes and are in the process of replicating it on-site for 25 of our departments and their community partners. We also are hoping to implement a faculty-community agency mini-grant project that will foster partnerships between faculty and community partners and provide resources to enhance what can be undertaken and accomplished via the service-learning project. Finally, we are committed to providing more venues for faculty and community agency representatives to meet, network, and learn about one another's needs and strengths. These activities are possible only with the ongoing, visible support of the academic leaders at the college. This support ranges from financial support to voicing clear expectations of department chairs to the leaders' own personal involvement in the activities.

Faculty Training and Development

Although we have done an adequate job in many ways, we must do more in this key arena. The chief academic officer (whether it be our provost or the campus's academic deans) can be a significant catalyst for this work. Through both words and deeds, the CAO can affirm that the academic mission of the college will embrace service-learning because it makes good educational sense. It is an effective and fair way to learn. His or her words can be in the form of written communications or personal addresses/conversations with other administrators, department chairs, and faculty members. Through the judicious assignment of resources, he or she can ensure that faculty members receive adequate professional development with service-learning. And through the influence of his or her office, service-learning can become integrated into the strategic planning processes of the college.

When this is done, as it is now being done at Miami-Dade Community College, we are able to do a better job of helping faculty become expert practitioners who appreciate that service-learning is much more complex than sending students into the community for a few hours and nominally connecting the service experience to the course. We will also find more ways to assist the faculty member in addressing the issues of civic engagement, social justice, and democratic citizenship.

Lessons Learned

What advice would we offer to those just starting a service-learning program? What lessons have we learned? What have been the keys to our success? One of the most rewarding and enjoyable aspects of the service-learning movement is the willingness of those involved to share their resources and expertise with others. The Corporation for National and Community Service, Brevard Community College, Campus Compact, the American Association of Community Colleges, and many others contributed to Miami-Dade's service-learning success. In turn, we have learned a great deal along the way and are eager to share these lessons.

Faculty training and development just may be the single most important factor in creating and sustaining a high-quality service-learning program, because service-learning demands much from the faculty member in many areas, from basic knowledge of the pedagogy to the development of specific, in-class facilitation skills. The chief academic officer must resist the temptation to assume that faculty members will naturally have these skills. By supporting a comprehensive program of faculty development, the CAO can assure high quality and excellent academic rigor.

Clearly defining service-learning and setting high standards differentiates it from volunteerism and internships. This is important because each stakeholder must understand what makes service-learning unique and what it requires (academic rigor, civic responsibility, mutually beneficial partnerships with community agencies, etc.). Once this definition and the subsequent standards have been established, the CAO should be the lead voice for the accurate use of the term service-learning.

Focus on quality rather than quantity by starting small with a limited number of faculty and community partners and staying true to the standards and definitions that you have created. When you do, support will come. The worst thing a program can do is to grow too fast and not pay attention to academic rigor and the other essential elements of service-learning.

Faculty leadership is critical. Identify a highly respected, key faculty member (or two or three) who can serve as the voice and leader of service-learning for other faculty members. Faculty listen to other faculty, and having a respected, knowledgeable faculty member to champion service-learning is invaluable in recruiting and supporting others. Formal designation in some form for this role from the college's academic leadership can do much to enhance the success of a service-learning effort.

Emphasize the reflective teaching strategies. Without reflection, there is no service-learning. When reflection is understood and utilized, service-learning is successful. It is advantageous when the academic leadership invests time and energy to become familiar with this concept. One easy activity would be to lead an invitational discussion on the concept of reflective teaching, perhaps using Silcox's (1995) A *How to Guide to Reflection.*

Create an infrastructure for the future. In order for service-learning to become a widely utilized teaching strategy, there must be space and staff allocated to coordinate and administer the program. To accomplish this may require that the CAO collaborate with the chief student services officer on campus.

Foster student leadership. Nothing is more powerful than student voices; utilize students as leaders, coordinators, and advocates for service-learning. Formal recognition from the CAO or president goes a long way here. This can be accomplished in a variety of ways, including invitations for student service-learning leaders to present to the cabinet and/or the board of trustees or inviting them to a luncheon or reception with college leaders.

Utilize community service Federal Work-Study funds. Seven percent of all Federal Work-Study funds must be utilized for community service. Coordinating a college's service-learning program is an approved use for these funds and the students so supported. Student assistants can handle much of the logistics involved with placing and supporting service-learners. Again, this will require collaboration with the chief student services officer regarding policies for financial aid, in that for each dollar used administratively there is less funding for individual student awards.

Document your success. Gather data on all program activities to demonstrate accomplishments and to constantly improve your program. This should be a routine component of the institutional research activities of the college. These data can also be a key input for strategic planning.

Provide training for agency partners on a regular basis. Agency supervisors generally are unfamiliar with service-learning and require training to ensure that they help students both serve and learn. Consider holding mandatory training sessions for your agency partners. It sends a very important message for an academic leader of the college to at least greet these agency representatives and welcome them to the campus.

Foster support from key administrators by consulting with and involving them from the beginning, as their support is critical to the viability and sustainability of the program. Again, collaboration with your peers in the student services and administrative services divisions of your college is a key to support for service-learning, as it does indeed cross many boundaries.

The Leadership Challenge: Seeing Another Picture Not Yet Actualized

As Mary Parker Follett writes, "the most successful leader of all is one who sees another picture not yet actualized. The leader sees things which belong in the present picture but are not yet there" (as qtd. in Rouche, Baker, & Rose, 1989, p. 1). We have achieved a tremendous amount with our service-learning program, and we are working hard to strategically improve every aspect of our program. However, our destination in say five years, or ten years, and our dreams for a model of excellence remain a work in progress. As has been true so far on this journey, the support, guidance, and leadership of our chief academic officer(s) will be one key to achieving the dream.

We believe that a chief academic officer influences the individual work of each faculty member through the expectations established for other academic leaders, faculty members, and ultimately for students. Through his or her active voice in the ongoing debate of what makes a quality education, the goals of service-learning can be a permanent part of the discussion. In a time of multiple, competing instructional methods, we believe that the CAO's support for service-learning is one that must be forever present.

With the support of the academic leaders of our college, we present a few of our dreams and some of the pictures not yet actualized.

- Every faculty member, administrator, and trustee will understand the fundamental differences between service-learning, volunteerism, and internships, and will recognize service-learning as an academically rigorous teaching-learning strategy that enhances classroom learning, meets community needs, and fosters a sense of civic responsibility.

- Faculty who utilize service-learning will be expert practitioners. They will be very purposeful in how they integrate service into their teaching; they will set clear service and learning objectives. They will thoroughly prepare students before they begin their service, and they will guide students throughout the service experience to connect course learning objectives with the service experience. They will help students think critically about the underlying societal issues that cause community problems. They will understand the concepts of civic responsibility and civic engagement as they help students understand these concepts and improve their civic skills and commitment. This expertise will be fully recognized within the promotion process of the college.

- Faculty will form relationships with a handful of community agencies—or even one—that result in long-term, sustained, mutually beneficial partnerships that continue semester after semester.

- Resources will be available to fund faculty-community service-learning partnerships (e.g., a pot of money that faculty, through their use of service-learning, could funnel back into the community via service-learning partnership projects).

- Every student who graduates from Miami-Dade Community College will participate in at least one service-learning experience. The effects of service-learning will be fully and consistently assessed for the specific purpose of improving the practice of service-learning.

- Every student who graduates from Miami-Dade Community College will understand the meaning and connections between civic responsibility, civic engagement, and a more just society. The students will see the essential role they play in bringing these concepts to life.

- Scholarships will be available to students who excel in service and service-learning.

- Students will be empowered to take an even greater role in the college's service-learning program and will lead campus-community engagement activities.

Conclusion

Leadership at many levels and in many ways is the key to success with service-learning. This is a simple truth, and yet we would be foolish if we ignored the fact that leadership from specific key positions and individuals plays an even greater role. Yes, we were fortunate to have had students willing to engage in the process and to tell others (other students, faculty members, and administrators) of their positive experiences. Yet these students would not have had this opportunity were it not for the courage of faculty members and their deans, vice presidents, campus presidents, and the college president. Yes, we have been fortunate to have exceptional leadership from our campus directors and specific agency personnel. Yet their efforts would have been for naught without the active support of midlevel academic managers and leaders. Even with all of this support and encouragement, we still believe that the single most important aspect of our success has been an unflagging dedication to seeing service-learning as an instructional strategy requiring much from every participant.

In this sense then, Miami-Dade's proud past—a past that is characterized by innovation and excellence, by dedication and experiment, and by hard work and dreams—and the leaders of its past truly laid the foundation for service-learning to take root and grow. We also know that Miami-Dade's tradition of access and excellence made this possible. Access and excellence is marked by a tradition of expecting that anyone and everyone, regardless of background or experience, can succeed in the arena of higher education.

It is important that we state here that the development of the service-learning program at Miami-Dade Community College was, from its very inception, a bold and far-reaching dream. Yet few of us could have ever conceived that the dream we had would become not only a reality, but so much more than our highest hopes. To achieve what has been accomplished is truly a testament to the right-heart attitude of compassion and the significant belief in the possibilities of others that has permeated Miami-Dade Community College from its very beginning. We owe a debt of gratitude to all who have done their share in making this dream so real for so many today, and to all who came before us at the college and developed a culture that not only allowed us to dream such a dream, but encouraged, even pushed us, to turn the dream into the daily reality. It is precisely this combination of heritage and tradition that fosters the innovative, caring, and daring leadership necessary for remarkable achievement, and our service-learning program has been the beneficiary of such leadership. In fact, it almost seems that the success of service-learning was a foregone conclusion, and yet we know that is not true. We know that it was, and remains, a journey rife with challenges as well as opportunities to fall short. We are grateful that we have successfully met the challenges so far, and yet we know that it is a journey that continues from today into tomorrow. We look forward to each step.

12 | San Jose City College: What Community College Chief Academic Officers Need to Know About Service-Learning

Louis S. Albert

Written from the perspective of a long-time advocate for service-learning in all sectors of higher education, this chapter has two purposes: 1) to offer a conceptual framework, and 2) to illustrate the application of that framework by examining nine factors that have contributed to the success of the San Jose City College Service-Learning Program. These can be found in almost every effective community college-based service-learning initiative, and they should be the subject of serious consideration by chief academic officers and other academic leaders who intend to develop service-learning programs.

Putting Learning First Among Competing Priorities

Like chief academic officers (CAOs) in other sectors of higher education, community college CAOs face a plate that is more than full. In far too many cases, the day-to-day activities of CAOs leave little time to deal with issues of student learning. Resolving personnel conflicts; attending endless staff meetings; completing and filing accountability reports; recruiting, hiring, and evaluating faculty; and making decisions about budget and resource deployment make it very difficult for the CAO to put learning first.

Despite these "other" demands on our attention and time, and despite the professional and career risks associated with advocating a new pedagogy that lacks broad-based faculty support, growing numbers of successful community college CAOs are finding ways to keep student learning in general and service-learning in particular at the top of their priority lists. These CAOs know how essential it is to encourage connections between disciplinary developments and the array of powerful pedagogies we now have at our disposal. They understand how student learning is deepened when instruction involves creating linkages between formal classroom study and practical experience. And they especially appreciate the kinds of connections between campus and community associated with the theory and practice of service-learning.

Service-Learning and the Community College Mission

The week after September 11, 2001, I asked about a dozen community college presidents and chief academic officers if they thought their institutional missions would have to change. The following statement from a president of a Midwestern community college summarizes their nearly unanimous responses to my probes about mission:

> Our mission, and the priorities that flow from that mission, offer the promise of building a more just, more compassionate, and more effective society. We've been doing the right thing; we just need to approach our work with an even greater sense of urgency and purpose.

As a CAO, I couldn't agree more. Our work in this post-9/11 world has never felt more important or relevant—for our communities, for our nation, for the world. Community colleges, and our four-year counterparts, share both a responsibility and a wonderful opportunity—through service-learning—to help our students develop the knowledge, skills, and values needed by both effective workers and responsible citizens during these very challenging times.

But the outcomes associated with service-learning often take a back seat to the accomplishment of other mission-level goals and objectives. The mission statements of every comprehensive community college almost always describe three core educational outcomes: the acquisition of basic skills in reading, writing, and mathematics; workforce development (both pre-service and in-service); and preparation for transfer to a four-year institution. Although many mission statements also contain language about educating students for responsible citizenship in a demo-cratic society, until the recent growth of the service-learning movement, investment in the civic mission of community colleges has primarily taken the form of rhetorical support instead of budgetary commitment.

Each of these mission-related lines of work places huge demands on us as CAOs—demands on our time, demands on the way we set priorities and make decisions, demands on how we deploy institutional resources. Trustees, administration colleagues, and faculty expect us to focus on providing support for basic skills education, workforce development, and transfer. They are less clear about their expectations for CAO leadership around the civic mission of higher education, and CAOs who engage this issue do so at some risk of losing support, especially from faculty members who have little or no experience with service-learning and related peda-gogies.

I am convinced that a growing number of community college CAOs are willing to take the risks associated with advocating for an educational agenda that often lacks broad support among the faculty. They are com-mitted to building a base of faculty support and ownership for service-learning and civic engagement because they believe the across-the-cur-riculum outcomes associated with the education of a next generation of responsible and engaged citizens are as important as the outcomes associ-ated with their institutional commitments to basic skills, career, and transfer education. Service-learning, done well, simultaneously enhances civic and social responsibility among students and faculty, contributes to the vitality of the communities we serve, and enhances student academic learning in their basic skills, career, and transfer programs. But for ser-vice-learning to have a deeper impact on our students, our graduates, and the communities we serve, community colleges are going to have to do a better job of integrating service-learning into the larger mission. That's where CAOs can and should exercise leadership!

Why CAOs Should Pay More Attention to Service-Learning

The centerpiece of our mission as community colleges is student learn-ing—learning that is deep and long-lasting, learning that is relevant, learning that transforms. Service-learning, when integrated into larger efforts to put student learning first on the institutional priority list, is one of the most powerful pedagogical strategies we can deploy.

Edward Zlotkowski, a senior scholar at both the American Association for Higher Education and Campus Compact, in his 1998 book *Successful Service-Learning Programs*, put it this way:

> Service-learning is positioned at that very point where two comprehensive sets of contemporary educational concerns intersect. On the one hand, it represents a pedagogy that extends our range of pedagogical resources beyond even such promising active learning strategies as cases, role playing, and simulations. . . . On the other hand, service-learning works with a second, intersecting axis: From knowledge as self-interest and private good, it creates a bridge to knowledge as civic responsibility and public work (Boyte & Farr, 1997). . . . Through service-learning, students can discover the possibility and the importance of simultaneously attending to their needs as individuals and as members of a community. By bringing public work into the very heart of the educational system—i.e., the curriculum—service-learning helps students avoid the schizophrenia of private advancement disassociated from public standards and public need. No longer does "doing well" hold center stage, while "doing good," if it exists at all, languishes somewhere off to the side. (pp. 3-4)

The arguments for adopting service-learning as an instructional strategy were strengthened by Janet Eyler and Dwight Giles, in groundbreaking research reported in their 1999 book, *Where's the Learning in Service-Learning.* Eyler and Giles discovered significant impact of service-learning on students in such areas as social and personal development, social skills and values development, academic learning, and career exploration.

Subsequent research by Paula Vaughn (2002) extended the work of Eyler and Giles. Vaughn developed a protocol and set of performance-based assessment rubrics that form the basis of interaction between instructors and students engaged in service-learning courses. In field-testing the assessment protocol and rubrics, Vaughn found evidence of service-learning's impact on personal growth, social growth, academic and intellectual growth, civic participation, career exploration, and ethical growth. Numerous other studies have yielded similar results.

Service-Learning at San Jose City College: A Case Study

The San Jose/Evergreen Community College District

The San Jose/Evergreen Community College District encompasses San Jose City College (SJCC) founded in 1922, Evergreen Valley College founded in 1974, and a contract training entity known as the Institute for Business Performance. Evergreen Valley College and SJCC each enroll about 11,000 full- and part-time students. The enrollment profile for the district approximates the profile at each college. Students average just over 29 years of age. Sixty percent of the students are women. More than 30% of the students are first-generation Americans. Approximately 44% of the district's students are Asian or Pacific Islander, 29% Hispanic, 16% White, 6% Black, 1% Native American, and 4% represent other categories including those of mixed origin.

In 1997, the board of trustees voted to eliminate academic and student affairs vice presidencies at each college, create a direct reporting line between the deans and their college presidents, and establish a new district-level vice chancellor for educational services to assist the chancellor and board in setting academic and student service policies and to provide support services to the presidents and their campus constituents. I was appointed as the district's vice chancellor for educational services in 1998, and came to the position with a 16-year history of advocacy for service-learning and other pedagogies in my role as vice president of the American Association for Higher Education.

Both colleges have active and growing service-learning programs. Both receive financial and staff support from my Office of Educational Services and from their campuses. Because the service-learning program at SJCC has a longer history, it was chosen for the case study that follows.

Service-Learning at San Jose City College: Getting Started

In an initiative organized prior to my arrival by the then vice president for student services, the concept of service-learning was introduced to the SJCC campus in spring 1996 through a series of brown-bag lunches.

The lunches were designed to foster understanding of the service-learning concept, develop initial faculty interest, and explore implementation at SJCC. These lunches were intended to introduce the concept of service-learning and promote first-level faculty interest in adopting service-learning in their courses.

In summer 1996, a team of administrators (including the vice president for student services) and faculty attended a Campus Compact three-day workshop. The team returned from the Campus Compact workshop as a newly constituted Service-Learning Steering Committee, and started work during the fall 1996 semester on a master plan for service-learning at SJCC. The committee procured the services of a consultant with extensive experience in the Santa Clara University Eastside Project, a comprehensive partnership between the university and community agencies on the east side of Santa Clara County. With help from the consultant, the committee conducted a needs analysis, interviewed faculty and potential community partners, and came up with a service-learning program design.

The following spring, the committee received support from SJCC's president for a reassigned time position for a faculty service-learning coordinator, and the college's academic senate also formally endorsed the college's fledgling service-learning program. In California, community college academic senates are responsible for approving all matters associated with curriculum and instruction, including the establishment of reassigned-time faculty positions. The approval of the service-learning coordinator position by the SJCC Academic Senate represented both increased legitimacy and visibility for the new program.

Ronald Levesque, a faculty member in the Language Arts Division, was appointed as service-learning coordinator in fall 1997. The coordinator's office was set up in the Job Placement Office, a decision that provided the coordinator with full-time logistical support from the job placement coordinator.

Program Profile

When the service-learning program at SJCC was first implemented, almost all of the early faculty adopters offered service-learning as in-course options. The majority of service-learning faculty still give students the option to pursue a service-learning project or do an alternative assignment, but the number of faculty who are making service-learning a course requirement for all students is steadily growing.

With patience and hard work on the part of the coordinator and the steering committee, the program has demonstrated slow but consistent growth. The District Office of Research and Planning started tracking the SJCC Service-Learning Program during spring 1999 and prepared a growth profile at the end of spring 2002 (see Table 12.1).

Table 12.1
Service-Learning at SJCC: Patterns of Growth

	Spring 1999	Fall 1999	Spring 2000	Fall 2000	Spring 2001	Fall 2001	Spring 2002
# Students	101	170	178	153	143	281	328
# Faculty	10	12	16	17	22	29	23
# Sections	18	24	30	28	37	44	38
# Courses	10	18	17	17	23	26	25

Within a full-time faculty of 160, about 40 SJCC faculty members (mostly full-time) representing a wide range of academic disciplines have now incorporated service-learning into their courses. As in most community colleges, these disciplines are housed in large multidisciplinary divisions headed by a dean. Some of the larger or more complex disciplines also organize as departments within their divisions (e.g., mathematics, biology, English, and English as a second language [ESL]). The disciplines represented through the spring 2002 semester are:

- Accounting
- Art
- Biology
- Child and Family Studies
- English
- ESL

- Guidance
- Health Science
- Mathematics
- Mexican American Studies
- Multimedia
- Psychology
- Sign Language
- Sociology
- Speech and Communications

SJCC partners with more than 50 community agencies. The service-learning coordinator, Ron Levesque, works closely with individual faculty members to help them identify appropriate community partners for their students. The following is a list of the types of service provided by the college's community partners.

- AIDS/HIV information and services
- Alzheimer's patient services
- Child abuse prevention
- Department of correction
- Disabled student services (at SJCC)
- Early childhood education assistance
- Emergency housing services
- Environmental services
- Immigrant services
- Mentoring/tutoring for elementary students
- Mentoring/tutoring for high school students
- Mentoring/tutoring for middle school students
- Mexican-American community services
- Migrant education
- Retired senior volunteer programs

Factors That Contribute to the Success of Service-Learning at SJCC

In its five years of operation, the Service-Learning Program at SJCC has created powerful learning opportunities for students, played a central role in shaping a more learner-centered faculty culture, and contributed significant service to the clients served by the college's community partners. Nine factors contribute to the success of the program. Each merits attention by CAOs.

1) Faculty ownership and innovation

2) Organizational infrastructure

3) Support from the board of trustees and administration

4) Board of trustees priorities that identify student learning as a core value

5) Support for professional development around issues of teaching and learning

6) Assessment and accountability

7) Active involvement of community partners

8) A web site accessible to students, faculty, and community partners

9) Advocacy and support from the CAO

Faculty ownership and innovation. The program coordinator for the SJCC Service-Learning Program is Ronald Levesque, a language arts faculty member who understands the academic nature of service-learning, patiently supports the adoption of service-learning by his faculty colleagues, and works overtime to bring the college's community partners into the academic equation. The coordinator's faculty status and his professional approach to the practice of service-learning lend credibility to his role and deepen his effectiveness in working with faculty colleagues.

But faculty ownership extends beyond the coordinator's faculty status. Created during the planning year (1996-1997), the SJCC Service-Learning Steering Committee includes a number of senior faculty members who make innovative use of service-learning in their own courses while simultaneously extending their wisdom and experience to their faculty colleagues. Meeting once a year as part of their formal advisory role, and as needed to provide support to the coordinator, faculty members serving on the steering committee have been a major factor in the adoption of service-learning as educational practice at SJCC. The steering committee also represents a pool of faculty from whom a next coordinator could be selected with minimal loss of momentum associated with a change in program leadership.

Organizational infrastructure. The service-learning faculty coordinator is supported with a 40% reassignment from his teaching load. The service-learning program office is physically located in the college's Job Placement Center. This organizational arrangement enables faculty members and students seeking information about service-learning or assistance with their service-learning placements to have access to the services of a full-time job placement coordinator on a 40-hour-per-week basis. Locating service-learning in the Job Placement Office has the added benefit of providing a one-stop service for students who are also looking either for part- or full-time employment or opportunities to serve and gain experience from a nonpaying community placement.

Support from the board of trustees and administration. SJCC president, Dr. Chui Tsang, has provided budgetary support and administrative advocacy for the Service-Learning Program since its inception in 1997. As vice chancellor (and the district's CAO), I became a member of the steering committee and committed additional district office resources to the SJCC Service-Learning Program after coming to the district in 1998. I have also provided funding through my office for both the Evergreen Valley College and the SJCC membership in Campus Compact.

Working with the service-learning coordinator and the president, I have used my position as vice chancellor to organize presentations for our board of trustees about the service-learning programs at both colleges. All of our board members have expressed enthusiastic support for service-learning. One of our board members even serves as a permanent member of the program steering committee at SJCC.

Board of trustees priorities that identify student learning as a core value. The SJCC Service-Learning Program is a direct response to the expectation of our board of trustees that student learning form the central commitment of our work as a district.

Each year, the board goes on retreat to review trends and developments in the nation, state, and local community, and to set priorities for the coming academic year. For the past three years (and for the foreseeable future), the board has focused on high quality student learning (with an emphasis on writing as a foundational skill for student success) as its first priority. The priority reads, "a commitment to high quality student learning and student success as well-rounded human beings is at the core of the mission of the SJ/ECCD and language competency is a foundational component of that core commitment to every student" (San Jose/Evergreen Community College District, 2002, p. 4).

With this first priority in mind, the board has instructed the chancellor, the presidents, and the faculty and staff to review and/or modify curricular content, instructional practices, student support services, and administrative procedures in an effort to ensure that all district employees are working in support of high quality student learning. They have even added language about service-learning in elaboration of their focus on student learning as a first priority. In support of this priority, the board has specifically asked the administration and faculty to:

- Advocate high quality learning as the primary goal of the district.
- Set and maintain high standards for student learning.
- Support new strategies for teaching and learning, and take steps to assure that those strategies are deployed to improve language competency for all students.
- Encourage and support active learning strategies.
- Provide a comprehensive student support system.
- Channel resources to support learning.
- Design staff development programs that focus on learning for all employees.
- Assess student learning and provide feedback to stakeholders.
- Expand our assessment of student learning to include both aggregate indicators of student achievement and assessment that tells us more about student knowledge, skills, and values.

Support for professional development around issues of teaching and learning. In addition to service-learning, the district and the colleges support a number of other pedagogical initiatives. Coordinators, with responsibilities similar to those assigned to the SJCC service-learning coordinator, are in place both at Evergreen Valley College and at SJCC for a learning communities initiative, for a peer-led team-learning initiative in the sciences, and for the development of online and web-enhanced instruction.

One of the initiatives I directed early in my tenure as vice chancellor was to create a district-funded Teaching and Learning Center that supports faculty work in service-learning and in the other above-mentioned powerful pedagogies. The Teaching and Learning Center also supports faculty work in project and problem-based learning, classroom assessment, and the scholarship of teaching and learning. Staff development committees at each college work closely with the Teaching and Learning Center in organizing professional development activities for faculty.

Assessment and accountability. Working closely with the district's Office of Research and Planning, headed by an associate vice chancellor for educational services, the program coordinator maintains detailed records about the number of students participating in service-learning projects, the number of courses offering service-learning options, faculty members and their disciplines, and hours of service provided by students. Using information provided by the Service-Learning Program coordinator, the Office of Research and Planning prepares annual accountability profiles for the board of trustees, faculty and staff, and community partners.

In addition to keeping track of these descriptive statistics, the Office of Research and Planning conducts annual assessments of student success rates (grades of C or higher) and persistence rates (successful movement from one course level to the next) in service-learning courses. The office is also working with selected service-learning faculty members to design focused studies of service-learning's impact on student learning and development. These studies are used by the board and administration for accountability and program evaluation, and by the faculty in their ongoing efforts to improve teaching and learning.

Active involvement of community partners. The SJCC Service-Learning Program maintains active relationships with more than 50 community partner agencies. The program coordinator meets with all of the partners on an annual basis and, more frequently, with those that serve as sites during a particular semester. The coordinator is very intentional about seeking the wisdom and advice of the college's community partners around issues of curriculum and pedagogical design. The coordinator also spends considerable time learning about the needs of the partner agencies and communicating those needs to faculty and students.

A web site accessible to students, faculty, and community partners. The Service-Learning Program's web site (www.sjcc.edu) has been designed to meet the information needs of students, faculty, and community partners and includes sections on program history; goals, mission, and educational philosophy; the role of the student; the role of the faculty; the role of the community partner; and a section on program evaluation.

The web site enables all program participants—students, faculty, and community partners—to operate from a common base of understanding about the program. It also serves as a source of professional information for colleges and other organizations seeking to learn more about SJCC's Service-Learning Program.

Advocacy and support from the CAO. I think most CAOs share my view about the importance of advancing a mission-level commitment to offering programs and services that promote civic responsibility and engagement. The problem for CAOs, as always, is the challenge of finding personal time and institutional resources to act on that commitment. A core focus on student learning, a deliberate effort to orchestrate connections between service-learning and other powerful pedagogies, and attention to each of the other eight factors listed above in almost every instance will result in a successful service-learning. Some of these factors will require "hard money" investments (e.g., in the service-learning coordinator's position, in support staff, in professional development services for faculty and staff). But, from my experience, the most critical role the CAO can play is analogous to that of the orchestra conductor—getting people to collaborate and leverage their individual talents and resources into a well-coordinated whole. In the case of the SJCC Service-Learning Program, in addition to the fiscal resources provided by my office, the success of the program is also enhanced by the personal time I spend working with the Service-Learning Program director and the efforts of both our associate vice chancellor for educational services and the coordinator of the district Teaching and Learning Center, two senior positions that report to me in my role as CAO. My work as a service-learning advocate with the board and chancellor, our college presidents, and academic deans also contributes to a supportive environment for the program.

Lessons for CAOs: Some Final Thoughts

Learner-centeredness! Putting learning first! Learning as a core value! Is there a chief academic officer who doesn't accept the priorities now so visibly assigned to learning by most community colleges? But with the competing demands for time and resources that form the day-to-day agendas of every CAO, finding a center of gravity for their work that fully integrates service-learning into the curriculum is not an easy task.

Most of the elements of a successful service-learning program are brought to life through the dedication and hard work of faculty members, service-learning program directors, and others. CAOs need to pay attention to these success factors to make informed decisions regarding the resources required to support these lines of work. But maybe the most important thing the CAO can do is to keep everyone focused on learning and to broker connections—between service-learning and other pedagogical efforts, between service-learning and campus-based volunteer service programs, between service-learning and the academic disciplines, and between service-learning and career development.

13 | University of Michigan: Dilemmas of Civic Renewal

Barry Checkoway

This chapter describes dilemmas of civic renewal at the University of Michigan, a large research institution whose civic renewal has intensified in recent years. It describes some of these civic activities, whose dilemmas arise partly from its institutional culture and status as a research university. It concludes that top administrators have been supportive of civic renewal, but that faculty members have been instrumental, and that without continuing faculty involvement, nothing lasting is likely to happen.

American research universities are strategically situated for civic renewal in higher education. They are civic institutions that were established with a public purpose and developed immense intellectual and institutional resources for research and learning. They produce much of the world's scholarly and scientific literature, prepare professors who populate the nation's colleges and universities, and educate students who teach other students and enter the workforce. They exercise disproportionate influence over other colleges and universities, and their initiatives spark changes in these other institutions. Renewing the civic mission of research universities can influence the entire educational system (Checkoway, 1991, 1997b, 2001).

However, as these universities have become powerful research institutions, they have multiplied their purposes and de-emphasized their civic mission. As a result, they have become the target of critics who charge that much classroom teaching does not develop civic competencies, that much academically—based research does not serve community needs, and that these universities have lost their sense of public purpose to become vehicles for private gain. In response, some educational and civic leaders have recognized their roles and shown stirrings of a movement for civic renewal in research universities (Bringle, Games, & Malloy, 1999; Ehrlich, 2000).

This chapter describes dilemmas of civic renewal at the University of Michigan, a large research institution whose civic activities have intensified in the past decade. It describes some of these activities and identifies unresolved issues that have arisen. It is written from my perspective as a faculty member, advocate, and administrator of a program that was established during this period.

Civic Renewal at Michigan

Civic renewal in higher education includes initiatives by students, faculty members, and other stakeholders to conduct institutional activities to strengthen the welfare of civil society. It can take the form of basic and applied research, teaching and learning, or a wide range of service activities; and it finds expression as civic engagement, community service, service-learning, university-community partnerships, or other rubrics. As long as stakeholders are taking initiative for the welfare of civil society, then civic renewal is taking place.

The University of Michigan is a public research university with more than 38,000 students and 20,000 faculty and staff members affiliated with 19 schools, colleges, institutes, centers, and educational programs. An annual budget of over $3 billion maintains an infrastructure of libraries, laboratories, telecommunications technology, and academic support facilities. It is more than an educational institution; it is a major employer, a provider and consumer of goods and services, and a powerful social and economic unit whose initiatives are worldwide.

The University of Michigan has a history of civic renewal, from the educational efforts of John Dewey in the 19th century, to its role in the founding of the Peace Corps, to the active involvement of thousands today. Michigan faculty and students have participated in every episode of the nation's civic development since the institution's founding. Given the university's size and complexity, no single form has characterized all approaches; there have always been many forms, and much mixing and phasing among them.

Task Force on Community Service

In 1992, Vice Presidents Maureen Hartford and Walter Harrison responded to faculty advocacy and appointed a University Task Force on Community Service of which I was chair. Hartford was vice president for student affairs with responsibility for student cocurricular activities and social development. Harrison was vice president for university relations with concern for government relations and community outreach. Both of them had long-term commitment to community service and civic engagement from their days as college students and into their professional careers. Neither of them was an academic affairs officer, and this perhaps made it easier for them to move this agenda at a research university.

We composed a task force of students, faculty and staff members, and community representatives. We assessed the campus and community situation, identified initiatives at peer institutions, and developed guiding principles for service-learning. We discussed many program ideas, discussed priority ones, and encouraged a student proposal for a center that might structure the effort. The task force was appointed by top administrators, but not without advocacy by faculty members. Shared ideological commitment enabled participants to communicate across institutional boundaries and formulate ideas for a common cause.

Michigan Neighborhood AmeriCorps Program

Michigan participated in the movement for national service that was surfacing in American society. Associate Vice President Thomas Butts worked closely with U.S. Representative William Ford, a Michigan democrat who chaired the congressional committee that formulated the national service legislation. Vice President Hartford and I were invited to the White House for its signature into law, and to testify in Representative Ford's congressional hearings on its regulations, with special emphasis on the proposed AmeriCorps national service program.

When AmeriCorps was conceived as a pre- or post-college experience, I was a strong advocate for an in-school approach that would extend national service to higher education, permit students to participate parttime in national service, and enable them to combine service and learning during their college years (Checkoway, 1993). We published op-eds in newspapers, organized a national conference and a campus think tank with new Corporation for National and Community Service CEO (and Michigan alumnus) Eli Segal, and hosted a White House Working Group to draft specific procedural language for an in-school approach (Checkoway, 1993, 1994a, 1994b, 1995). Michigan views itself as a national institution, maintains a permanent Washington staff, and involves academic administrators and faculty advocates in federal affairs as part of its role in higher education.

Once the new national service program was in place, faculty members and community partners prepared a successful proposal for the Michigan Neighborhood AmeriCorps Program, a unique collaboration of graduate professional schools—for example, Architecture and Urban Planning, Business, Public Health, Public Policy, Social Work—and community-based organizations associated with the Michigan Neighborhood Partnership in Detroit neighborhoods. Working together in teams, university students and community residents addressed unmet economic, educational, environmental, health, housing, and human service needs in neighborhoods citywide.

Our AmeriCorps program not only got things done in neighborhoods; it also had educational effects on the students and established a new institutional infrastructure for service and learning on campus and in the community. It established a campus committee bringing together faculty and staff members for planning and coordination of activities campus-wide, and a campus-community committee that brought them together with community-based partners who themselves found a new vehicle for planning and coordination. On a campus whose units often operate like autonomous little villages rather than as a coherent institutional whole, these structures built relationships, stimulated creative thinking, and generated new program possibilities (Checkoway 1997a; Krzyzowski et al., 2001).

For example, AmeriCorps enabled the College of Architecture and Urban Planning to build relationships with community-based organizations and increase involvement in Detroit neighborhoods. It enabled the School of Public Health to increase interaction with public health agencies and community-based organizations and propose new partnerships. It enabled the Department of Psychology to conduct community-based research and develop courses involving students in urban communities. University units built on these relationships and generated new sources of external funding. There has been no calculation of external funding attributable to AmeriCorps, but it is estimated that the program to date has generated $10 million of such funds.

AmeriCorps remains a unique campus-community partnership that has continuing individual, institutional, and community effects, but it is important to recognize the importance of university administrators in the process. Faculty members and community partners proposed the program, but Vice Presidents Hartford and Harrison were strongly supportive and persuaded President James Duderstadt to provide substantial funding for the institutional match required by the federal government.

There was agreement that the university should participate in any national service program in accordance with its role in society, although it was uncertain which institutional unit would sustain fiscal responsibility. University vice presidents remained supportive of AmeriCorps in subsequent years, and several deans joined them in support of efforts from which their students would benefit. Deans can play powerful roles in a decentralized institution whose executive officers often seek their approval, and their willingness to share the costs, of an initiative. Graduate school deans whose own students learn from community experience as part of their professional training were especially willing to give funds from their own budgets.

Center for Community Service and Learning

Building on increasing interest in national service and institutional momentum, I prepared a successful proposal for a comprehensive campus-wide center which would strengthen student learning, involve the faculty, and build university-community partnerships (Checkoway et al. 1996b). Provost Gilbert Whitaker, a former dean of the business school who believed in philanthropy and voluntarism, and who was convinced by campus and community leaders that this was an idea whose time had come, approved the proposal. The provost provided start-up funds that would decrease over a five-year period with the expectation that the center would have continuing support from the vice presidents for student affairs and university relations, to whom its director would report. These executive officers designated a building for the new center and appointed me as its founding director.

The Center for Community Service and Learning was established in order to 1) strengthen student learning and leadership through community service, civic participation, and academic study; 2) engage faculty members in research and teaching which involve and develop communities; and 3) build university-community partnerships that improve the quality of life and enhance the educational process. We brought together established curricular and cocurricular programs with expectation of new initiatives, conducted a planning process, and prepared a mission statement for launching the enterprise (Ginsberg Center Long Range Planning Committee, 2001).

The center established a new institutional infrastructure for leadership and management. The national board included distinguished alumni and civic leaders with commitment to its purposes and ability to position its programs and assist with fund development. Eli Segal served as national chair; Olivia Maynard (elected university regent and former lieutenant governor) and Ronald Weiser (influential businessman and future ambassador) as cochairs; and Provost Whitaker, Vice President Hartford (future president of Meredith College), Vice President Harrison (future president of the University of Hartford), and I rounded out its executive committee. The faculty council included leading scholars and top administrators who assured the intellectual integrity of our work and strengthened support in campus politics.

In a brief period, the center had an impressive list of activities and accomplishments. It brought together under one umbrella some of the nation's largest and oldest curricular and cocurricular programs, and established new programs to strengthen service and learning on campus and in the community. It enabled faculty to increase interdisciplinary interaction, learn from one another, and build mutual support for research and teaching innovations. It contributed to university-community collaboration by involving students and faculty members in rural and urban communities. It organized national meetings of higher education leaders, and expanded the only national peer-reviewed journal of service-learning.

We were highly entrepreneurial, prepared a large number of proposals for new initiatives, and received recognition through funding from public agencies and private foundations. With guidance from Vice President of Development Susan Feagin, the family of alumnus Edward Ginsberg endowed the center as a way to honor his civic accomplishments, with the written promise that the provost would make permanent his annual allocation, and that the vice presidents for student affairs and university relations would continue their allocations in perpetuity. By December 2002, the center had an endowment worth more than $7 million, grants and contracts more than $1 million, and general fund allocation more than $750,000 annually.

Provost's Seminar on Community Learning

As part of our strategy of building constituency support, we formed alliances and convened meetings of campus and community stakeholders. For example, Provost Nancy Cantor invited key faculty members to a Provost's Seminar on Community Learning for a Diverse Democracy. Our purpose was to promote dialogue about community learning, identify pedagogical and institutional issues, and enable faculty to learn from each other and build mutual support.

More than 100 participants from all schools and colleges shared ideas about this important pedagogy and how it contributes to the civic mission. Sessions focused on learning and teaching, scholarship of engagement, faculty roles and rewards, bridging diversity and democracy, and university-community partnerships.

Provost Cantor closed the seminar with a stirring speech about the importance of community learning and a compelling charge to tackle this fundamental mission of public higher education. With passion and specificity, she cited many efforts of faculty members, and drew them together under a unified and renewed mission to construct a university that is fundamentally engaged with the public and that sees itself as a public resource with deep societal responsibilities. She was eager for students to fully engage in their educational experiences and confirmed her commitment to community learning for a diverse democracy. She viewed community learning as part of the intellectual diversity that was her passion and expanded on this theme in conjunction with the institutional commitment to save affirmative action as a vehicle for educational excellence.

Provost Cantor received an enthusiastic response from faculty members whose comments were noteworthy. Most faculty were pleased to increase interaction with others who shared common cause, confirm their sense of a growing movement, and express their desire for more institutional involvement. However, some perceived that there were few rewards for civic renewal at a research university and that there was need for stronger support at the highest levels of the institution (Ginsberg Center for Community Service and Learning, 2001a). Faculty perceptions of insufficient incentives and rewards for civic initiatives are widespread in research institutions, even when there is evidence that these initiatives can contribute to quality research and teaching (Checkoway, 1998a; Marver & Patton, 1976; Patton & Marver, 1979).

Symposia on University-Community Partnerships

We followed the seminar with a series of symposia on university-community partnerships in Detroit neighborhoods. Held in Ann Arbor and Detroit, the symposia were convened by Earl Lewis, vice provost and dean of the graduate school, and me. Our purpose was to assess present partnerships and develop strategies for sustaining partnerships in the future.

More than 125 campus and community representatives participated in these symposia, including community and civic leaders, university administrators, faculty members, and others with commitment to partnerships. Sessions featured discussion of Making Contact/Bridging Commentaries, Working Together, Roles and Rewards, Community-Based Participatory Research, and Formulating a Comprehensive Strategy. Participants formulated specific strategies for strengthening partnerships and some guiding principles for university-community collaboration.

Again, participants appreciated an opportunity to meet with campus and community partners and again identified unresolved issues. They recognized real resources on campus and in the community, but also questioned a lack of commitment at the highest university levels and a lack of communication among community-based organizations. They expressed the need to prepare people for entering communities and working across cultural boundaries, establish centers or points of entry and contact on campus and in the community, form a campus-community advisory group for planning and coordination of partnership activities, discuss issues of common concern, and formulate guiding principles for collaborative research and other partnership activities (Ginsberg Center for Community Service and Learning, 2001b).

Local and National Momentum

As momentum built, students, faculty, and staff members came forward with new institutional initiatives. Imagining America, a consortium of universities and cultural institutions to support the civic work of artists and humanists, and Arts of Citizenship, a program with funds for humanists to conduct community-based projects, received support from President Lee Bollinger. Michigan Community Scholars Program, a living-learning program for undergraduates, received funding from the vice president for student affairs and dean of the College of Literature, Science, and the Arts. With faculty advocacy, deans created offices for university-community partnerships establishing a new layer of campus-community liaisons and signifying new levels of institutional support.

University faculty and staff also reached out to national constituencies. They conducted research projects on relevant themes and integrated new content into teaching and training. They presented their ideas in national conferences and published books and articles in journals. They took leadership positions and influenced initiatives in a range of public agencies and private associations, such as the American Council on Education, American Association for Higher Education, and Association of American Colleges and Universities. National outreach of this type is a normal workload expectation at a research university like ours.

As part of our outreach, we convened higher education and civic leaders in a national symposium series titled "Strategies for Renewing the Civic Mission of the American Research University" at Wingspread in Racine, Wisconsin. The Johnson Foundation, Association of American Universities, American Association for Higher Education, American Council on Education, Association of American Colleges and Universities, Campus Compact, New England Resource Center for Higher Education, and University of Pennsylvania Center for Community Partnerships cosponsored these symposia, with support from the W. K. Kellogg Foundation.

Symposia participants were current or potential leaders of a movement to promote civic renewal in research universities. They included presidents, provosts, deans, and faculty members with extensive experience in higher education and others who had played civic roles and worried about the future of universities from outside their walls, such as leaders of civic agencies, professional associations, and private foundations (Checkoway, 2000a).

Symposia participants drafted the Wingspread Declaration on Renewing the Civic Mission of the American Research University. The declaration formulated the idea of an engaged university, which would view research as a public good, integrate civic content into the curriculum, and make knowledge more accessible to the public. Such an institution would engage the faculty, modify the reward structure, change the academic culture, and develop leaders who could implement these goals. Its students would develop their civic competencies, faculty members would promote public culture at their institutions, staff would contribute to community building, and administrators would articulate the purpose of research universities as agents of democracy (Campus Compact, 1999b).

> Research universities and leaders from all levels of our institutions need to rise to the occasion of our challenge as a democracy on the edge of a new millennium. We need to help catalyze and lead a national campaign or movement that reinvigorates the public purposes of civic mission of our great research universities and higher education broadly. (Campus Compact, 1999b, ¶ 1)

Diversity and Democracy

Michigan's top administrators contributed to civic renewal despite constant changes in their composition. In 1996, President James Duderstadt resigned his office and was followed by all of his vice presidents within two years. Lee Bollinger became president in 1997 and appointed an entirely new group of executive officers. In 2001, President Bollinger became a finalist for the presidency of Harvard University; Provost Cantor was a finalist for the presidency of the University of Wisconsin, and she resigned to become chancellor of the University of Illinois. President Bollinger himself resigned to become president of Columbia University by the end of the year, followed thereafter by resignations of three other vice presidents. Top administrators play important roles in universities like ours, and this turnover affected major movements in the institution.

Concerned about maintaining the momentum of civic renewal, we approached Senior Vice Provost for Academic Affairs Lester Monts, the highest ranking academic affairs administrator to remain in place, to establish a Provost's Faculty Committee on Education for a Diverse Democracy. President Duderstadt had emphasized social diversity during his administration, invested institutional resources, and stimulated substantial work in this area. President Bollinger and Provost Cantor continued the commitment and led the defense of affirmative action in higher education during their administration, at the end of which there was a core constituency of people who were uncertain about the future.

The Provost's Faculty Committee on Education for a Diverse Democracy was established to renew the university's civic mission, reintegrate democracy and diversity as complementary educational objectives, and reestablish the leadership of the faculty. Committee members included several faculty leaders, including the senior provost, deans, department chairpersons, center directors, and former foundation officials. In a brief period, committee members were planning new initiatives and building constituency support.

Committee members shared commitment to democracy and diversity as complementary objectives. They assumed that because democracy is about the participation of the people, and the people are increasingly diverse, then education for democracy must include education for diversity. For democracy to function effectively in the future, students must be prepared to work with people who are different from themselves and to build bridges across social and cultural boundaries en route to a more diverse democratic society.

Dilemmas of Renewal

By almost any measure, the University of Michigan has a great deal of civic engagement activity. Thousands of students learn from their involvement in curricular and cocurricular activities. Faculty members conduct research and teaching that involve and develop communities, and build university-community partnerships that contribute to the quality of life and enhance the educational process. Academic administrators show commitment to civic renewal and provide funding support for its achievement. As an institution, Michigan has immense resources that are or might be available for this purpose. Taking all relevant research, teaching, and curricular and cocurricular service activities together, Michigan's expenditures for these purposes amount to more than $30 million annually.

Despite its resources, however, Michigan has dilemmas of civic renewal that have become apparent in recent years. These dilemmas—which arise both from its own institutional culture and from its status as a research university—do not necessarily limit the scope of activity, but may affect its quality or impact, and surely will affect its future.

For example, Michigan undergraduate students learn from their involvement in some of the nation's oldest and largest curricular and cocurricular activities, and graduate students are placed in diverse communities as an integral part of their professional training. Although they learn a great deal from their involvement, too few of them receive formal preparation for entering the community, or for working with people who are different from themselves, or for critical reflection on their experience, or for making the connection between direct service and civic participation.

Indeed, Michigan students participate in more than 100 for-credit service-learning courses—two of which are 40 years old and place hundreds of students in dozens of communities—and in a dizzying number of cocurricular activities with a strong social purpose (Checkoway, 1996a). Although students in one course were shown to develop greater awareness of societal problems from their community involvement (Markus, Howard, & King, 1993), too few students aspire to civic leadership or strengthen their civic competencies through higher education, a problem that Michigan shares with higher education in American society (Checkoway, 2000b).

Michigan faculty members have increasing interest in research and teaching that involve and develop communities, and some faculty have received national and international recognition for this work. But most faculty operate in isolation from one another, or lack information on relevant research methodologies or pedagogies, or perceive that there are few rewards for this type of work in the academy. There are faculty change agents who are exceptional in their civic commitments and who comprise a talented cadre of the professorate, but they are not typical.

In research universities like ours, faculty perceptions are shaped by an academic culture that does not emphasize civic renewal. Most faculty are trained in graduate schools whose required courses ignore civic content, and they enter academic careers whose gatekeepers dissuade them from spending much time in the community. They are socialized into a culture whose institutional structures shape their beliefs and cause behaviors that are consistent with their conditioning. They perceive that civic engagement is not central to their roles, and that it might even jeopardize their careers in the university. This is what many faculty believe; this is their dominant culture. The dilemma is that without the faculty, nothing lasting is likely to happen.

Michigan's university-community partnerships are numerous, with many mutual benefits on campus and in the community. These partnerships can strengthen student learning from real-world experience, contribute to the quality of faculty research and teaching, and help the institution to fulfill its civic mission, at the same time as they benefit the community (Dewar & Isaac, 1998; Schulz et al., 1998). However, university units also have partnerships that lack adherence to true partnership principles or commitment to collaboration over the long haul. Lacking a strategy for sustainability, the learning benefits are lost (Checkoway, 1998b).

University executive officers and academic administrators show commitment to civic renewal and provide funding support for its achievement. Presidents, provosts, vice presidents, and other administrative officers make public presentations, form task forces and committees, bring key stakeholders to the table, convene important meetings, and provide funding for initiatives that develop.

But presidents, provosts, and vice presidents are limited in what they can accomplish in an institution whose present structure is best understood as a loosely coupled federation of decentralized units, each of which is relatively autonomous, rather than a unified institution with a single mission. This, too, is a characteristic that Michigan shares with other research institutions, whose decentralization both facilitates and limits innovation.

For example, research universities are organized around academic departments and professional schools whose prestige is often measured by their rankings in national peer hierarchies. Their present reward structure—including promotion and tenure—places emphasis on research performance and production of new knowledge for publication in scholarly journals. Even if a president or provost wanted to modify his or her institution's reward structure to increase incentives for contributions to

223

civic renewal rather than to the knowledge base in an academic discipline, he or she would be limited by structures that reinforce the status quo. Innovation is possible, to be sure, but wanting will not make it so (Alpert, 1985).

University executive officers and academic administrators can be instrumental to civic renewal in higher education, but these officers operate in an institutional arena in which faculty members are a powerful constituency that may or may not organize for this purpose.

Our recent experience is that top administrators can leave a mark on the institution, but that they come and go, and that without the faculty, nothing lasting is likely to happen.

Research University for What?

The University of Michigan was established with a public purpose that continues today, but the institution has multiplied in its purposes, and civic work is only one among them. It is an important purpose, to be sure, but only one, and there are dilemmas in its realization.

It is possible to imagine a research university whose president expresses a clear civic mission for higher education, views the university as an instrument for democracy, and takes public positions in a civil society. It is possible to imagine a provost who has a strong spirit of democracy and leads academic policies, strategic planning, and budgetary decisions with unyielding civic values. There is nothing a priori to prevent the president, provost, executive officers, and deans from formulating a comprehensive strategy for reaffirming the civic mission, restructuring the institution, and refocusing its dominant culture. They could start this tomorrow, if this were their will.

But the reality is that there are civic dilemmas in the research university, and these are illustrated in the University of Michigan. For example, it is difficult to conceive of a comprehensive strategy for civic renewal in an institution that has constant turnover in its succession of presidents, provosts, and executive officers in recent years. Such turnover can be expected to increase insecurity in any large institution, and it amplifies the significance of what was accomplished in this period.

At a more fundamental level, the University of Michigan shows the inherent tensions that arise from its establishment as a civic institution with a public purpose, and its evolution into a powerful research engine that has undergone major changes in its objectives and operations, research paradigms and pedagogical methods, and internal infrastructure and external relationships. The modern research university responds to interests inside the institution and outside its walls, and it serves multiple masters in a society dominated by a range of public and private forces in various political and economic arenas.

Conclusion

By almost any measure, the University of Michigan has immense resources and an impressive list of civic activities over the long haul. Its presidents, provosts, and other academic administrators have been instrumental to its accomplishments. But the institution is not at its founding, and the present focus of institutional allegiance is not civic.

In the final analysis, the University of Michigan shows that faculty members can play key roles in the civic work of the research university. Michigan has faculty who prepare students for active participation in a democratic society, who conduct research that involves and develops communities, and who build collaborative partnerships that contribute to the quality of life and enhance the educational process. These faculty conceive of research and teaching as forms of civic scholarship, construct their roles in terms of the benefits to civil society, and strive to change the dominant culture of the institution. They are not necessarily typical of their peers, but they demonstrate that the civic purpose is alive and that institutional change is possible nonetheless. If their numbers were to grow, the results would be extraordinary (Checkoway, 2002).

These faculty members will continue to raise unanswered questions about civic renewal in the research university, such as: What civic competencies are needed to prepare students for active participation? What are some ways of increasing the involvement of faculty members? What should be the civic mission of the research university in a diverse democratic society? Research university for what?

Unanswered questions like these will be raised inside and outside the institution. The president, provost, vice presidents, and other academic officers will be part of their answer, but only part, for the future of the research university is beyond any single individual. Without the faculty, nothing lasting is likely to happen, but what is, or will be, the civic work of the faculty in the research university of the future?

14 | University of Minnesota: Renewing the Land-Grant Promise

Victor Bloomfield
Dale A. Blyth
Harry C. Boyte
Robert Bruininks
Susan Engelmann
Edwin Fogelman

Robert J. Jones
Catherine A. Solheim
Craig Swan
Billie Wahlstrom
Steven R. Yussen

When we try to pick out anything by itself, we find it hitched to everything else in the universe.

(John Muir, 1911, p. 211)

When the University of Minnesota celebrated its 150th year in 2000, a rededication was made to being an engaged university, renewing the land-grant tradition of public purpose and public work. This chapter discusses the university's system-wide initiatives: creation of a high-level task force, establishment of an outstanding community service award, strategic use of technology, aligning public engagement initiatives with the university's planning and budget processes, and the development of performance indicators for civic engagement efforts. The deeper requirements for civic engagement include creating broad and deep understanding of critical philosophical principles and values, recognizing the importance of cultural celebration and recognition, aligning civic commitment with institutional planning and resources, launching effective initiatives that link the human resources of higher education to community issues, and incorporating civic engagement commitments and strategies into institutional systems of governance and accountability.

Institutional Culture and Values: Civic Engagement Initiative

In spring 2001, in an address to the University of Minnesota's Board of Regents, President Mark Yudof captured both the moment—a fierce battle in the state legislature over the university's budget—and longer term trends: "I see across America a gradual withering of the covenant or understanding that the work of public research universities is a public good." The work of civic engagement and other initiatives to revitalize the public purposes and activities of the university directly counters the discouragement and uncertainty that attend such withering at many institutions, including our own.

In the first years of the new century, a systematic effort has emerged to strengthen and rebuild the University of Minnesota's connections with the citizenry of Minnesota. The effort has included the creation of a high-level Civic Engagement Task Force (www.umn.edu/civic). The task force has its roots in a research project by the university's Center for Democracy and Citizenship. At the request of the Kellogg Foundation in 1997-1998, the center undertook an examination of the possibilities for renewing the university's public land-grant mission. As part of that effort, Ed Fogelman, professor of political science, and Harry Boyte, senior fellow in the Hubert H. Humphrey Institute of Public Affairs, interviewed dozens of faculty, administrators, staff, and students at the University of Minnesota, as well as stakeholders in the broader community. More than expected, the interviews revealed widespread desire for much more public engagement as a constituting dimension of regular professional work. Moreover, the strong interest in deepened public relevance of teaching and research was not simply an individual desire but was echoed in broad, if often invisible, disciplinary sentiments. "Our whole department feels too cloistered," said one department chair in the College of Liberal Arts. "There is a broad desire to engage more deeply in the urban scene, and the broader public world."

Over the next two years the center worked with Executive Vice President and Provost Robert Bruininks, Vice Provost for Undergraduate Education Craig Swan, and Vice Provost for Research Victor Bloomfield on strategies for strengthening public engagement. In fall 2000, the Civic Engagement Task Force was appointed and charged by Provost Bruininks with clarifying the meaning of civic engagement and recommending practical measures for renewing the university's land-grant mission across the full range of university activities, including scholarship, teaching, and work with communities.

The task force defined civic engagement in a broad and comprehensive way. In its view, civic engagement is best understood not as a discrete set of activities, but as a deepening "institutional commitment to public purposes and responsibilities intended to strengthen a democratic way of life in the rapidly changing Information Age of the 21st century" (Bruininks, 2003). This perspective is a very broad rendering of public commitment, affecting all of the primary functions of the university and suggesting a long-term process of culture change that builds on existing efforts.

To begin catalyzing action and sustained intellectual attention to the practical meaning and implications of such a view, the task force undertook work on many fronts. It sponsored an inventory of civic engagement activities at the university. It made connections with higher education institutions and groups across the country. Through new funds, it sponsored a number of initiatives and organized public forums and discussions with stakeholders inside and outside the university. Finally, its working groups gave sustained attention to the meaning of civic engagement for scholarly activities individually and in disciplines and fields, for teaching, and for connections of the university with communities. This is an enormous set of intellectual and practical challenges that have been inaugurated. To continue such work, the task force proposed a continuing Council on Public Engagement.

Meanwhile, associated efforts took shape on a number of other fronts. In spring 2002, more than a dozen public forums were organized at colleges and coordinate campuses. The Faculty Senate Committee on Educational Policy organized a university-wide effort to develop a strategy for expanding civic and community learning opportunities—an effort strongly endorsed and supported by many student groups as well. Colleges and departments established their own work groups on civic engagement. The Kettering Foundation sponsored a project to interview leading scholars on their views of public scholarship. The Career and Community Learning Center, based in the College of Liberal Arts, expanded its efforts to promote service-learning across the Twin Cities campus, and several other colleges initiated important service-learning activities.

Overall, these civic engagement efforts amount to the beginnings of sustained, long-term, deep, and comprehensive conversations and action strategies to renew the land-grant tradition of public purpose and public work. No one imagines that the process of culture change and public engagement will be easy or quick. But there is once again emerging the vision of a university, in the words of former president Lotus Coffman, "of the commonwealth, by the commonwealth, and for the commonwealth."

Creating and Sustaining a Culture of Engagement: Centrality of Recognition

Celebrating excellence and high achievement is important for healthy organizations. At the University of Minnesota, we celebrate excellence in teaching and service to students and the university, and we also celebrate service to the community through the Outstanding Community Service Award. This award, established by action of the board of regents, honors the accomplishments of faculty, staff, and members of the greater university community who contribute their time and talent to make substantial and enduring contributions to the community and to improving public life and the well-being of society. A peer review panel of faculty and staff, appointed by the provost, selects six awardees annually from a group of about 30 nominees.

Awards are presented at an annual university-wide celebration and dinner that includes six to ten people who have worked with each honoree. In accepting the award, each honoree introduces his or her project and the significant community members. The award takes the form of an attractive plaque and a significant and permanent salary augmentation. Working with citizens and community organizations in the University of Minnesota land-grant tradition, award recipients have extended and exchanged their unique knowledge by applying their expertise to community issues. Their contributions have resulted in long-term and lasting changes for the public good and demonstrated an unusual commitment to the university and to the greater Minnesota community. The Outstanding Community Service Award Program not only recognizes significant community contributions but, equally important, signifies the university's critical and reciprocal engagement with the broader community.

Aligning Civic Commitment With Institutional Planning and Resources

In fall 1998, the University of Minnesota began to make substantial changes in its strategic planning and accountability process. Noteworthy is a system of public agreements, or compacts, between the administration and each of the campuses and colleges, as well as many of the university's support units. The compact process is designed to align the goals, directions, and overall investment strategy established by the president and the board of regents through the capital request, the academic supplemental request, the biennial request, and institutional evaluation measures.

At its essence, a compact is a written agreement between the campus/college/support unit and the administration, explaining how the unit and the university together will address strategic issues to advance the teaching, research, outreach, and internal service responsibilities of the University of Minnesota. Compacts delineate directions and actions, respective responsibilities, investments, outcomes, and mutual expectations for accountability within the university and the unit's long-range plan. The compacts contain specific measures and indicators of progress (linked to the university's critical measures) and emphasize specific outcomes (e.g., quality, impact, efficiency, effectiveness, and service). The agreements are developed and written annually and jointly by the unit and the administration.

The compact process provides extensive data on the performance of all units in relation to university-wide goals and performance profiles and goals of the local unit. The process also governs the flow of new resources through an all-university investment pool and the targeted reduction of resources.

During the past several years, the compact planning and budget process has emphasized the integration and alignment of important public engagement initiatives with the university's research and education priorities. This process has led to an academic audit of the public engagement initiatives of all colleges and campuses of the University of Minnesota. Future work will focus more sharply on the most important and feasible measures of institutional performance, with the goal of recommending to the Council on Public Engagement and to the provost a set of assessment criteria that can be used for the University Plan, Performance, and Assessment Report. This report emphasizes the development of institutional evaluation measures to assess the university's investment progress, impact, and cost effectiveness of its commitment to public scholarship and civic engagement.

Selected Strategies for Aligning and Integrating Research

Career and Community Learning Center

The Career and Community Learning Center (CCLC) assumed responsibility for the Twin Cities campus-wide service-learning infrastructure in 1992. At that time there were four faculty members offering service-learning courses; now more than 75 faculty and instructors teach courses integrating service-learning in more than 25 departments and seven colleges. Financial support and increased visibility of CCLC service-learning efforts, from Vice Provost for Undergraduate Education Craig Swan, has played a key role in this growth.

On behalf of the campus, CCLC develops and maintains reciprocal relationships with over 100 community partners to work with service-learning courses and the Community Empowerment through Learning and Leadership (CELL) program, described below. The contributions of community partners are central to this work and occur in the following ways:

- Helping to guide the development of the CELL program.

- Playing a crucial role in the creation and implementation of the pre-service orientation and training program.

- Collaborating with CCLC staff to create a set of expectations and responsibilities for participants involved in service-learning.

- Presenting in service-learning courses each semester.

- Participating in gatherings with faculty to discuss their roles as co-educators in the service-learning process.

- Educating new faculty on their experiences working with service-learning.

CCLC introduced an Outstanding Community Partner Award in 2002 to highlight the work of organizations and their staff representatives.

Student leadership is also a core value of CCLC service-learning efforts. Students launched the CELL program in 1998 with support by staff and community partners. This program was responsible for establishing and cultivating relationships with 50 community organizations in the Twin Cities to create meaningful opportunities for over 250 students yearly. Student leadership has also been crucial in supporting the growth of service-learning courses. Students play a central role in coordinating the logistics of 25 to 30 classes a semester, involving approximately 1,300 service-learning students each year. The CCLC web site (www.cclc.umn.edu) also maintains a listing of service-learning courses. Over 500 service-learning course students and CELL members participate in the "Get Up, Get Into It, Get Involved" interactive training session to prepare for their community experiences. Vice Provost Craig Swan invited CCLC to develop and coordinate a living-learning housing program for incoming first-year students dedicated to community work.

The increase in service-learning on campus is attributable to many factors, including heightened national attention to service-learning and civic engagement, increased outreach efforts by CCLC staff and faculty advocates of service-learning, and the consistent voice of support by Vice Provost Craig Swan. In 1998, Vice Provost Swan created the Service-Learning Advisory Committee to recommend ways to further develop and support service-learning on the Twin Cities campus. Faculty advocates on the Service-Learning Advisory Committee made several key recommendations that proved successful when supported and acted on by Vice Provost Swan:

- Provide funding for Service-Learning Faculty Fellows Program to encourage more faculty to develop service-learning courses (eight faculty grants awarded 2002-2003).

- Provide encouragement for service-learning to be included as part of the Center for Teaching and Learning Services programs (Preparing Future Faculty, Early Career and Mid-Career Faculty Programs, and Teaching Enrichment Series).

- Increase financial support for hiring of an additional staff member in CCLC to expand service-learning to departments and colleges not currently participating.

- Continue to support existing efforts by highlighting work done by departments on campus, for example, by supporting the sociology and English departments' participation in the National Campus Compact Engaged Department Summer Institute.

These efforts have been successful in expanding service-learning on campus. The infrastructure provided by CCLC continues to be mentioned by faculty as the key ingredient that allows them to integrate service-learning into their curricula.

University Reads Program

Minnesota has an exemplary pre-K–12 education system. Despite its successes, our system and our state face serious economic, language, education, and literacy gaps that will lead to a critical competition gap in the global society and economy of the 21st century. Improving reading, language, and writing literacy in the early years is the single most powerful educational intervention that can produce great long-term dividends in raising school achievement and basic standards for all children.

The Minnesota Model for Promoting Early Literacy spells out action steps to help children throughout Minnesota learn to read and write competently. Led by the University of Minnesota in partnership with local and state education leaders, this model calls for collaboration among the full range of stakeholders—local education districts; the Department of Children, Families, and Learning; public and private colleges and universities; community groups; business leaders; families; and policymakers—using all resources in the state to improve early literacy. It builds on the ideas and community partnerships developed at a literacy summit, organized by the university in fall 1999.

The first phase of the model focuses on urban public school districts in the Twin Cities, where currently there are 25,000 K-6 students and 1,800 elementary teachers in St. Paul schools, and 29,500 K-6 students and 2,500 elementary teachers in the Minneapolis schools. In the second phase, the model will be expanded to involve schools statewide and to include work on improving literacy in the middle grades.

An excellent example of the collaborative activities that link the university to the community is a tutoring program that specifically targets early and emergent readers (typically kindergarten to grade three students). The program, part of the America Reads Program, has recruited, trained, and placed over 1,000 reading tutors in schools and community centers. Plans are currently underway to expand the tutoring program by disseminating the program model to other educational institutions and community organizations across the state. The replication strategy includes creating and distributing training materials.

Jane Addams School for Democracy

For the past seven years, diverse units of the University of Minnesota, organized by the Center for Democracy and Citizenship/Humphrey Institute and the College of Liberal Arts, have been partners with new immigrants and others in the Jane Addams School for Democracy (JAS). JAS is a community-based education and social action initiative located at Neighborhood House, a 105-year-old settlement house on St. Paul's West Side. The JAS mission is to improve literacy among new immigrants and to develop civic capacity among all neighborhood participants.

The JAS aims to create a multitextured tapestry of learning for all generations. Everyone, from the youngest child to the college professor, is considered a teacher and a learner. The learning method draws on the ideas of nonprofessional learning partnerships and uses the immediate goal of literacy to encourage active citizenship. Language learning and cultural exchanges take place in three learning circles—the children's circle, the adult Hmong circle, and the Spanish-speaking circle. Faculty from more than 20 departments and more than 800 University of Minnesota students have been involved, helping to create a variety of neighborhood art and theater projects with children, working to improve education at the local high school, helping with a community wellness project, and organizing, with immigrants, new initiatives for citizenship, health care, and housing. One project under consideration is a College House in which students involved in the JAS would live on the West Side.

The JAS has acted as a catalyst and resource to other organizations and residents. In the last two years, residents of the West Side and participants of the JAS created the concept of the Neighborhood Learning

235

Community, a four-year initiative recently funded by the DeWitt Wallace Readers Digest Fund. Says Nan Skelton, associate director of the Center for Democracy and Citizenship and principal investigator on the project, "Our belief . . . is that the work of creating a culture of learning is organic, developing sometimes in surprising places and unexpected ways" (Creating a Culture of Learning, 2002, p. 7). "But a collaboration like this, one that evolves and is self-sustaining, is rare" (Creating a Culture of Learning, 2002, p. 7).

Undergraduate Leadership Minor

The Undergraduate Leadership Minor is a cross-disciplinary collaboration between the College of Education and Human Development, the Hubert H. Humphrey Institute of Public Affairs, and the Office for Student Affairs. The program is designed to assist undergraduates to develop the leadership and social change skills requisite for their role as engaged citizens on the campus and in their larger, global community. Senior faculty and professional staff from the three collaborating units teach core courses in which students examine multiple leadership frameworks, leadership and social justice, community building, systems thinking, and social change within the context of an inquiry-, experiential-, and competency-based instructional design. Students interview and "shadow" leaders, conduct and present research on systems and policies that affect perceptions of leadership, participate in service-learning, and create a comprehensive portfolio. A two-credit field experience provides the opportunity for students to apply the theories they have learned.

The Undergraduate Leadership Minor is a vehicle for students to incorporate a leadership and citizenship component into their academic program as they prepare for the workplace and meaningful life in the community.

University of Promise: Realizing the University's Promise for Minnesota Youth

Under the leadership of General Colin Powell, the 1997 President's Summit for America's Future launched America's Promise with the mission of mobilizing people from every sector of American life to build the character and competence of our nation's youth by fulfilling five promises: to mentor, protect, nurture, and teach them and to offer them opportunities to serve their communities. These promises were grounded in extensive theory and research on youth development. Colleges and universities were invited to join America's Promise by becoming a University of Promise to serve as catalysts, conveners, providers, partners, innovators, and civic generators and to play a crucial role in the successful transition to adulthood. In June 2000, on the occasion of its 150th birthday, the University of Minnesota became the first land-grant university to join America's Promise as a University of Promise.

The university has a long history of research, teaching, and outreach in the field of child and family development and is widely recognized for its pioneering work in defining standards for healthy development. Over the last two years, it has engaged its four campuses, six research and outreach centers, extension offices in all 87 counties, and statewide network to touch the lives of thousands of children and youth, from mentoring newly arrived Somali high-school students, to tutoring young children at community sites, and from training teens as peer leaders in healthy futures programs, to engaging third graders as full citizens in public projects they design and lead themselves. Links to many of these projects can be accessed on the University of Promise web site (http://www.promise.umn.edu/). The university is happy to join with many community partners already committed to the five promises, most notably Minnesota Alliance with Youth and Minneapolis Promise for Youth.

As a University of Promise, the University of Minnesota pledges to deepen the understanding of what Minnesota children and youth need to succeed through better research and evaluation, to communicate the needs of youth to improve programs and public policies, and to strengthen and expand outreach efforts that directly touch the lives of children and families.

Journey Toward Engagement in the College of Human Ecology

In light of current challenges and opportunities facing higher education—demographic changes, technological advances, changes in public expectations and funding—the College of Human Ecology (CHE) embarked on a journey to understand its scholarly mission in the 21st century. In the fall 2000, the dean appointed three multidisciplinary faculty committees to address broad themes of scholarship across the college: discovery/research, learning/teaching, and engagement/outreach. Each group identified key trends, current strengths, and areas for improvement. This process resulted in a guiding document titled "Discovery, Engagement, Teaching: Toward an Understanding of the College of Human Ecology's Scholarly Mission in a New Age." The college is taking several action steps toward its goal of engagement.

First, the college is clarifying issues relating to the balance of scholarship, particularly in relation to outreach or engagement endeavors. A task force is specifically charged to develop standards for definitions, meanings, and measures of outreach/engagement scholarship, which will provide the basis for meaningful dialogue regarding expectations for outreach/engagement within the college's tenure and promotion process. Second, the college is developing a cohesive system for gathering data that will incorporate systematic reporting of engagement activity in annual faculty reports. These data will be used in publications to communicate CHE's balanced scholarship agenda to stakeholders. Third, the college is strengthening its partnerships with the community through two college-wide vehicles. The annual CHE Scholarship Dialogue features faculty and graduate students who share current discovery projects and engage community partners and extension educators in a roundtable dialogue to explore how newly generated knowledge applies to family and community needs. The CHE Fabric of Community seminar series connects cutting-edge discovery, teaching, and outreach scholarship to expressed needs of diverse communities of professionals.

Nonprofit Management Task Force

The field of nonprofit management education in the U.S. has expanded quickly, growing from 16 to 180 college or university-based programs in the last 15 years. Many undergraduate and graduate students at the University of Minnesota have expressed an interest in pursuing nonprofit management education, and the university has many resources that are applicable to nonprofit management activities. Leaders of nonprofit organizations have also expressed a strong desire to collaborate with the university in addressing issues and problems related to the management of nonprofit organizations. There is a clear need for coordination across academic programs and community outreach efforts.

In fall 2000, Provost Bruininks charged a Nonprofit Management Task Force, comprised of faculty, staff, students, and community experts, to investigate the feasibility of developing a range of programs related to the interests and needs both of students and of nonprofit employers in Minnesota. After extensive information collection and focus group discussions, the task force developed a set of recommendations for the creation of nonprofit management programs and initiatives at the university.

The task force recommended that the university provide support for a coordinating unit for internal resources and programs relating to nonprofit management and for members of the external nonprofit community. They recommended development and implementation of an undergraduate minor in nonprofit management as well as credit and noncredit certificate programs and workshops. Rather than a separate graduate degree in nonprofit management, they advised concentrations of coursework within various university professional schools. Other recommendations include development of a process for providing technical assistance to nonprofit organizations, an incentive program for action research to advance both theory and practice in the field, and a method for convening roundtables, workshops, and institutes to explore how the work of nonprofits contributes to a democratic way of life and seeks a broader purpose in advancing civil society. The university is currently implementing these recommendations in collaboration with community and statewide organizations.

Distributed Learning

In 2000, Provost Bruininks established a system-wide task force on distributed education, charged with developing a strategic plan for instructional technology that would align teaching and learning technologies with other university initiatives and foster land-grant values of access and accountability. That task force was institutionalized the following year as the Technology Enhanced Learning (TEL) Council under the leadership of Vice Provost Billie Wahlstrom. The TEL Council works to build consensus for systematic and strategic use of technology to enhance learning, to remove obstacles to the use of learning technologies, and to improve access to the university's intellectual assets through programs with statewide reach. TEL initiatives are under way to

- Create communities of learners (including first-year residential students and students of color).

- Extend access to university libraries and other digital collections to learners throughout the state.

- Support new faculty in the effective and strategic uses of learning technologies in their disciplines.

- Extend educational programs—particularly in health professions education—beyond the campus to the community.

- Leverage resources by coordinating learning technology investment in colleges, centers, departments, and initiatives.

- Support the university's unique contributions to workforce education through the State of Minnesota's ISEEK (Internet System for Education and Employment Knowledge) Solutions, of which the university is a founder and charter member.

The University of Minnesota's Portal Strategy Initiative, which is underway, redefines and extends what engagement can be and do. Seen from the beginning as a university-wide effort and led by a broadly representative committee called the Web Integration Group, the Portal Initiative is designed to carry forward the land-grant mission and serve those inside the institution as well as those outside.

Because users can customize their portal to serve their needs and support their university or community role, the university can do a better job of efficiently providing people with access to specific resources that they need. The university portal gives everyone a window on the university, but the landscape each user sees is modified by his or her interests and needs. Therefore, technology can be used to create and support learning communities around issues of interest instead of more centering on subject or departmental affiliation.

Portals offer educational institutions an opportunity to alter the typology by which they define themselves and by which the community knows them. Instead of organizing themselves traditionally by listing hundreds of departments, centers, and degree programs in alphabetical order in a directory, portals allow the university to describe itself thematically, focusing, for example, on points of engagement with the community. At the University of Minnesota, a lifelong learning channel can bring together information about opportunities for citizens to engage with the university beginning with programs for children, such as Farm in the City or 4-H, and continuing through retirement in the Vital Aging Network. Using the portal, citizens can gain access to the university's resources on Community Partnerships or K-16 programs without having first to master the arcane language of departmental nomenclature.

Lastly, the university, along with other academic and community institutions, has long been a part of organizations like the Democracy Collective, which is designed to foster the values of democracy and a civil society. Using its portal structures, the university is now better equipped to be a voice on topics where its research can provide balanced information needed by the community. Just as important, it can provide an electronic forum where the community can engage in conversations about issues of local and global significance. The university's portal strategy includes "green space" where citizens can voice their opinions and offer direction to the institution. Combining these forums with the university's intellectual assets such as the library means that citizens can draw on many of the university's digital resources by using their local library card to gain access to things they hear about online, and they can do this wherever they are in the state.

Institutional Governance and Accountability

Administrative Advisory and Ad Hoc Regents Committees

In the fall 2001, Provost Bruininks appointed two groups to provide recommendations for addressing key issues in public/civic engagement and outreach. These groups were the Administrative Advisory Committee on Public Engagement/Outreach, with membership of deans, chancellors, and vice presidents, and the continuation of the Civic Engagement Task Force. The board of regents appointed a third group: the Regents Ad Hoc Committee on Outreach. Numerous common themes and recommendations emerged from reports submitted by the three groups in May 2002 to the board of regents.

Terminology: What is it? Each report uses "engagement" or "engaged university" to replace the terms "outreach" and "public service." The word "engagement" emphasizes the importance of two-way communication. Engagement means more than the university reaching out. It includes "in-reach" from the public, citizenry, and community.

Scope: How big is it? The magnitude of engagement at the university is immense. Engagement is not compartmentalized as a separate activity distinct from other core missions of the institution; rather, it is integral to teaching and research missions and critical to the survival of some colleges. The University of Minnesota is a leader on the regional and national scenes in its comprehensive approach to being an engaged university.

Value: Why do we do it? Engagement directly benefits both the university and external groups and communities. The benefits to the university include enhancing its core missions, by promoting public scholarship and civic learning as engaged forms of research and teaching, and involving the university in positive relationships with members of the public. The benefits to communities and external organizations include promoting common purposes, addressing real needs, and creating public spaces in which citizens and communities have a voice and where university professionals and citizens can wrestle with pressing, sometimes controversial issues. As engagement with citizenry increases, the university's capacity to address important societal issues will increase.

Implementation: Who does it? Colleges, campuses, and units need their own customized strategies for integrating engagement into their goals. Every discipline has a public dimension. Every college and campus has partnerships. Identifying best practices distinctive to different collegiate units is necessary to assess quality, utility, and effectiveness. The compact process helps address and promote this customization and integration.

Assessment: How well do we do it? Engagement needs to be among the performance indicators of institutional accountability. Indicators should be identified that can help evaluate engagement work, and measures should be developed to assess how the University of Minnesota will be different in five years as a result of engagement. The university should analyze the resources devoted to engagement in the practice of teaching and research, as well as in explicit engagement activities. Such an analysis might well identify an unexpectedly large current institutional investment in engagement. Engaged activities, programs, and scholarly work should be considered in discipline-appropriate ways in recruitment, merit, promotion, and tenure decisions. Such practices are already in place on a limited basis in some units.

Improvement: How can we improve what we are doing? The university should be proactive in communicating with internal and external audiences about engagement. The extent of the university's engagement efforts is not widely understood. Results, as well as activities and improvement efforts, should be featured. Expanding the community of learners and enhancing access to the university's intellectual assets through distributed learning and the university's portal are noted as key strategies for improving both outreach and in-reach.

Each report recommends that engagement be part of the portfolio of one and preferably more senior administrators, who would advocate for it among university priorities and provide coordination of our manifold activities. Following their recommendations, the provost appointed a Council on Public Engagement, comprised of faculty, staff, administration, community representatives, and students, to initiate, facilitate, coordinate, and publicize engagement work.

The University Plan, Performance, and Accountability Report

The university uses its primary planning document, the University Plan, Performance, and Accountability Report, to identify areas in which it intends to excel, to define strategic actions and investments to accomplish its goals, and to measure the impact of these initiatives. This accountability document focuses on the three core missions of the university—research and faculty excellence, student experience, and engagement—together with three supporting areas—human resources, facilities, and institutional efficiency and effectiveness. The prominence of engagement in this plan and in the university's accountability reporting reflects the institution's commitment to measuring and improving performance in this area.

Our goal of becoming an engaged university is translated into a diverse array of access and outreach activities that, taken together, benefit Minnesotans across every community in the state. As described earlier in this chapter, engagement is about more than bringing the university into communities or using its resources to meet needs and solve problems. Beyond these important contributions, the university intends to act more as an active citizen, along with our fellow Minnesota citizens, considering and taking action on issues of mutual interest and importance. At the same time, it faces the pressing issue of financing outreach as sources of public support decrease and as it moves toward a hybrid financing model. Between 1998 and 2001, the university centrally invested nearly $3 million in research-linked, engagement-related activities in addition to the wide range of college and campus-based activities that take place every year.

Two specific goals focus university priorities and measures of performance related to engagement. First, through surveys, the university annually assesses satisfaction of Minnesota citizens and key constituency groups with the university's performance and contributions to the state. Second, to assess progress in increasing the university's successful interactions with, and benefits to, its external constituencies, it uses such diverse measures as library holdings and service, numbers of students participating in community service, and transfers of metropolitan-area students to the university. For the future, the university will synthesize recommendations from the Civic Engagement Task Force, the Administrative Advisory Group on Outreach/Public Engagement, and the Regents Ad Hoc Committee on Outreach to determine what additional measures might be used to analyze its progress in meeting its engagement goals.

Concluding Observations

One striking pattern in Fogelman and Boyte's interviews was the silence about civic motivations, a silence many faculty felt obliged to maintain. The desire for public engagement in scholarly and other activities was widespread. But an equally widespread comment went something like, "I could never discuss this with my colleagues." The pattern pointed to broad cultural norms at the University of Minnesota and across the landscape of higher education. Public activities were seen as "on the side," or even as disadvantageous to one's success as a distinguished researcher and scholar.

The last several years of civic engagement efforts at the University of Minnesota have not completely changed these norms by any means, but they have significantly raised questions, debate, and conversation about the issue in many parts of the university. "Public scholarship," "engaged inquiry," "the epistemology of first-rate research," and a challenge to the conventional continuum of "applied to basic" research have become increasingly common topics.

A striking feature of this ferment is both its decentralization and fragmentation. It is clear that public engagement "looks different" in different units. The College of Architecture and Landscape Architecture, with its focus on educating and empowering communities to create built environments of vibrant and human quality, is different than the College of Biological Sciences, with its stress on educating communities to understand and manage wisely the revolution in biological sciences. The College of Liberal Arts in the Twin Cities has emphasized, among other things, community-based learning opportunities, while the Morris Campus stresses the importance of learning in the context of small towns and rural development. What does civic engagement mean for different disciplines? What are the civic skills and capacities developed by different fields of study and knowledge?

While decentralization has many strengths, it can contribute to the loss of an overall sense of public purpose and institutional civic identity. Thus, a number of issues are also central to revitalizing the land-grant mission of the institution. The Civic Engagement Task Force has proposed concepts of "public scholarship," "civic learning," and "community partnership" as broad themes for continuing development and discussion. A number of related questions arise. What is a scholarship of assessment in which communities become true partners? What are the university's contributions to a "democratic way of life" in the Information Age—and what does it mean, in theoretical as well as practical terms, to talk about democracy as a way of life, not simply a set of formal public institutions and electoral procedures?

These questions illustrate a few of the deep intellectual and theoretical challenges of public engagement that face a great public, land-grant, urban research university as the new century dawns. They are not questions that can be answered quickly, easily, or in isolation. Increasingly, people at the university have come to recognize the need to create collaborations involving peer institutions, disciplines, and the larger landscape of higher education and K-12 education in the state, the nation, and the world in order to begin to adequately address challenges of public engagement. Moreover, the work of knowledge creation and dissemination at the core of the university requires, for its full development, robust, respectful partnerships with a variety of communities, organizations, and public institutions.

In many ways, this effort is at an early stage. But it has already generated wide attention. As a lead editorial in the *Star Tribune* put the matter
recently:

> An identity crisis is at the core of the University of Min-
> nesota's trouble winning support from the Minnesota legis-
> lature in the last decade . . . [As its] great, overarching pub-
> lic mission . . . the university could dedicate itself to
> strengthening the democratic way of life. It could teach the
> skills needed for civic participation and conduct research
> that solves public problems. It could disseminate knowl-
> edge, and share human and physical resources with those
> who need them the most. It could nourish pluralism and
> enter partnerships with others committed to the public
> good. (2001)

The editorial judged that such a course "has much to recommend it."
Many inside and outside the University of Minnesota agree. As a participant in one of the public forums put it, "The whole future of the state of
Minnesota is bound up with the university. If the university recovers its
public purposes, it will have an impact everywhere."

Through its civic engagement initiative, its recognition and reward
programs, and special committees looking at engagement and outreach,
the University of Minnesota is on the brink of the kind of dramatic culture change the *Star Tribune* describes. Programs described here—University Reads, the Career and Community Learning Center, the Jane
Addams School, the Leadership Minor, Nonprofit Management and Distributed Learning initiatives, University of Promise, the College of
Human Ecology's journey toward engagement—exemplify the thousands
of ways in which the university is already deeply connected in two-way
engagement with communities throughout the state of Minnesota and
beyond its borders. As it looks to the future, the university recognizes
that it must continue to state the value of engagement as a cornerstone
of its public, land-grant mission; seek creative approaches to investing in
these activities; measure and reward success in strengthening and
expanding its engagement-related initiatives; and develop effective com-

munication tools to inform the entire community about the wealth and impact of these activities. President Robert Bruininks and Provost Chris Maziar have identified the work of the Council on Public Engagement as a priority under their leadership.

15 | University of San Diego: A Commitment to Collaboration

Francis M. Lazarus
Judith S. Rauner
Cynthia Villis

Service-learning and all of the programs of the Office for Community Service-Learning at the University of San Diego (USD) commit to a collaborative approach with faculty, students, community partners, and staff. Actively supported by the provost, all have benefited from networking and learning through national, state, and regional initiatives. A diversity initiative, also based in the provost's office and a vital component in all USD programs, has significantly influenced USD's development of service-learning.

The University of San Diego (USD) is an independent Roman Catholic institution of higher education located on 180 acres overlooking San Diego's Mission Bay. The university is best known for its commitment to teaching, the liberal arts, the formation of values, and community service. USD was founded on the singular philosophy that a university should be an inspiring place where students not only receive an excellent liberal arts education, but also learn values and participate in public service projects that empower them to pursue careers, and lives, benefiting their communities.

In addition to the dollar figures reported in its economic impact study, the university provides other valuable resources to the San Diego region. Each year USD students, faculty, and staff contribute more than 50,000 hours to volunteer community service programs. Creating opportunities for community service is an integral part of USD's mission and allows students, faculty, and staff to enrich their lives while making this life better for many.

History and Influences: Program Development

The Office for Community Service-Learning (formerly Volunteer Resources) was inaugurated in 1986 by former President Dr. Arthur Hughes, an early member of Campus Compact, and by Sr. Sally Furay, provost and vice president for academic affairs. The provost had formed a small faculty group that became the Social Issues Committee; the president had joined Campus Compact and wanted to expand community service. Together, they envisioned a staff member who could expand programming in these areas and further activate USD's institutional mission. Dual reporting to the vice presidents of academic affairs and student affairs was established, with fiscal connection to the former. Within a few years, Associated Students (AS) leaders expanded Cocurricular Community Service from one to 15 ongoing projects. The Social Issues Committee, with student involvement, initiated a Speakers Series and an annual Conference. Faculty members formed an Ad Hoc Experiential Education Committee (EEC), which became a permanent advisory committee to the provost's office. In 1994, EEC sponsored the development of a service-learning program. Dual reporting strengthened communication and programming for all three committees (Social Issues, Cocurricular Community Service, and Experiential Education).

In 1995 and 1996 respectively, a new president, Dr. Alice Hayes, and a new provost, Dr. Frank Lazarus, brought leadership, expertise, and commitment to community outreach, reinforcing the vitality of service-learning in USD's academic mission. By this time, networking at national conventions and through grants had given staff, faculty, and students a sound theoretical foundation, inspiration, and practical ideas. Every grant that USD proposed was funded, largely due to Office for Community Service-Learning (CSL) initiatives. USD institutionalized its fiscal commitment to CSL and forged a strong reciprocal relationship with its widely diverse Linda Vista neighborhood. The university's willingness to supplement grant funds and its strong history of institutionalizing grant programs in its base budget strongly influenced continuing support from public and private sources.

Annual California Campus Compact grants funded summer institutes in the mid-1990s. Campus teams developed strategies for effective service-learning programs; CSL developed growth strategies at one such program. USD was invited to participate in two Campus Compact–sponsored Wingspread Conferences, including one in 1998 where the provost, a faculty member, a community partner, and the CSL director contributed to an exploration of democratic partnerships between universities and their communities. *Benchmarks for Campus/Community Partnerships* (Campus Compact, 2000) documented these outcomes.

USD and community partners became one of three sites for a National Society for Experiential Education (NSEE) National Community Development Program, identifying issues and strategies in the development of sustainable university-community partnerships. Several publications from that study profiled USD faculty, community partners, and staff in service-learning that engaged college students with elementary and high school students. USD and Linda Vista students formed a multi-aged service-learning group, Youth Empowered through Service (YES), a program in which participants linked the service that they planned and implemented to their academic work. USD matched grant funds with other San Diego colleges and universities when hosting numerous service-learning institutes, networking, and special events.

Role of Academic Leadership

The first priority of an administrator includes reviewing the costs and benefits of a service-learning office, to determine the degree to which the program fulfills the academic mission of the institution. If the program demonstrably promotes both general and specialized educational goals, then it deserves a measure of support proportional to any other effective pedagogy. The importance of such a determination is both to convince casual observers of the legitimacy of the undertaking and to emphasize to faculty and students who participate that they are accountable for effective learning taking place in the service-learning components of the courses offered.

Deans and provosts have special responsibility for reflection on behalf of the faculty. They must uphold the academic integrity of the programs they sponsor, including service-learning, online education, independent study, and internships. Each of these learning modalities must be able to demonstrate support of the unit's educational objectives, and, when it has done so, each modality deserves the support and encouragement of the administration and faculty. Without such support, both internal and external constituents could reasonably question the legitimacy of such programs as credible sources of intellectual development and legitimate sources of academic credit. Administration demonstrates its commitment to support service-learning in a number of ways, but never more importantly than by supporting faculty development in integrating service-learning components into courses across the curriculum. This work lies at the core of the academic process and speaks directly to the quality of learning and teaching at the institution. This support should include the tenure and promotion processes, although faculty peer support for professors who use service-learning pedagogy is equally critical in this respect.

A second level of support for service-learning emanates from the administration's articulation of the institution's relationship to its community. Service-learning has to demonstrate effective service as well as effective learning. Without a mutually beneficial relationship between community and university, there is no opportunity for legitimate service to be performed or legitimate learning to take place in a community setting. The university has a special responsibility to share its intellectual, human, and fiscal resources with its community and to ask for and expect similar and proportional sharing in return. The university teaches students civic responsibility best by providing examples from its own interaction with its community.

Finally, there must be organizational and financial support for service-learning within the structure of the university. Such support is easy to provide when there is an excellent relationship between institution and community; when faculty invest themselves with the responsibility to prepare for, plan, and execute service-learning opportunities in their classes; and when students appreciate and can articulate the intellectual, social, and moral values that derive from this kind of learning. What academic leader would not want to support such a learning paradigm?

Provost and CSL Staff: An Ongoing Team Approach

Service-learning professionals can most effectively seek the support of their faculty and administrative colleagues by demonstrating their commitment to the same principles of effective learning articulated above:

promoting both general and specialized education goals as well as an effective pedagogy. This argument wins approval from leaders who have the best interests of their students and faculty at heart, and, attracts faculty who have not tried service-learning to look seriously into providing such opportunities to students.

From the vantage point of a CSL director, top administrative support brings credibility to CSL in the eyes of all USD collaborators: faculty, staff, students, and community partners. This direct reporting, initially to the provost and then through an associate provost, links major campus initiatives and affirms the academic value of service-learning. This link was evident when USD proposed an Irvine Foundation grant linking service-learning and diversity initiatives. It expanded with USD's participation in the California Campus Compact Community/University IDEAS (Initiatives on Diversity, Equity, and Service) grant. A national campus service-learning reputation increases exponentially when the president, provost, and other academic administrators support service-learning at regional and national levels. Provost Lazarus attended a 1998 Wingspread Conference, California Consortium for Provosts, and California Campus Compact IDEAS Institute, held at USD. At each event he articulated both the theoretical and practical advantages of active service-learning programs and emphasized the need for institutional support to ensure their success.

The president and provost have welcomed participants and affirmed their support at USD events, institutes, conferences, and with groups of educators visiting CSL. USD CSL's national reputation was enhanced when the provost and director presented a case study at the California Consortium for Provosts, and through the Wingspread Conference publication, *Benchmarks for Campus/Community Partnerships*.

Service-Learning as a Collaborative Process

USD collaborators engage in short- and long-range planning; their grant proposal development process involves faculty, students, community partners, and staff. Staff facilitate the process, but the synergy of collaboration generates shared vision and creativity. All collaborators implement programs and institutionalize grant-funded projects, provide conference opportunities, and contribute to information exchange with other institutions. An advisory committee helps to determine the CSL office's direction and serves as an oversight group. Committee members include equal numbers of faculty, students, community partners, and administrators who regularly interact with the CSL office (counseling, career services, financial aid services, student affairs).

CSL staff support faculty, student, and community partner leaders. An experienced faculty member assumes responsibilities as service-learning liaison: recruiting faculty to incorporate service-learning, facilitating curriculum development workshops, and supporting CSL faculty participation. A staff community liaison develops and maintains partnerships with community agencies and schools, working with experienced CSL community leaders to offer workshops for newer agencies and school liaisons. The CSL director and experienced student mentors facilitate student leader recruitment and ongoing seminars and encourage faculty/student leader teams who support students in service-learning classes. All collaborators implement service-learning reflection and evaluation.

Course-based service-learning means commitment to enriching learning through integrated service, academic content, and peer mentoring for faculty, students, and community partners. Infusing diversity awareness, knowledge, and skills in the context of social justice is intrinsic to service-learning and CSL programs. Ongoing improvement is made through evaluation and responses to the information generated.

Overlapping layers of departments, programs, and staff lending support to community service-learning indicate the nutritive institutional support that academic leaders can provide, within ordinary budgeted resources, to service-learning. At USD, staff enthusiastically collaborate in service-learning implementation. Cooperation reflects their perception that USD's mission is linked to service-learning. University Ministry cosponsors social issues events and reflection, attended by many service-learning participants. Residence life actively encourages service-learning participation. Academic deans cosponsor faculty development programs. Financial aid services assigns 20 work-study students to coordinate projects at several placement sites and refers 70 America Reads and America Counts work-study students. Career services facilitates student leader seminars. The counseling center helps students resolve service-related issues. The health center administers tuberculosis tests and provides verification cards. Human resources provides risk management information. Public relations keeps USD's community aware of service-learning programs. Public safety coordinates security, traffic flow, and parking for community partners, speakers, and special events. The registrar facilitates student leader seminar registration after student leaders are chosen from the service-learning classes.

Staff and faculty hope to have service-learning adopted throughout the USD schools and arts and sciences departments, with a high proportion of students experiencing it. Ongoing effort increases the quality of support given to faculty and students. As faculty institutionalize service-learning in their courses, many develop sustainable connections to community.

USD's collaborative model is grounded in mutual exploration of theory and practice, and it involves staff, faculty, student leaders and participants, and community partners. This process is ongoing through conference attendance, planning, evaluating, and networking with other campuses, especially through the regional San Diego Service-Learning Network. As the first and only local campus to initiate and maintain institutional funding, USD supported early and ongoing collaboration. USD and the University of California-San Diego (UCSD) have collaborated most consistently, though not connected through centralized service-learning contacts.

Faculty from San Diego campuses connect through regional service-learning institutes and programs. Internship program staff encourage faculty participation in regional service-learning programs. USD and UCSD teacher education faculty work together in community-based service-learning programs such as Fifth Dimension, where students link service-learning and research. Finally, San Diego presidents and chancellors of higher education meet quarterly to discuss issues of mutual concern, including a common response to community needs such as college and university outreach to public schools.

USD Service-Learning Organization and Administration

Faculty assume leadership in the organization and administration of USD CSL through an Experiential Education Committee (EEC), open to all faculty who engage in any form of experiential teaching and learning.

255

The EEC sponsors all service-learning–related grant proposals, including a 1994 Learn and Serve America grant from the Corporation for National Service. Faculty serve on the CSL Advisory Committee, facilitate curriculum development, and team with student leaders from their classes to support student participation in service-learning.

A director and two assistant directors staff the USD CSL. With overall responsibility for the CSL program, the director develops planning and evaluation; works with faculty and student mentors to recruit, prepare, and support faculty and student leaders; and oversees funding needs, including grant proposal development and implementation.

One assistant director facilitates academic service-learning; the other facilitates student activities-community service. The academic affairs assistant director liaises with community partners, contacts agencies and schools to determine sites where reciprocal learning can take place that corresponds to faculty learning goals, and acts as the primary agency contact throughout the year. Linked to school outreach, he runs the America Reads and America Counts programs.

The student affairs assistant director facilitates the service-related diversity initiative and advises the Associated Student Community Service coordinators, including some who are service-learning participants engaged in service placements. He and the director jointly advise and support the Social Issues Committee, providing programming relevant for service-learning participants.

All three staff share advising of the AmeriCorps site coordinators and three graduate students, preparing them to facilitate site-based orientation, training, and reflection. The CSL administrative assistant, in addition to providing overall support to programs, supervises work-study students who drive shuttle vans, taking service-learning and America Reads students into Linda Vista.

The USD CSL student staff includes three graduate assistants, 20 work-study students (part-time AmeriCorps site coordinators), and six to eight Service-Learning Associates (advanced service-learning leaders). About 20 student leaders team with faculty to integrate service-learning into courses each semester. Associated Students has two student directors and 20 student coordinators. Student leadership continues to expand in scope and depth. One experienced student leader joined students from other U.S. campuses to plan and implement the Raise Your

Voice Campaign, increasing student participation in public life and mobilizing higher education to encourage civic engagement. The student also organized Civic Engagement Week at USD and on a regional level.

The cocurricular program operates from the University Center, adjacent to other AS directors' offices; service-learning is in academic affairs space. Both equally support students interested in service-learning.

Program Implementation

In 2001, the CSL Advisory Committee revised the mission statement for all programs, providing a new foundation to implement. USD CSL facilitates learning with the community through service by

- Supporting reciprocal learning: People help each other within sustainable partnerships.

- Promoting social justice and leadership development

- Valuing diversity, inclusiveness, and the dignity of each individual.

- Encouraging a lifelong commitment to community.

Faculty and student leadership is key. The **faculty liaison**, receiving one course reassigned time, facilitates the curriculum development workshop, supports and guides faculty, and works closely with CSL staff to plan and write grant proposals through the Advisory and Experiential Education Committees.

Student and community partner leadership development parallels this approach: Experienced leaders coach new leaders. Before classes begin, faculty who plan to incorporate service-learning in upcoming semester courses meet with the director to identify placements where learning goals can be met. Agency and school liaisons are contacted by the CSL community liaison to confirm availability of site placements. Over 35 agencies and schools provide regular placements.

In the first few days of classes, **student leaders** are recruited from service-learning courses. Each faculty member chooses a student leader from those who apply. Throughout the semester, student leaders attend a Leadership through Service-Learning seminar, and faculty/student leader teams facilitate service-learning participation through contact with community partners and CSL. Student leaders lead reflections, track logistics, and facilitate evaluation. The midsemester faculty/student leader lunch gives teams opportunities to share strategies that work in reaching those learning goals. It encourages faculty and student leaders to help students in service-learning classes to identify issues and strategies of their placement sites. Problems faced by programs are explored, and students are asked how they can respond to community issues. Community partners play strong roles in advisory groups and collaboration, including grant projects designed to identify the strategies necessary to sustain partnerships.

Agency staff and school liaisons outline needs with the service-learning assistant director and discuss how student participants' knowledge, skills, and time can meet the identified needs of the community and whether services initiated through a class will meet the academic learning goals. CSL prepares USD students to interact effectively with diverse populations, learning reciprocally with the child or adult served and participating in service that links to academic learning.

Sometimes **academic learning goals** result in students developing programs; for example, a media criticism class team planned a workshop with a teacher that responded to specific student needs. Service-learning hours vary according to the learning goals established by faculty; most expect 12-15 hours per semester. Some classes introduce community service-learning, and this requires at least eight hours beginning in mid-semester. These classes are generally freshmen preceptorial classes or those in which students need to develop skills before engaging in service-learning (e.g., engineering workshops in schools).

Faculty are compensated for two days' participation in curriculum development workshops. One day is devoted to a review of foundation and theory; across a semester, the equivalent of the other day permits the faculty member to integrate service-learning. Workshops cover syllabus construction and strategizing links between clear learning goals and the service experience. In addition to faculty/student leader seminars, speakers, and conference opportunities, faculty can look to the experienced faculty liaison for coaching and support. Experienced colleagues have attended and presented at national conferences (funded by grants and USD faculty development). Faculty are also compensated for revising their curricula and writing evaluations. A critical mass of USD faculty are committed to service-learning as a viable pedagogy. They support each other in practical and theoretical implementation.

Social issues forums offer additional content for class reflection. While reflection is a clearly stated expectation, it occurs more effectively in some courses than others. Agency or school liaisons and service-learning site coordinators, often part-time AmeriCorps members, are prepared to enhance site orientation, training, and reflection that reinforce reflection that happens in the classroom (see Figure 15.1).

Figure 15.1
A Team Approach to Service-Learning

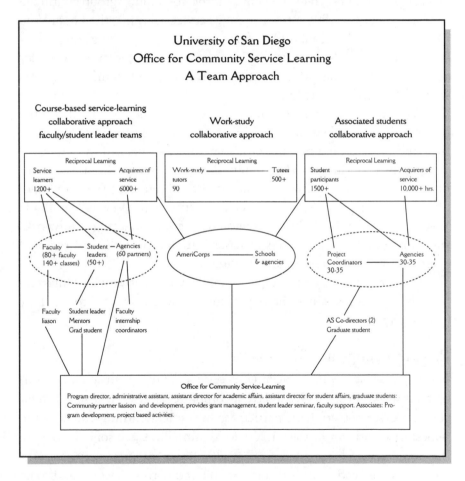

Campus and Community Relations

USD invited existing community partners, especially from its Linda Vista neighborhood, to an informational meeting at the beginning of its Learn and Serve America Higher Education Enhancement grant to discuss dimensions that service-learning added for partners. Community agency and school staff members heard that they would help students meet academic learning goals, and that these students would have expectations beyond those of students engaged in cocurricular service activities. The meeting generated such excitement that the community group continued to meet. Since the 1994 introduction to service-learning, the Linda Vista Collaborative has met monthly to map assets, engage in long-range planning, and successfully partner in grant proposal development with and for agencies and schools. Many partners have received significant grants with USD as their collaborator.

CSL staff regularly invite partners to speak to the community on the benefits of service-learning. Faculty are encouraged to visit placement sites and meet community liaisons; some have succeeded in significant ongoing relationships. A Community Partner Resource Book is distributed to community partners and updated each semester. CSL staff, faculty, and students remain active in community groups, especially in Linda Vista. Staff attend San Diego Regional Network meetings and workshops. National organizations provide valuable conferences, regional meetings, written materials, and funding.

The president's membership in Campus Compact provides information about national issues and opportunities for the director to regularly meet with the president.

Program Scope and Evaluation

Seventy-four faculty have taken USD service-learning curriculum development workshops; 67 (90%) have incorporated service-learning in their courses. Over 600 students participate in service-learning courses each semester; slightly fewer than 1,200 do so annually, since some take more than one service-learning class. Over 70 classes integrate service-learning across the academic year; some are offered both semesters, and some have more than one section. Courses are offered in the Schools of Business and Education and in many arts and sciences departments: communication studies, English, fine arts (music and dramatic arts), foreign languages (French, German, Spanish, Japanese), gender studies, history, computer science and math, political science, psychology, and sociology. Service-learning is incorporated in biology, philosophy, and theology and religious studies, but less frequently. Business courses in economics, information systems, and engineering regularly include service-learning. Most School of Education service-learning courses are in teacher preparation, through an integrated approach.

Results from evaluation and assessment of the service-learning program inform the CSL system, and include:

- **Participants:** Evaluation results are tabulated by class and composite, and then forwarded to faculty and agencies. CSL reviews the results for planning.

- **Student leaders:** Interactive journals are exchanged among student leaders and the director. Journal entries focus on participants' leadership experiences and the process of meeting self-identified seminar goals. Students' written evaluations of seminars help implement changes as necessary and appropriate. End-of-semester focus group interviews reveal the impact of students' experiences.

- **Community partners:** Phone calls are made at the beginning of the semester to confirm placements and also assess student effectiveness, so that problems are identified. The results of surveys and interviews with the partners at the end of the semester are taken into consideration when making plans for the next semester.

- **Faculty liaisons/facilitators:** Written reports from semester's end are reviewed for issues and questions.

- **Overall assessment of diversity** infusion throughout CSL programs: Issues related to diversity are addressed in all evaluations and surveys. (Service-learning students participated in institutional research, establishing norms for the USD Model for Inclusion.) Each semester, assessment outcomes are considered through student self-reporting.

Improvements have occurred in all areas assessed from 1995 to the present. The strongest outcome expressed through assessment was that students could "work productively with persons you might not otherwise encounter," and that judgment was complemented by such expressions as "think about yourself as a resource to the community and the community as a resource to you," "challenge stereotypes, assumptions, and prejudices," "examine your values," and "identify and analyze complex social problems." One student responded, "the service-learning experience was eye-opening . . . I saw things that I thought were just myth or just not there"; another "learned how to put aside my judgments and learn how to meet people and understand them from the inside."

Student assessment clearly indicates unhappiness when the expectation of their reflection is not realized. When students do not perceive their community experience to be integrated with course content, they are disappointed and resent the incongruity.

Faculty who evaluated their course qualitatively the first time they incorporated service-learning saw positive outcomes for themselves and their students. One faculty member said,

> I have never asked students to apply their theoretical knowledge to the day-to-day experiences of community members. Overall, the use of community service-learning improved my course. Not only do the students have a stronger grasp of the complex political world, but I do also.

Another indicated "my intent to confront USD students with reality different than the one they normally live everyday was accomplished over and over."

Program Challenges: Closing Thoughts From the Director

Every program, including those with strong institutional support, faces challenges.

The number of students who can be referred to some popular placements face limits; those interested in a Juvenile Hall literacy project from which they tell peers about their emotionally powerful experience cannot all be accepted as participants.

A few community placements fail to meet academic learning goals or have logistical problems that can't be resolved in a timely fashion. In response, the placement is changed or staff help the students incorporate ambiguity as part of their learning experience. Faculty members and staff can thereby make less-than-ideal service experiences emerge as powerful learning about funding pressures, community agency vulnerability, and the ways in which staff and clients are challenged.

Each semester's beginning is always hectic: recruiting and preparing student leaders for the classroom-based team approach, facilitating placements, presenting orientations and training, and preparing for service-learning experiences to begin within three weeks. Difficulties in recruiting student leaders may occur in some classes where faculty attempt this team approach. When faculty choose to not have a student leader, staff and student mentors provide liaison with CSL.

Institutional procedures must be in place to address rare but potential academic integrity issues. These include written agreements between student and placement liaison, time records which must signed by agency/school staff, and student site coordinators (part-time AmeriCorps members) who provide structure and support that the agency or school cannot.

Students face constraints when they wish to take more than one service-learning course during a semester. A service-learning designation is included in the class schedule, allowing students to make informed decisions about service-learning classes. However, each faculty member must identify the service-learning designation, and when this does not happen, the course catalogue list is incomplete. Students can sometimes change classes or work with faculty to increase the number of hours and fulfill requirements that connect the course content and community experience for each course.

The quality of classroom reflection varies. Faculty who use the faculty/student leader team approach find that leaders initiate discussion about the community experience.

Faculty who integrate service-learning are strong proponents of the meaningful learning experiences for their students, but other faculty still question whether service-learning will maintain academic rigor. Reportedly they discourage untenured faculty from incorporating service-learning. The Experiential Education Committee supports the value of service-learning in the tenure and review process as an extremely important issue on institutional and national levels.

USD has not faced one challenge that plagues many other programs. From the outset of the Social Issues Committee and service-learning, top USD administrators contributed limited institutional funds and provided the necessary space for effective, collaborative administration. The transition from a budget largely proportioned in grant funds to one of institutional funds took time and effort, stemming not from lack of commitment but from fiscal realities. Administrative financial support, however, has been consistent from the outset.

Seeking grant funds remains important, including small incentive grants that became more available than the development grants that helped to start the program. The early grants provided incentive and time needed for fiscal institutionalization. The energy, creativity, and community building that occur when collaborators envision possibilities, design strategies, and commit themselves to continued improvement still happen when even the smallest grants are written and awarded.

Program Challenges: Closing Thoughts From the Provost

My first experience with service-learning occurred at Marquette University in 1994 when I learned that a member of our philosophy faculty was teaching "The Philosophy of Community" and incorporating student service projects as a required component of the course. I was initially skeptical about the idea of providing credit for work that included service, which I have always considered a function of genuine altruism or, at least, of honest volunteerism. I had such respect for this faculty member's integrity and intelligence, however, that I withheld my skepticism and waited to see what would happen. What happened, of course, was an explosion of interest and activity in a mode of learning that struck a responsive chord in hundreds of faculty and thousands of students across the nation within a mere couple of years.

I share this anecdote because I firmly believe that the best catalyst to effective service-learning is a passionately committed faculty member or group of faculty who understand how real learning can and should emerge from community service, and who recognize the distinctive value of this kind of learning. This kind of interest and commitment cannot be dictated, imposed, or cajoled into existence. It depends, as does most good pedagogy and all good scholarship, on the intelligence, curiosity, and persistence of faculty who search for the best ways to help students develop their intellectual abilities and moral character.

There is more required than simply some committed faculty, though, and activities similar to those already mentioned assist us in providing the organizational and financial resources necessary to sustain a service-learning program over time. As provost, I profited immensely from the Wingspread Conference, at which I encountered a broad series of examples of service-learning and community interaction. I am very comfortable at defining the objectives and articulating the theory of service-learning, but the participants at Wingspread opened my eyes to kinds of service projects and levels of institutional involvement in community development that I had not imagined. There is great value in learning from others.

One of the most attractive aspects of service-learning is the creativity demonstrated by faculty and students across the country in developing new ways to integrate service into the curriculum. Sending faculty, students, and professional service-learning staff to regional and national conferences offers them the same opportunity I had at Wingspread to experience new and challenging ideas for student projects, faculty development, and collaborative efforts with other institutions. There are no secrets about the decisions necessary to provide service-learning programs with the tangible resources they need to accomplish their mission. Faculty alone cannot sustain a service-learning program over time, and community organizations require easily accessible contact with university personnel to respond to their legitimate needs. These needs are as real and compelling as the need for production staff in online distance education, for laboratory assistants in the basic sciences, and for directors of co-op and internship programs.

There is always a need to establish priorities and to allocate resources to follow those priorities. Grants have played a large role in the development of many service-learning programs, but, like all government and most foundation support, these sources of funds are not reliable over extended periods of time. The work of scholars such as Alexander Astin and Thomas Ehrlich has clearly established the value of service-learning in developing public virtue and civic responsibility, and it argues persuasively for the continuing support of service-learning programs in institutional base budgets. And once a critical mass of resources has been established, the staff itself can and should demonstrate numerous opportunities to leverage institutional support in the community to expand the reach and effectiveness of partnerships and collaborative efforts. Service-learning programs are generally not expensive to establish or develop to the point of critical mass, and they supply, for the investment, a higher return on learning (to say nothing of community advertising and good will) than any of the other types of pedagogy I mentioned previously.

The question of the value of service-learning on the resume of faculty members, especially those who are not tenured, is and will remain an unresolved issue. That question relies for an answer on the effectiveness of peer review at each institution that supports service-learning. Although administration can affect tenure and promotion review processes at certain points and with respect to some institutional policies, it cannot and should not substitute its own judgment for peer evaluation. What it must insist upon, however, is true peer evaluation, and that should include in the review process a consideration of the faculty member's performance and effectiveness with service-learning, rendered by a review committee that includes other faculty members experienced with service-learning.

I agree with the list of challenges that remain, but I want to expand two issues that are implicit in what has already been suggested. The first is the challenge for faculty and staff involved with service-learning to remain true to the liberal values that attend to service-learning. I do not mean the term "liberal" in a partisan sense, but in the most general social and political sense. The act of rendering service to fellow citizens in need is truly a liberating experience, with or without the more disciplined reflection and articulation of intellectual values that service-learning demands from students. We have become much better at assisting students in intelligent reflection upon their service experiences and in their articulating those values in a meaningful fashion. These efforts have been central to strengthening the overall acceptance of service-learning among faculty, students, and administrators alike, and we should continue to encourage additional development of these skills in our students. I hope that we do not lose sight, however, of the original purpose for developing the service-learning paradigm: the promotion of a genuine altruism that lies at the heart of rendering service without concern for recompense. That altruism teaches students a great deal about the character of liberal learning and establishes a firm foundation for subsequent civic responsibility.

A second challenge is the need for institutions to maintain a sense of modesty and gratitude toward the communities that they serve. Modern American universities possess a daunting array of intellectual, human, and financial resources in the eyes of the communities in which they reside and which they seek to serve. It is not difficult to understand how our communities can be confused by our organizational structure, uncertain of what services and resources are available, and unclear about how to access what they need. Communities, after all, exist to a considerable extent as confederations of small and vulnerable organizations, frequently dependent on volunteer staff and usually underfunded, but also with a clear sense of what their constituents need to improve the quality of individual and communal life.

In the face of such organizations, it is altogether too easy for a university and its representatives to want to impose solutions rather than to offer assistance. Best practices in service-learning make clear that representatives of universities should avoid such tendencies, but it is all too easy to err by trying to help too much and thereby to undermine the credibility, the mission, or the very existence of the organizations we seek to help. Universities, and those representing the service-learning organizations in them, must always bear in mind that we, like the students, are engaged in a learning experience in our communities, and we must discipline ourselves to reflect upon what we can learn from the communities we serve and to render thanks for the privilege of service. Faculty, students, our community partners, and USD administrators have very strong commitments to our Community Service-Learning program, and to the collaborative process that makes our program succeed. Our dedication to continuous improvement keeps us challenged to reflect upon what we do and why we do it.

16 University of Southern Mississippi: Student and Academic Affairs Collaboration for Service-Learning

Myron S. Henry
Joseph Paul
Thomas J. Schnaubelt

The development and evolution of service-learning at the University of Southern Mississippi and at the Board of Trustees of State Institutions of Higher Learning is a case study of collaboration between student and academic affairs. Service-learning is traced from the creation of a Volunteer Resource Center in 1992 to the current coexistence of a campus Office of Community Service-Learning and a statewide Center for Community and Civic Engagement. The authors articulate themes that emerged from a review of institutional documents, from interviews with key personnel, and from personal experience.

The University of Southern Mississippi is in a somewhat unique situation because it hosts the Office of Community Service-Learning (OCSL), which is probably the most well-developed, formal service-learning program of any postsecondary institution in Mississippi, and it hosts the Mississippi Center for Community and Civic Engagement (CCCE, or the center), an extensive-scope center sanctioned by the public university governing board to provide service-learning leadership for the entire state. Both the institutional and state-level service-learning structures were derived from, and continue to rely upon, significant relationships between student affairs and academic affairs. Two institutional stories intersect.

The University of Southern Mississippi

The University of Southern Mississippi (USM) was founded as a normal school in 1910 and is now a multi-sited comprehensive university with its major residential campus in Hattiesburg. Other university sites are primarily along the Mississippi Gulf Coast, including campuses at the John C. Stennis Space Center, Long Beach (a four-year, nonresidential campus), and Ocean Springs (one of two primary locations for the USM College of Marine Sciences). The institution offers doctoral programs in more than 20 fields and is classified as a Doctoral/Research Extensive University by the Carnegie Foundation for the Advancement of Teaching. Between 1996 and 2002, USM's external grant and contract activity nearly tripled (from $17.8 million to $51.1 million).

About 15,500 students are enrolled at USM, and approximately 23% of these students are from underrepresented populations. The mean age of the student population is 25, and 83.4% of undergraduates are less than 25 years old. The university is home to several centers and institutes, including the Mississippi Polymer Institute, the Mississippi Gulf Coast Research Laboratory, and the Center for Economic and Community Development. With the establishment of the statewide Center for Community and Civic Engagement, the university is building on existing service-learning activities and providing new learning opportunities for students through service in communities throughout Mississippi.

The more than 600 tenure-track faculty of the university (about one-third of whom are women) come from virtually every location in America and from many corners of the world. Ten percent of faculty is from races other than Caucasian. Virtually all faculty are involved in the instruction of undergraduate students.

Mississippi, a rural state with a per capita income well below the national average, has struggled with many social and cultural challenges. Much progress on many fronts is evident, but the Magnolia State remains a virtual laboratory to study and accelerate progress on societal issues such as health care delivery, poverty, race relations, community building, and educational attainment in economically disadvantaged areas. With its several sites throughout the most populous part of the state, USM is in an ideal location for the incorporation of service-learning and community engagement into academic curricula. The university recognized the need for more pervasive and direct involvement in addressing societal issues in Mississippi when it created the Volunteer Resource Center in 1992, which in 1995 was renamed the Office of Community Service-Learning (OCSL). The university reaffirmed the growing importance of service as an integral ingredient to learning when it established the more extensive, statewide Mississippi Center for Community and Civic Engagement (CCCE) in October 2000.

Case Study Process

This case study is the product of three modes of inquiry. First, the authors reviewed important institutional documents, proposals, annual reports, and other service-learning–related artifacts. Second, interviews were conducted with past and current administrators, faculty, and staff who were instrumental in the development of service-learning at the state and institution levels. These individuals represent a variety of perspectives that vary both in time (when they were involved) and in place (the positions from which they influenced the development of the programs). The specific interviewees, their roles, and the times of their involvement are included in Table 16.1. The authors used a standard, guided interview format. The authors also reflected upon their roles in the evolutionary process and drew upon their own experiences.

Table 16.1

Interviewees, Roles, and Dates of Involvement

Interviewee	Role: Position	Date(s) of Involvement
Ms. Deanna Berg	Professional staff: service-learning coordinator	1997 - 1999
Dr. Richard Conville	Faculty member: professor, speech communication & service-learning faculty liaison	1996 - present
Dr. Myron Henry	Administrator: provost	1998 - 2001
Dr. Jim Hollandsworth	Administrator: associate provost	1992 - present
Dr. Joe Paul	Administrator: vice president for academic affairs	1992 - present
Ms. Barbara Ross	Administrator: director of union & student activities	1992 - present
Mr. John Wyble	Professional staff: assistant director of union & student activities (service-learning director)	2000 - present

What follows is a composite of the various perspectives obtained through a review of documents, interviews, and personal reflection. Our goal was to provide an accurate account of the development of service-learning, with attention to several observations and themes that emerged regarding how the relationship between student affairs and academic affairs impacted the development process. We have intentionally included successes, failures, and tensions, and avoided a more Panglossian description. The authors recognize that educational environments differ among institutions, and therefore we caution readers to extrapolate only those lessons that are applicable to their particular institutional circumstance.

The Volunteer Resource Center (1992-1995)

By all accounts, the institutionalization of service-learning at USM began within Student Affairs. Ms. Barbara Ross, the director of Union and Student Activities, spearheaded the initial effort by creating the Volunteer Resource Center (VRC) in the fall of 1992. Ms. Ross credits a workshop sponsored by the Association of College Unions International and the University of Pittsburgh for inspiring her initial enthusiasm and ideas. She noted that the VRC was filling two voids, which she perceived to be interconnected. First, there was no coordinated effort to promote volunteerism in the local community. Second, Ms. Ross believed the leadership program that her unit had been implementing had not been successful due to prior compartmentalization of efforts, and she believed that service might be a possible alternative, and more effective way to foster leadership skills in students.

Dr. Joe Paul, the vice president for student affairs, welcomed the concept of creating the VRC, but for slightly different reasons. His support for the initiative was derived from a strong belief in experiential learning and a desire to combat the image (whether real or perceived) of the college student as having become overly self-centered and disengaged from public and community life. Dr. Paul and Ms. Ross both acknowledged significant pressure from students for the creation of the VRC and the students' responsibility for nearly every aspect of its initial development.

According to a progress report dated March 30, 1994, the original purpose of the VRC was to "encourage civic responsibility among university students and to promote community in the Hattiesburg area." For the first two years, Counseling Psychology graduate assistants served as part-time staff for the VRC and reported directly to Ms. Ross. During this time, activities included investigating how other colleges and universities developed and operated community service programs, soliciting student organizations for support, and conducting an audit of the need for volunteers at local area community agencies. The VRC organized its first community service project—refurbishing a playground at a local housing project—on National Youth Service Day in April 1993. By the end of the 1992-1993 academic year, 24 community-based agencies had been identified as needing volunteers, 20 student organizations had affiliated with the VRC, and approximately 100 individuals had volunteered in and through the VRC. By the end of its second year, the VRC had identified volunteer needs in 30 community-based agencies, 23 student organizations had affiliated, and the number of student volunteers had doubled to approximately 200. Ms. Ross attributes strong connections with the local United Way to rapid growth in agency partnerships, and all those who were interviewed about the initial development of the VRC cited strong student support as a factor that contributed to early successes.

While student involvement dramatically increased during the first two years, faculty involvement in the VRC was neither ubiquitous nor well organized. For instance, when the VRC invited faculty from across campus to participate in a service-learning videoconference sponsored by the National Association for Student Personnel Administrators, only two faculty members attended. Actually, faculty who attended from other institutions outnumbered the USM faculty. Through her active involvement in a variety of Hattiesburg organizations, Ms. Ross was able to develop relationships with several key faculty who were interested in community work; however, no formal or systematic effort was made to develop a faculty role. These faculty shared predispositions to being involved in community service work (and had perhaps been doing service-learning under another name), and as they became aware of the VRC, they began to coalesce into a small, informal support network. This small group—comprised of about five individuals—can be referred to as "green light" faculty.

These green light faculty did not represent a critical mass, but they did serve an important informal role in guiding the program's focus from an exclusively community service orientation toward a focus on *academic service-learning.* This guidance included authoring a United Way grant proposal to support the VRC, developing a position description, and assisting with the selection of a full-time service-learning coordinator.

Although unrelated to these developments, another serendipitous event took place that would ultimately impact the connection between academic and student affairs. Dr. Richard Conville, a highly respected, tenured professor of speech communication, audited an undergraduate service-learning course taught by Harvard professor Robert Coles at the Center for Documentary Studies at Duke University in winter 1994. Although Conville's initial interest in the course was motivated by Coles' use of narrative methods, his first exposure to service-learning was as a participant. As part of the documentary writing course, Conville helped teach a 55-year-old general equivalency diploma student arithmetic in downtown Atlanta. The power of this experience was transformative. Upon his return to USM, Dr. Conville began integrating service-learning into Honors College courses (Narrative Community and Communications). Conville would ultimately play an essential role in increasing faculty participation in service-learning and creating a bond between academic and student affairs.

From the formation of the VRC through the 1993-1994 academic year, there had been a rather uncoordinated and somewhat serendipitous new emphasis on academic service-learning (as opposed to exclusively community service). In a spring 1994 report, VRC graduate students described a need for grant funding, reported having contacted all the academic deans, and made a vague reference to having "set goals of acquiring academic credit for student volunteers." This report also included the first reference to and a tacit recommendation for the creation of a full-time coordinator position.

Formal Expansion (1995-1996)

A year after the recommendation for a full-time coordinator was made, the University of Southern Mississippi became the first institution in the state to create and fill a full-time professional position to support service-learning. Shortly after assuming the role of service-learning coordinator at USM in June 1995, Mr. Thomas Schnaubelt initiated a name change: the VRC became the Office of Community Service-Learning (OCSL). The change reflected a more comprehensive purpose that included efforts to integrate service into the undergraduate learning experience—

particularly through service-learning coursework. During Mr. Schnaubelt's year at USM, a student organization dedicated exclusively to leadership and service was created (VISION), and USM became the first public university in Mississippi to affiliate with Campus Compact. Mr. Schnaubelt made numerous presentations to faculty and administrators and had some success bridging student affairs and academic affairs, particularly through support of faculty in social work and general studies who had a predisposition to service-learning as a pedagogy. Although he served as the service-learning coordinator for only one year, the basic structure and foundation laid by Mr. Schnaubelt remains. Furthermore, Schnaubelt continued to have a direct impact on the OCSL through his work at the state college board office, where he directed an academic affairs unit responsible for providing state-level oversight and resources for service and outreach.

Expanding Academic Connections (1997-1999)

The service-learning coordinator position remained vacant for nearly a year. During this time, undergraduate students in the fledgling student organization VISION, a graduate student assistant, and AmeriCorps members in the new Campus Link program, maintained—to a limited extent—the OCSL. Ms. Ross provided administrative leadership while programmatic matters were managed by a graduate assistant. In the spring of 1997, Ms. Deanna Berg was selected to fill the vacancy. Like Mr. Schnaubelt, Ms. Berg had been active in postsecondary service-learning initiatives elsewhere as a student (Schnaubelt at the University of Michigan, Berg at California State University-Chico).

Unprecedented growth occurred during Ms. Berg's tenure. During this period the OCSL developed or strengthened numerous programmatic partnerships, including connections with AmeriCorps, the Freshman Year Experience office, fraternities and sororities, and the local United Way. Other specific accomplishments included:

- Reinvigorating the VISION student service organization, including the development of a clear organizational structure with progressive student leadership opportunities.

- Securing administrative support staff.

- Assisting in the establishment of a faculty liaison position.

275

- Developing a Fund for the Improvement of Postsecondary Education (FIPSE) faculty fellows grant proposal (which was ultimately funded).

- Expanding the OCSL's physical presence (both metaphorically and in terms of square footage).

- Establishing a process by which community members were able to utilize the OCSL volunteer clearinghouse.

- Providing summer volunteer opportunities—specifically through a VolunTeens program.

- Establishing a campus-wide service council.

More important, formal connections between academic affairs and student affairs flourished. There were at least three contributing factors: 1) There was a change in academic affairs leadership, 2) formal involvement of respected faculty increased service-learning's academic credibility, and 3) the institution undertook an extensive strategic planning process—a process that enabled significant communication between student and academic affairs. Although several efforts had been made to engage academic affairs (or at least build awareness of OCSL efforts), there had been little tacit support from a top-down perspective prior to 1998. Dr. Myron Henry was appointed to the provost position in 1998, and he brought with him a proactive receptiveness to Ernest Boyer's (1990) concept of the engaged campus. USM faculty were also catalyzed by the September 1998 visit of Dr. Edward Zlotkowski, a senior fellow at the American Association for Higher Education and Campus Compact. He spent several days with key faculty to provide theoretical foundations and practical applications, and he met with top-level academic administrators.

The establishment of a service-learning faculty liaison position provides tangible evidence of an evolving relationship between student affairs and academic affairs during this period. The concept of the faculty liaison position was developed and proposed by Ms. Berg and Dr. Conville, whom Provost Henry then appointed to the position. The faculty released time was initially paid for by student affairs, but ultimately this cost was shifted to academic affairs. Dr. Conville's role was to assist

Ms. Berg in efforts to reach, orient, and support faculty interested in implementing service-learning. Student affairs recognized the need for academic legitimacy, and academic affairs found value in the community partnerships, student enthusiasm, and logistical support that could be provided by the OCSL. Although the relationship between student affairs and academic affairs during this period can be characterized as productive and amicable, several interviewees also described some tension regarding program ownership.

One of the assignments for then Provost Myron Henry in 1998-1999 was to lead the institution in the development of its first comprehensive strategic plan. USM's involvement in service-learning was already a priority, due in large measure to the leadership of Vice President for Student Affairs Joe Paul. In recognition of past and ongoing commitments by USM to service-learning, the 1999 strategic plan, titled The University of Southern Mississippi: A National University for the Gulf South, contained a major section on cocurricular activities. A prominent phrase from that section reads:

> The concept of service-learning is based upon the supposition that the interaction of knowledge and skills with experience is the key to learning. . . . students learn when they apply what they have gained from classroom experiences to real issues of importance, and when the community becomes the field laboratory. (p. 29)

The strategic plan also contained several relevant goals, including:

- Expand faculty knowledge of, and professional development in, service-learning approaches, especially in academic fields that lend themselves to these experiences.

- Increase the opportunities for students to enroll and participate in service-learning experiences. (p. 29)

Continued Expansion and Strengthening Academic Connections (2000-Present)

After Ms. Berg's departure, university-wide budget concerns delayed the filling of the service-learning coordinator position for another year. Fortunately, the faculty service-learning liaison and the full-time administrative staff person were able to provide a degree of continuity, and they were able to maintain—and in fact build upon—some of the basic and essential programs during the vacancy. In September 2000, Mr. John Wyble was selected to serve as assistant director of union and student activities—a new position title representing an increase in responsibilities and nature of the position.

Mr. Wyble inherited several advantages. First, the OCSL now had a history on campus. Although not ubiquitously known, the OCSL and its mission were now familiar to students, faculty, staff, and the community agencies. Second, while previous coordinators came to a position that had very few established programs, the OCSL now had several externally funded projects that were either already operating or about to unfold. These programs included maintenance of a volunteer clearinghouse, advisorship of the VISION student organization, coordination of a FIPSE faculty fellows program (spearheaded by Eastern Michigan University), local oversight of a team of Campus Link AmeriCorps members, and administration of a new Learn and Serve America sub-grant to establish a service-learning, after-school program with a K-12 and community-based partner.

Mr. Wyble's primary task was to provide a structure to ensure coherence, comprehensiveness, and effectiveness. Wyble's resourcefulness led to the development of several new programs at USM, including:

• A SCALE-funded (Student Coalition for Action in Literacy Education) literacy program to improve tutoring effectiveness in local K-12 schools.

• The development of a Community Council (which helps ensure coherence, comprehensiveness and effectiveness).

• Preparing Tomorrow's Teachers to use Technology (PT3) program that brings together technology and service-learning to prepare students in education for integrating technology into instruction in an experiential process.

Although the OCSL provides technical assistance to faculty across the university who are interested in developing or implementing service-learning courses, its formal connections to academic affairs are derived from the service-learning faculty liaison position and the FISPE faculty fellows program. Each semester, faculty from across the university are selected to participate in a fellowship seminar. Participants are expected to lead similar workshops within their unit or department, thereby "cascading" awareness and involvement in service-learning as a pedagogy.

Evolution of Service-Learning in Mississippi (State-Level Leadership)

While USM's service-learning program continued to develop after his departure from USM in July 1996, Mr. Schnaubelt changed position to lead a new effort at the Board of Trustees of State Institutions of Higher Learning (IHL) in Mississippi. His work focused on the development of service-learning and the creation of partnerships between student affairs and academic affairs at several Mississippi colleges and universities. Mr. Schnaubelt initially directed a statewide AmeriCorps program (Campus Link), a program that sought to establish campus/community partnerships as well as student affairs/academic affairs partnerships at 18 postsecondary institutions throughout Mississippi. The success of this initiative prompted the creation of the Academic Service Programming unit within the Division of Academic and Student Affairs at IHL.

In 1999, all three state education agencies, the Mississippi Commission for Volunteer Service, and a variety of service-learning practitioners engaged in a strategic planning process. The group met periodically during the year to discuss how service-learning could be made a more central part of Mississippi's formal and informal education processes. Among other things, the group articulated the need for a statewide higher education–based center to foster growth in educator awareness of service-learning and to support its growth through training and resource development. The group—formally known as the Mississippi Alliance for Community Service-Learning—developed and submitted several proposals for external funding. The success of these proposals enabled the establishment of a new Mississippi Center for Community and Civic Engagement (the "center") to be based on a campus.

After USM responded favorably to a call for proposals from chief academic officers to establish the center at its Hattiesburg campus, a meet-

279

ing was convened with Dr. Myron Henry (provost), Dr. Joe Paul (vice president for student affairs), Dr. Richard Conville (service-learning faculty liaison), Dr. Don Cotten (vice president for research), and Dr. Carl Martray (dean of the College of Education and Psychology) to discuss how the center would operate and be supported. It was decided that each of the three vice presidents, in addition to the IHL Office of Academic and Student Affairs, would contribute financially to the initial development of the center.

Dr. Thomas Schnaubelt was offered and accepted appointment at USM as the director of the center in August 2000. In the context of the 1999 strategic plan, USM Provost Henry envisioned that the USM-based center would become the agent for the state college board office for an extensive array of statewide service programming. In Dr. Schnaubelt's letter of appointment, it was made explicit that he would be expected to work in "collaboration with staff at the Institutions of Higher Learning on appropriate statewide initiatives." Indeed, Dr. Schnaubelt's initial duties as director of the center included overall management for two statewide Learn and Serve America programs, including a multi-institution higher education consortium (comprised of USM, Delta State University, Hinds Community College, Jackson State University, and the University of Mississippi).

The partnership with IHL was further advanced when Dr. William McHenry, assistant commissioner for academic and student affairs of IHL, and Dr. Henry agreed that IHL would support 10% of the compensation package for the director of the center. Draconian budget reductions to all Mississippi public universities and to the IHL central budget, and Dr. Myron Henry's January 2001 departure from the USM provost's office, eventually altered initial understandings between the IHL central office and USM. However, because of Assistant Commissioner McHenry's commitment to a statewide agenda in service programming and Dr. Schnaubelt's regional leadership, the center has, in fact, become the agent for the state college board office on many statewide initiatives. The center provides statewide leadership for the Learn and Serve America Lighthouse Partnership program, the Mississippi AmeriCorps*VISTA Service-Learning Initiative, Reading Is Fundamental, Campus Link AmeriCorps, and the Pew Partnership for Civic Change Leadership Plenty program. Each of these initiatives involves multiple K-12, postsecondary, and community-based partners across the state. Although IHL was unable to provide financial support to the center during its first two years of operation, significant support is being provided during the 2002-2003 academic year.

The role of Dr. Joe Paul, vice president for student affairs, was as important in establishing the center as it was in creating the OCSL in 1995. Drs. Henry and Paul agreed that the director of the center would have a joint reporting responsibility to the provost and the vice president. In order to give the center higher visibility among faculty and to encourage further incorporation of service-learning concepts into curricula, it was decided that the director's position would be fully budgeted through the provost's office. However, the vice president for student affairs was to underwrite a portion of the costs annually (the vice president for research also agreed to underwrite a portion of the center's cost for the first year of its existence). The OCSL would continue to report through the vice president for student affairs but would work in tandem with the more extensive-scope center.

The center and the OCSL are currently connected through a variety of the initiatives previously mentioned, including Learn and Serve America, Campus Link, and AmeriCorps*VISTA. In each of these cases, the center provides similar resources and programmatic opportunities to the OCSL that are provided to other Mississippi postsecondary institutions. In other cases, the two offices operate more collaboratively. For instance, the OCSL and the center comprise the leadership team for the first annual Gulf South Summit on Service-Learning, Community Engagement, and Higher Education, and they share responsibility for the development of the American Humanics program. The relationship between the center and the OCSL is perhaps similar to that of a state Campus Compact office housed at an institution that also has a community service-learning office.

Lessons Learned

Perhaps the most telling lesson in this case study is that the views from various perspectives were remarkably similar. For instance, the view that student affairs served as the initial catalyst was confirmed by the provost and associate provost. Although discrepancies between accounts existed, more often than not the discrepancy related to when something happened as opposed to who was responsible, or how or why a particular event happened. Upon further analysis and reflection, the following themes were developed based on the consistency among interview responses.

Planned Serendipity

Nearly all of the interviewees suggested that serendipity or auspicious timing played a role in the development of service-learning at USM or in Mississippi, or in the development of partnerships between academic and student affairs. However, a more appropriate term might be "planned serendipity." As described by the Hardwood Group (1998), which developed the term based on interviews with 65 community organizers across the U.S., the seemingly paradoxical notion of "planned serendipity" is "actively setting the stage for fortuitous circumstances to come together" (A Different View, ¶ 1). Each of the individuals involved in Mississippi was able to think of the unimagined, build relationships where barriers or complacency once existed, and learn or discover what was previously unknown.

The Importance of Capitalizing on Inherent Strengths and Weaknesses

Another factor contributing to the success of service-learning partnerships was the ability of each of the parties to recognize their own inherent strengths and weaknesses, and to collaborate when necessary to maximize strengths or circumvent weaknesses. Robert Putnam's (2000) concepts of bonding and bridging social capital help illustrate this point. Bridging social capital is described as having broader identity and reciprocity, linking to external assets, and being more flexible. Conversely, bonding social capital consists of dense, often exclusive or narrowly defined groups and networks. In social situations, bonding social capital is glue, while bridging social capital is WD-40.

The institutionalization of service-learning demands both bridging and bonding social capital. Descriptions by those interviewed indicate that the nature of USM academic affairs was akin to bonding social capital, while the currency of student affairs was that of bridging social capital (here, as throughout, we seek only to describe USM and are not seeking to generalize to other institutions or higher education as a whole). For instance, being less constrained by the academic calendar and course rotations, student affairs personnel have been able to develop more (though not necessarily "better") relationships with community agencies. The strengths and weaknesses, as articulated in the interviews, are summarized in Table 16.2. The view that academic affairs provided glue, while student affairs served as a lubricant, is consistent with the widely held perception that student affairs provided the catalyst for service-learning at USM.

Table 16.2
Perceptions of Strengths/Weaknesses of USM Academic and Student Affairs Units

	Strengths	Weaknesses
Student Affairs (Bridging Social Capital)	• Funding flexibility (auxiliary funds) • Programming flexibility (able to pilot new programs; not bound by semester) • Close connections with student organizations and leaders	• Lack explicit or formal connection to classroom/curricula • Lack academic credibility
Academic Affairs (Bonding Social Capital)	• Academic credibility • Dense networks and interaction with community partners and students • Expertise in narrowly defined areas	• Rigid schedule • Institutionally conservative (slow to change or adopt something new)

Again, these observations are not intended to be generalizations. They are common perceptions of people interviewed for this particular case study. In our experience—at both the institution and the state level—academic service-learning would not have naturally evolved from a volunteer clearinghouse housed solely in student affairs divisions; nor did the academic affairs units have the flexibility or vast local social/community networks to catalyze the growth seen at USM or in Mississippi. Simply stated, each unit (student affairs and academic affairs) was able to identify their strengths and opportunities and subsequently provide access to these resources (grant writing, access to student leaders, access to respected faculty, etc.) to strengthen service-learning. More generally, the importance of maintaining connections with more than one area—to tap into inherent strengths and overcome weaknesses—is essential for long-term, transformational success.

The Importance of Sustained Leadership From Upper-Level Administrators

It is no secret that leadership from upper-level administration is key not only for establishing a major center such as the Mississippi Center for Community and Civic Engagement, but also for ensuring that service-learning flourishes. When many institutions and leaders might have shied away from a major new investment during tough times, Drs. Henry and Paul from USM and Dr. McHenry from the state college board helped foster the creation of the center under difficult fiscal circumstances for higher education in Mississippi.

While an initial investment in service-learning was important, the sustained leadership provided by key individuals was absolutely essential. Despite dramatic turnover in administrative posts at USM, Drs. Paul and McHenry have continued to support service-learning in visible and essential ways from positions that they held when these initiatives began. Other key senior level administrators, most notably Drs. Henry and Hollandsworth, played important roles during the administrative transition by successfully garnering the continued support of the new administration. While these two individuals now serve in different capacities at USM (Dr. Henry as president-elect of the faculty senate and Dr. Hollandsworth as the dean of the graduate school), both continue to provide indirect support for the development of service-learning.

USM's two watershed events provide the basis for our final lessons: the creation of an administrative unit staffed by full-time professionals and the establishment of the faculty liaison position. Edward Zlotkowski (1998) and others (Morton & Troppe, 1996) have already described the importance of having strong program advocates. While Zlotkowski calls for a "specific leader, an individual willing and able to serve as program champion and program visionary" (p. 10), Morton and Troppe indicate that a team of faculty and administrators needs to serve as a core group committed to service-learning. In USM's case, two individuals were needed—one from student affairs and one from academic affairs, each

with distinct roles, but working in tandem—to make the program successful.

The Importance of Service-Learning Professional Staff

It is self-evident that it takes good people to make service-learning work.
Indeed, a common theme from interviews (particularly with top-level
administrators) was the belief that USM's success in service-learning was
in large part due to the abilities and enthusiasm of the three service-
learning coordinators. This observation raises a new question: what kind
of people are good people to coordinate service-learning programs? All
three of the service-learning coordinators interviewed were dynamic,
energetic, systems-thinking individuals. Each was also relatively young,
ambitious, relatively inexperienced, and aspired to long-term careers in
academia (all were enrolled in graduate degree programs during their
tenure).

Service-learning, viewed as a form of institutional renewal, requires a
great deal of sustained, almost "booster-like" energy in its initial stages of
development. For professional staff, it also requires an understanding of
academic culture and limited respect for its processes and purposes. By
"limited" we mean that the individual must simultaneously challenge and
respect the traditional notion of academic culture. Though each
approached his or her responsibilities differently, all three USM coordinators demonstrated considerable ability in communicating within both the
academic and the nonprofit (or community-based) cultures in which
they needed to operate. Having said this, thus far the tenure of service-
learning coordinators has lasted less than three years. This turnover has
undoubtedly impeded program growth, and draws attention to the need
to provide appropriate compensation, professional development, and
advancement opportunities to attract and retain service-learning coordinators.

The Importance of Sustained Involvement of Senior-Level Faculty

Interviews also made clear that although USM's service-learning program germinated from within the student affairs division, stagnation—or
at least stunted growth—would have occurred without significant and
sustained involvement from academic affairs. Specifically, the creation of
a faculty service-learning liaison and the appointment of a senior, well-

respected faculty member, provided an injection of energy at precisely the right time. To use Putnam's term, this person was able to provide bonding social capital within the academic world. Moreover, Dr. Conville has fostered a greater understanding of the principles of service-learning and has helped clarify the distinction between service-learning and experiential learning (practica, internships, etc.) and community-based work (community service, volunteerism, etc.). His involvement has been particularly effective in promoting and ensuring the high standard of academic integrity and rigor needed to combat the common misconception that service-learning is pedagogical "fluff." Perhaps Dr. Conville's greatest contribution was his sustained involvement through periods of administrative transition. Dr. Conville was able to help provide programmatic continuity and garner support from the new administration.

Future Directions

As was noted earlier, service-learning in Mississippi and at USM has not "crossed the finish line." Future plans—for both the center and the OCSL—in large part involve acting upon the lessons learned above. For instance, Mr. Wyble articulated future plans to build internal support to develop positions that focus on three key areas: academics, students, and community. The OCSL plans to continue growth by focusing on developing a more coordinated and efficient approach to implementing existing programs. Wyble articulates a vision of strengthening support for service-learning at USM—particularly as a mode of teaching and learning.

For its part, the center hopes to emulate the grassroots, organic process that has made service-learning successful at USM and other institutions participating in its higher education consortium. Plans are currently underway to establish senior level service-learning faculty liaisons at four other postsecondary institutions to work with their service-learning coordinators. Members of the center's higher education consortium (which includes USM) will also be involved in two assessment efforts during the 2002-2003 academic year. First, coordinators at each campus will conduct institutional self-assessments to informally gauge institutionalization of service-learning at their respective campus. The self-assessments will be based on a process designed by Dr. Andrew Furco at the University of California-Berkeley: "Self Assessment Rubric for the Institutionalization of Service-Learning in Higher Education."

Second, the center plans to coordinate a multi-institutional survey of faculty to assess the breadth and scope of service-learning involvement. Other goals include intensifying efforts to emphasize service-learning in faculty roles and reward structures; working with more faculty members and departmental chairs to expand the use of service-learning in more departments, colleges, and institutions throughout the state; and expanding the number of institutions participating in the higher education consortium.

Because of the need to be a household word at grassroots levels of the university, USM's service-learning advocates now seek to raise the level of awareness of department chairs and faculty leaders about its activities. This type of visibility is paramount for the long-term success of service-learning, especially as it relates to increasing faculty involvement and curriculum development at postsecondary institutions throughout Mississippi.

Sustained faculty involvement will also be enhanced by recognition that service-learning and community engagement that utilize academic expertise count in the faculty roles and rewards structure of the university and IHL. The USM 1999 strategic plan contains a major section titled "Scholarship: All Encompassing." Service is a featured subsection, and scholarship in service to society is described through several examples. A central statement reads, "Whenever USM faculty draw upon their professional expertise to aid people and organizations, or when students are engaged in service-learning through class, then faculty are engaging [in scholarship] in service to society." Another statement reads, "Paraphrasing [Ernest] Boyer's words, 'building bridges between theory and practice' is an essential activity for faculty to engage in and is the basis for scholarship in service to society" (p. 36). USM's service-learning advocates must ensure that these statements are brought to life more completely by making faculty scholarship in service to society an activity that is rewarded—in tenure and promotion and in salary increases. Changes in senior administrative leadership at USM have been numerous since the development of the 1999 strategic plan and the creation of the Mississippi Center for Community and Civic Engagement (e.g., there have been three presidents and three provosts, and several deans and an associate provost have left). Turnover at senior administrative levels makes it even more apparent that the department chairs are a key leadership group with whom practitioners must connect in more pervasive ways. Simply stated, service-learning must be in the consciousness of leaders among faculty and department chairs if it is to enjoy maximal, long-term success.

Finally, the future evolution of service-learning at USM has undoubtedly been impacted by recent turnover in USM's cabinet-level posts. This transition requires that service-learning advocates continuously build awareness and seek involvement/investment from new administrators, and in turn has prompted discussion about the possible administrative reorganization of service-learning (including the relationship between student affairs and academic affairs). Each of the people interviewed for this case study recognized that administrative changes provide an opportunity for a quantum leap—the question is simply in which direction that leap will be.

Resources

Below are a number of resources—web, print, and people/organizational—that will assist academic leaders interested in advancing service-learning and civic engagement on their campuses. These resources are divided into three categories: general, which includes a wide variety of helpful resources for any campus; sector-specific, which are tailored to particular types of higher education institutions; and topic-specific, which offer guidance on particular subjects, many of which are also addressed in the main text of this book. Again, we strongly encourage you to pursue these helpful and plentiful resources.

General Resources

American Association for Higher Education Service-Learning Project/Service-Learning in the Disciplines (20-Volume Monograph Series)
http://www.aahe.org/service/series_new.htm
This site includes program models and extensive information about the American Association for Higher Education's groundbreaking series on service-learning in the disciplines, an invaluable resource for faculty and departments in 20 discipline areas.

Astin, A. W., Vogelgesang, L. J., Ikeda, E. K., & Yee, J. A. (2000). *How service learning affects students.* Los Angeles, CA: University of California-Los Angeles, Higher Education Research Institute.

Boyer, E. L. (1996). The scholarship of engagement. *Journal of Public Service & Outreach, 1* (1), 11-20.

Bringle, R. G., Games, R., & Malloy, E. A. (Eds.). (1999). *Colleges and universities as citizens.* Boston, MA: Allyn & Bacon.

Campus Compact
www.compact.org
Arguably the most comprehensive web site on civic engagement in higher edu-

cation in the world, Campus Compact's site includes a wide range of information, including "Strategies for Creating an Engaged Campus: An Advanced Service-Learning Toolkit for Academic Administrators" (http://www.compact.org/advancedtoolkit/default.html), as well as an extensive resources section containing service-learning syllabi, definitions, principles of best practices, program models, online databases, statistics, links, listservs, funding and grant opportunities, and more. Many of the web, print, and people/organizational resources listed below can be accessed via Campus Compact's web site.

Campus Compact/American Association for Higher Education
Service-Learning Consulting Corps
http://www.compact.org/faculty/consulting-corps.html
Corps members include 20 senior teacher-scholars with expertise in different institution types and representing a variety of disciplines. A unique resource offered by Campus Compact and AAHE to assist institutions in becoming more effective vehicles of academically based civic engagement.

Colby, A., Ehrlich, T., Beaumont, E., & Stephens, J. (2003). *Educating citizens: Preparing America's undergraduates for lives of moral and civic responsibility.* San Francisco, CA: Jossey-Bass.

East/West Clearinghouses on the Scholarship of Engagement/National Review Board for the Scholarship of Engagement
www.scholarshipofengagement.org
The National Review Board provides external peer review and evaluation of a faculty's scholarship of engagement. Other clearinghouse services include consultation, training, and technical assistance to campuses that are seeking to develop or strengthen systems in support of the scholarship of engagement; forums, programs, and regional conferences on related topics; and a faculty mentoring program with opportunities for less experienced faculty to learn from the outreach experiences of more seasoned scholars.

Ehrlich, T. (Ed.). (2000). *Civic responsibility in higher education.* Phoenix, AZ: Oryx Press.

Hollander, E., & Saltmarsh, J. (2000, July/August). The engaged university. *Academe,* 86(4), 29-31.

Jacoby, B., & Associates. (1996). *Service-learning in higher education: Concepts and practices.* San Francisco, CA: Jossey-Bass.

The Journal of Public Affairs, Vol. VI. (2002). Supplemental Issue 1: Civic Engagement and Higher Education.

Michigan Journal of Community Service Learning
http://www.umich.edu/~mjcsl/
A national, peer-reviewed journal, with articles written by faculty and service-learning educators on research, theory, pedagogy, and issues related to the service-learning community.

National Service-Learning Clearinghouse
www.servicelearning.org
Originally more K-12 focused, the clearinghouse, supported by the Corporation for National and Community Service, now includes significant higher education resources, as well a searchable program models database.
(http://128.121.127.1/servicelearning/resources_tools/program_directory/index.php)

Campus Compact. (1999). *Presidents' Fourth of July declaration on the civic responsibility of higher education.* Retrieved October 13, 2003, from http://www.compact.org/presidential/plc/declaration.html

Kenny, M. E., Simon, L. A. K., Kiley-Brabeck, K., & Lerner, R. M. (Eds.). (2001). *Learning to serve: Promoting civil society through service learning.* Boston, MA: Kluwer.

Sirianni, C., & Friedland, L. (2001). *Civic innovation in America: Community empowerment, public policy, and the movement for civic renewal.* Berkeley, CA: University of California Press.

Zlotkowski, E. (Ed.). (1998). *Successful service-learning programs: New models of excellence in higher education.* Bolton, MA: Anker.

National Service Resource Center
www.nationalservice.org/resources/epicenter
This site includes examples of projects funded by the federal Corporation for National and Community Service, which offers grants once every three years to individual campuses and to consortia to advance service-learning and civic engagement.

Sector-Specific Resources

American Association of Community Colleges
http://www.aacc.nche.edu/
This site includes contact resources, numerous online and print publications, grant opportunities, conferences and events, and links to other useful sites. The following address offers lessons learned from the association's Horizons Project, a three-year service-learning initiative: http://www.aacc.nche.edu/Content/ContentGroups/Project_Briefs2/sustainability.pdf. And the association's eight-

page brief, "Sustaining Service Learning: The Role of Chief Academic Officers," can be found at www.aacc.nche.edu/servicelearning (click on "publications").

American Democracy Project
www.aascu.org or mehaffyg@aascu.org
A partnership between the American Association of State Colleges and Universities (AASCU) and *The New York Times*, this project is aimed at undergraduates enrolled at institutions that are members of AASCU. Goals include increasing the number of undergraduate students who understand and are committed to engaging in meaningful civic actions and focusing the attention of policy makers and opinion leaders on the civic value of the college experience.

Campus Compact Indicators of Engagement Project
http://www.compact.org/community-colleges/indicators/
From 2002-2005, Campus Compact is gathering exemplary practices from three specific types of higher education institutions:

- Community Colleges (2002-2003)

- Minority-Serving Institutions (2003-2004)

- Comprehensive Universities (2004-2005)

This site provides such information as a project summary, upcoming presentations, project updates, and community college exemplars.

Center for Liberal Education and Civic Engagement
http://www.compact.org/faculty/CLECE/default.html
A partnership between Campus Compact and the Association of American Colleges and Universities (AAC&U) that serves as a catalyst and incubator of new ideas, campus-based innovations, research, and collaborations. The center seeks to deepen understandings of the relation of liberal education to service and civic responsibilities.

Community College National Center for Community Engagement
http://www.mc.maricopa.edu/other/engagement/
This site includes referrals to resources, model programs, online and print publications, conference papers, grant opportunities, and other resources on service-learning at community colleges.

Council of Independent Colleges' Engaging Communities and Campuses Project
http://www.cic.org/caphe/grants/engaging.asp
This Council of Independent Colleges' (CIC) program assists independent col-

leges and universities to establish partnerships with community organizations that can enhance experiential learning activities while addressing community needs. The program is comprised of three separate but related activities— regional teaching and learning workshops, the creation of a web-based effective practice network, and a national grant program administered by the Consortium for the Advancement of Private Higher Education, a grant-making unit of CIC.

Doermann, H., & Drewry, H. N. (2001). *Stand and prosper: Private black colleges and their students.* Princeton, NJ: Princeton University Press.

Holland, B. A. (2002, January). Private and public institutional views of civic engagement and the urban mission. *Metropolitan Universities, 13*(1), 11-21.

Merisotis, J. P., & O'Brien, C. T. (Eds.). (1998). *New directions for higher education, No. 102. Minority serving institutions: Distinct purposes, common goals.* San Francisco, CA: Jossey-Bass.

National Association of State Universities and Land-Grant Colleges. (2000). *Returning to our roots: Executive summaries of the reports of the Kellogg Commission on the future of state and land-grant universities.* Retrieved October 13, 2003, from http://www.nasulgc.org/publications/Kellogg/Kellogg2000_ RetRoots_execsum.pdf

Maine Campus Compact

www.mainecompact.org
As this book goes to press, Maine Campus Compact, along with Michigan, Montana, North Carolina, and Vermont Campus Compacts, is exploring creation of a national rural campus network around civic engagement. Contact Maine Campus Compact at the above address for more information.

Stevens, C. S. (2003, Winter). Unrecognized roots of service-learning in African American social thought and action, 1890-1930. *Michigan Journal of Community Service Learning, 9*(2), 25-34.

Zimpher, N. L., Percy, S. L., & Brukardt, M. (2002). *A time for boldness: A story of institutional change.* Bolton, MA: Anker.

Topic-Specific Resources

Battistoni, R. M. (2002). *Civic engagement across the curriculum: A resource book for service-learning faculty in all disciplines.* Providence, RI: Campus Compact.

Battistoni, R., Gelmon, S., Saltmarsh, J., Wergin, J., & Zlotkowski, E. (2003). *The engaged department toolkit.* Providence, RI: Campus Compact.

Campus Compact. (2000a). *Establishing and sustaining an office of community service.* Providence, RI: Author.

Campus Compact. (2000b). *Introduction to service-learning toolkit: Readings and resources for faculty.* Providence, RI: Author.

Campus Compact. (2003). *The service and service-learning center guide to endowed funding.* Providence, RI: Author.

Driscoll, A., & Lynton, E. A. (1999). *Making outreach visible: A guide to documenting professional service and outreach.* Washington, DC: American Association for Higher Education.

Eyler, J., & Giles, D. E., Jr. (1999). *Where's the learning in service-learning?* San Francisco, CA: Jossey-Bass.

Eyler, J. S., Giles, D. E., Jr., Stenson, C. M., & Gray, C. J. (2001). *At a glance: What we know about the effects of service-learning on students, faculty, institutions and communities, 1993-2000* (3rd ed.). Washington, DC: Corporations for National and Community Service. Available online at http://www.compact.org/resource/aag.pdf

Gelmon, S. B., Holland, B. A., Driscoll, A., Spring, A., & Kerrigan, S. (2001). *Assessing service-learning and civic engagement: Principles and techniques* (Rev. 3rd ed.). Providence RI: Campus Compact.

Heffernan, K. (2001). *Fundamentals of service-learning course construction.* Providence, RI: Campus Compact.

Holland, B. A. (1999). Factors and strategies that influence faculty involvement in public service. *Journal of Public Service and Outreach, 4*(1), 37-43.

Holland, B. A., & Gelmon, S. (1998, October). The state of the "engaged campus": What have we learned about building and sustaining university-community partnerships? *AAHE Bulletin, 51*(2), 3-6.

Hollander, E., Saltmarsh, J., & Zlotkowski, E. (2001). Indicators of engagement. In Simon, L. A. K., Kenny, M., Brabeck, K., & Lerner, R. M. (Eds.), *Learning to serve: Promoting civil society through service-learning.* Norwell, MA: Kluwer Academic Publishers.

Jacoby, B., & Associates. (2003). *Building partnerships for service-learning.* San Francisco, CA: Jossey-Bass.

Lynton, E. (1995). *Making the case for professional service.* Washington, DC: American Association for Higher Education.

Maurrasse, D. J. (2001). *Beyond the campus: How colleges and universities form partnerships with their communities.* New York, NY: Routledge.

Oates, K., & Leavitt, L. H. (2003). *Service-learning and learning communities: Tools for integration and assessment.* Washington, DC: Association of American Colleges and Universities.

O'Grady, C. R. (Ed.). (2000). *Integrating service-learning and multicultural education in colleges and universities.* Mahwah, NJ: Lawrence Erlbaum.

Rhoads, R. A., & Howard, J. P. F. (Eds.). (1998). *New directions for teaching and learning, No. 73. Academic service learning: A pedagogy of action and reflection.* San Francisco, CA: Jossey-Bass.

Zlotkowski, E. (2001, January/February). Mapping the new terrain: Service-learning across the disciplines. *Change, 33*(1), 25-33.

Zlotkowski, E. (2002). *Service-learning and the first-year experience: Preparing students for personal success and civic engagement.* Columbia, SC: University of South Carolina, National Center for the First-Year Experience and Students in Transition.

Bibliography

Alpert, D. (1985). Performance and paralysis: The organizational context of the American research university. *Journal of Higher Education, 56*, 241-281.

American Association of Community Colleges. (n.d.). *Horizons service learning project.* Retrieved October 28, 2003, from http://www.aacc.nche.edu/Content/NavigationMenu/ResourceCenter/Projects_Partnerships/Current/HorizonsServiceLearningProject/HorizonsServiceLearningProject.htm

American Association of State Colleges and Universities. (2002). *Stepping forward as stewards of place: A guide for leading public engagement at state colleges and universities.* New York, NY: Author.

American Association for Higher Education, American College Personnel Association, & National Association of Student Personnel Administrators. (1998, June). *Powerful partnerships: A shared responsibility for learning.* Retrieved October 1, 2003, from http://www.aahe.org/assessment/joint.htm

Astin, W. A. (2000). The civic challenge of educating the underprepared student. In T. Ehrlich (Ed.), *Civic responsibility and higher education* (pp. 124-146). Phoenix, AZ: Oryx Press.

Austin, A., Sax, L., & Avalos, J. (1999). Long-term effects of volunteerism during the undergraduate years. *Review of Higher Education, 22*(2), 187-202.

Barber, B. (1991, Spring). Mandate for liberty: Requiring education-based community service. *The Responsive Community, 1,* 46-55.

Battistoni, R. M. (2002). *Civic engagement across the curriculum: A resource book for service-learning faculty in all disciplines.* Providence, RI: Campus Compact.

Beckham, E. (1994). *Opening remarks.* Paper presented at the Ford/UNCF Conference, Atlanta, GA.

Bell, R., Furco, A., Ammon, M. S., Muller, P., and Sorgen, V. (2000). *Institutionalizing service-learning in higher education: Findings from a study of the Western Region Campus Compact Consortium.* Bellingham, WA: Western Washington University, Western Region Campus Compact Consortium.

Boyer, E. L. (1990). *Scholarship reconsidered: Priorities of the professoriate.* Princeton, NJ: The Carnegie Foundation for the Advancement of Teaching.

Boyer, E. L. (1994, March 9). Creating the new American college. *Chronicle of Higher Education*, p. A48.

Boyer, E. L. (1996a). From scholarship reconsidered to scholarship assessed. *Quest*, 48(2), 129-139.

Boyer, E. L. (1996b). The scholarship of engagement. *Journal of Public Service & Outreach*, 1(1), 11-20.

Boyte, H., & Farr, H. (1997). The work of citizenship and the problem of service-learning. In R. Battistoni & W. Hudson (Eds.), *Experiencing citizenship: Concepts and models for service-learning in political science* (pp. 35-48). Washington, DC: American Association for Higher Education.

Bringle, R. G., Games, R., Foos, C., Osgood, R., & Osborne, R. (2000). Faculty Fellows Program: Enhancing integrated professional development through community service. *American Behavioral Scientist*, 43, 882-894.

Bringle, R. G., Games, R., & Malloy, E. A. (Eds.). (1999). *Colleges and universities as citizens.* Boston, MA: Allyn & Bacon.

Bringle, R. G., & Hatcher, J. A. (1995). A service-learning curriculum for faculty. *Michigan Journal of Community Service-Learning*, 2, 112-122.

Bringle, R. G., & Hatcher, J. A. (2000). Institutionalization of service-learning in higher education. *Journal of Higher Education*, 71(3), 273-290.

Bringle, R. G., & Hatcher, J. A. (2002). Campus-community partnerships: The terms of engagement. *Journal of Social Issues*, 58, 503-516.

Bringle, R. G., Hatcher, J. A., & Games, R. (1997). Engaging and supporting faculty in service-learning. *Journal of Public Service and Outreach*, 2(1), 43-51.

Bruininks, R. (2003). *About public engagement.* Retrieved October 29, 2003, from http://www1.umn.edu/civic/about/index.html

California State University-Monterey Bay. (1994). *Vision statement.* Seaside, CA: Author.

Campus Compact. (1999a). *Presidents' Fourth of July declaration on the civic responsibility of higher education.* Retrieved October 13, 2003, from http://www.compact.org/presidential/plc/declaration.html

Campus Compact. (1999b). *Wingspread declaration on renewing the civic mission of the American research university*. Retrieved October 27, 2003, from http://www.compact.org/civic/Wingspread/wings3.html

Campus Compact. (2000). *Benchmarks for campus/community partnerships*. Providence, RI: Author.

Campus Compact. (2002). *Service statistics: Highlights of Campus Compact's annual membership survey*. Retrieved October 16, 2003, from http://www.compact.org/newscc/2002_Statistics.pdf

Campus Compact. (2003). *Definitions of service-learning*. Retrieved September 28, 2003, from http://www.compact.org/faculty/definitions.html

Checkoway, B. (1991). Unanswered questions about public service in the public research university. *Journal of Planning Literature, 5*, 219-225.

Checkoway, B. (1993). *In-school national and community service: The challenge ahead for higher education*. Ann Arbor, MI: University of Michigan.

Checkoway, B. (1994a, May 11). AmeriCorps is coming. *Education Week, 24*.

Checkoway, B. (1994b, June 7). With new programs, a legacy can be left to shape the future. *Chicago Tribune*, p. 11A.

Checkoway, B. (1995, May 21). Inner-city hopes will die if AmeriCorps is cut. *Detroit Free Press*, p. 34.

Checkoway, B. (1996a). Combining service and learning on campus and in the community. *Phi Delta Kappan, 77*, 600-607.

Checkoway, B. (1996b). *Commitment to collaboration: Toward a center for learning through community service at the University of Michigan*. Ann Arbor, MI: University of Michigan, Office of the Vice President for Student Affairs.

Checkoway, B. (1997a). Institutional impacts of AmeriCorps on the University of Michigan. *Journal of Public Service and Outreach, 2*, 70-79.

Checkoway, B. (1997b). Reinventing the research university for public service. *Journal of Planning Literature, 11*, 307-319.

Checkoway, B. (1998a). Professionally related public service as applied scholarship. *Journal of Planning Education and Research, 17*, 358-360.

Checkoway, B. (1998b, January 7). Should the University of Michigan have a Detroit strategy? *Michigan Chronicle*, p. A7.

Checkoway, B. (2000a). Public service: Our new mission. *Academe, 86*, 24-28.

Checkoway, B. (2000b, November 6). Schools must lead youths to civic engagement. *Detroit Free Press*, p. 11A.

Checkoway, B. (2001). Renewing the civic mission of the American research university. *Journal of Higher Education, 72*, 125-147.

Checkoway, B. (2002). *Strategies for involving the faculty in civic renewal.* Ann Arbor, MI: University of Michigan.

Conville, R. (2000, Spring). *Faculty involvement in service-learning at the University of Southern Mississippi.* Unpublished manuscript, University of Southern Mississippi.

Cooper, D. D. (2002). Bus rides and forks in the road: The making of a public scholar. In Kettering Foundation (Ed.), *Higher education exchange* (pp. 24-36). Dayton, OH: Kettering Foundation.

Corporation for National and Community Service. (n.d.). *Learn and serve.* Retrieved October 28, 2003, from http://www.learnandserve.org/about/service_learning.html

Creating a culture of learning: The west side neighborhood learning community. (2002, Spring). *Research Review,* 6-7. Retrieved October 29, 2003, from http://www.cyfc.umn.edu/communities/resources/Neighborhood_Learning.pdf

Dewar, M., & Isaac, C. (1998). Learning from difference: The potentially transforming experience of community-university collaboration. *Journal of Planning Education and Research, 17,* 334-347.

Dewey, J. (1916). *Democracy and education.* New York, NY: Macmillan.

Dewey, J (1927). *The public and its problems.* New York, NY: Henry Holt.

Dewey, J. (1929). *Experience and nature.* Chicago, IL: Open Court.

Dewey, J. (1938). *Experience and education.* New York, NY: Macmillan.

Dewey, J. (1964). Need for a philosophy of education. In R. D. Archambault (Ed.), *John Dewey on education* (pp. 194-204). New York. NY: Random House.

Driscoll, A. (2000, June). *Putting faculty scholarly portfolios to work.* Paper presented at the American Association for Higher Education Conference, Charlotte, NC.

Driscoll, A., & Lynton, E. A. (1999). *Making outreach visible: A guide to documenting professional service and outreach.* Washington, DC: American Association for Higher Education.

Edgerton, R. (1997). *Higher education white paper.* Unpublished paper for the Pew Charitable Trusts.

Ehrlich, T. (Ed.). (2000). *Civic responsibility and higher education.* Phoenix, AZ: Oryx Press.

Ewell, P. T. (1997, December). Organizing for learning: A new imperative. *AAHE Bulletin, 50*(4), 3-6.

Eyler, J., & Giles, D. E., Jr. (1999). *Where's the learning in service-learning?* San Francisco, CA: Jossey-Bass.

Ferrari, J., & Worrall, L. (2000, Fall). Assessments by community agencies: How "the other side" sees service-learning. *Michigan Journal of Community Service-Learning, 7*, 35-40.

Foos, C. L., & Hatcher, J. A. (1999). *Service-learning curriculum guide for campus-based workshops.* Indianapolis, IN: Indiana Campus Compact.

Francis, M. C., Mulder, T. C., & Stark, J. S. (1995). *Intentional learning: A process for learning to learn in the accounting curriculum.* Sarasota, FL: American Accounting Association.

Furco, A. (2002a). Institutionalizing service-learning in higher education. *Journal of Public Affairs, 8*, 32-47.

Furco, A. (2002b). Is service-learning really better than community service? In A. Furco & S. H. Billig (Eds.), *Service-learning: The essence of the pedagogy* (pp. 23-50). Greenwich, CT: Information Age Publishers.

Ginsberg Center for Community Service and Learning. (2001a). *Community learning for a diverse democracy.* Ann Arbor, MI: University of Michigan, Ginsberg Center for Community Service and Learning and Center for Research on Learning and Teaching.

Ginsberg Center for Community Service and Learning. (2001b). *Symposium on university-community partnerships in Detroit neighborhoods.* Ann Arbor, MI: University of Michigan, Ginsberg Center for Community Service and Learning and Rackham Graduate School.

Ginsberg Center Long Range Planning Committee. (2001). *Strengthening community service and learning at the University of Michigan.* Ann Arbor, MI: University of Michigan, Ginsberg Center for Community Service and Learning.

Glassick, C. E., Huber, M. T., & Maeroff, G. I. (1997). *Scholarship assessed: Evaluation of the professoriate.* San Francisco, CA: Jossey-Bass.

Gray, M. J., Ondaatje, E. H., Fricker, R. D., & Geschwind, S. A. (2000, March/April). Assessing service-learning: Results from a survey of Learn and Serve American, Higher Education. *Change, 32*(2), 31-39.

Gray, M. J., Ondaatje, E. H., Fricker, R. D., Geschwind, S. A ., Goldman, C. A., Kaganoff, T., et al. (1998). *Coupling service and learning in higher education: The final report of the evaluation of the Learn and Serve America, Higher Education.* Santa Monica, CA: The RAND Corporation.

Gray, W. (1994). *HBCUs and community service.* Paper presented at the Ford/UNCF Conference, Atlanta, GA.

Hardwood Group. (1998). *Planned serendipity: Executive summary.* Richmond, VA: University of Richmond. Retrieved June 27, 2002 from http://www.pew-partnership.org/pubs/serendipity/summary.html

Harkavy, I. (1996). Back to the future: From service-learning to strategic, academically based community service. *Metropolitan Universities, 7*(1), 57-70.

Harkavy, I. (2002). *Honoring community, honoring place.* Retrieved September 28, 2003, from www.compact.org/publication/Reader/Fall_2002.pdf

Hatcher, J. A. (Ed.). (1999). *Service-learning tip sheets: A faculty resource guide.* Indianapolis, IN: Indiana Campus Compact.

Hatcher, J. A., Bringle, R. G., & Muthiah, R. (2002). Institutional strategies to involve first-year students in service. In E. Zlotkowski (Ed.), *Service-learning and the first-year experience: Preparing students for personal success and civic responsibility* (pp. 79-90). Columbia, SC: University of South Carolina, National Resource Center for the First-Year Experience and Students in Transition.

Holland, B. A. (1997). Analyzing institutional commitment to service: A model of key organizational factors. *Michigan Journal of Community Service-Learning, 4,* 30-41.

Holland, B. A. (1999a). Factors and strategies that influence faculty involvement in public service. *Journal of Public Service and Outreach, 4*(1), 37-43.

Holland, B. A. (1999b). From murky to meaningful: The role of mission in institutional change. In R. G. Bringle, R. Games, & E. A. Malloy (Eds.), *Colleges and universities as citizens* (pp. 48-73). Boston, MA: Allyn & Bacon.

Holland, B. A. (2000, Fall). Institutional impacts and organizational issues related to service-learning. *Michigan Journal of Community Service-Learning,* [Special issue], 52-60.

Holland, B. A. (2001). Toward a definition and characterization of the engaged campus: Six cases. *Metropolitan Universities, 12*(3), 20-29.

Holland, B. A., & Gelmon, S. (1998, October). The state of the "engaged campus": What have we learned about building and sustaining university-community partnerships? *AAHE Bulletin, 51*(2), 3-6.

Hollander, L. (2001). *What is an engaged campus? Scholarship and civic responsibility in the 21st century.* Presentation at the 9th Annual American Association for Higher Education Conference on Faculty Roles and Rewards, Tampa, FL.

Howard, J. (1993). Community service-learning in the curriculum. In J. Howard (Ed.), *Praxis I: A faculty casebook on community service-learning* (pp. 3-12). Ann Arbor, MI: OCSL Press.

Hutchings, P. (Ed.). (1995). *From idea to prototype: The peer review of teaching, a project workbook.* Washington, DC: American Association for Higher Education.

The International Partnership for Service-Learning. (n.d.). *Mission and activities.* Retrieved October 13, 2003, from http://www.ipsl.org/organization/organization.html

Jackson, F. (1993). Evaluating service-learning. In T. Kupiec (Ed.), *Rethinking tradition: Integrating service with academic study of college campuses* (pp. 128-132). Providence, RI: Campus Compact.

Jacoby, B., & Associates. (1996). *Service-learning in higher education: Concepts and practices.* San Francisco, CA: Jossey-Bass.

Kelly, P. (1994, April 14). Johnson C. Smith University wants volunteering to be mandatory. *Charlotte Observer,* p. 4.

Kenny, M. E., Simon, L. A. K., Kiley-Brabeck, K., & Lerner, R. M. (Eds.). (2001). *Learning to serve: Promoting civil society through service learning.* Boston, MA: Kluwer.

Kilpatrick, W. H. (1918). The project method. *Teachers College Record, 19,* 319-335.

Kimball, B. A. (1995). Toward pragmatic liberal education. In R. Orrill (Ed.), *The condition of American liberal education: Pragmatism and a changing tradition* (pp. 3-122). New York, NY: The College Board.

Kimball, B. A. (1997). Naming pragmatic liberal education. In R. Orrill (Ed.), *Education and democracy: Re-imagining liberal learning in America* (pp. 45-67). New York, NY: The College Board.

Knight Higher Education Collaborative. (2000). Disputed territories. *Policy Perspectives, 9*(4), 1-8.

Kramer, M. (2000). *Make it last forever: The institutionalization of service-learning in America.* Washington, DC: Corporation for National Service.

Krzyzowski, M., Checkoway, B., & Gutierrez, L. (2001). *Educating community workers for collaborative practice: The Michigan Neighborhood AmeriCorps program*. Ann Arbor, MI: University of Michigan, School of Social Work.

Levine, A. (1980). *Why innovation fails: Institutionalization and termination of innovation in higher education*. Albany, NY: State University of New York Press.

Lynton, E. (1995). *Making the case for professional service*. Washington, DC: American Association for Higher Education.

Marchese, T. (1996, March). The search for next-century learning. *AAHE Bulletin, 48*(7), 3-6.

Markus, G. B., Howard, J. P. F., & King, D. C. (1993). Integrating community service and classroom instruction enhances learning: Results from an experiment. *Educational Evaluation and Policy Analysis, 15*(4), 410-419.

Marver, J. D., & Patton, C. V. (1976). The correlates of consultation: American academics in "the real world." *Higher Education, 4*, 319-335.

Maurrasse, D. J. (2001). *Beyond the campus: How colleges and universities form partnerships with their communities*. New York, NY: Routledge.

Meister, R. J. (1996, Spring). Expectations and visions. *Academic Affairs Quarterly, 2*(2), 1-4.

Meister, R. J. (1997, Fall). Future directions: "Make no little plans." *Academic Affairs Quarterly, 3*(3), 1-3.

Meister, R. J. (2002, July). *Vision 2006—maintaining the momentum*. Unpublished keynote address, DePaul University Academic Affairs Retreat.

Mill, J. S. (1962). Civilization [1836]. *Essays on politics and culture*. New York, NY: Doubleday. (Original work published in 1836)

Morton, K. & Troppe, M. (1996, January). From the margin to the mainstream: Campus Compact's project on integrating service with academic study. *Journal of Business Ethics, 15*(1), 21-32.

Muir, J. (1911). *My first summer in the sierra*. Boston, MA: Houghton Mifflin.

National Association of State Universities and Land-Grant Colleges. (2000). *Returning to our roots: Executive summaries of the reports of the Kellogg Commission on the future of state and land-grant universities*. Retrieved October 13, 2003, from http://www.nasulgc.org/publications/Kellogg/ Kellogg2000_RetRoots_execsum.pdf

National Service-Learning Clearinghouse. (2001). *Service-learning is . . .* Retrieved September 28, 2003, from http://www.servicelearning.org/ article/archive/35/

Newman, F. (2000). *Saving higher education's soul*. Providence, RI: The Futures Project.

Palmer, P. J. (1996, March/April). Divided no more: A movement approach to educational reform. *Change, 24*(2), 10-17.

Parker, I. (1977). *Community involvement*. Unpublished manuscript, Johnson C. Smith University, Charlotte, NC.

Patton, C. V., & Marver, J. D. (1979). Paid consulting by American academics. *Educational Record, 60*, 175-184.

Perry, W. G. (1970). *Intellectual and ethical development in the college years*. New York, NY: Holt, Rinehart, and Winston.

Pew Charitable Trusts. (2002). *Public policy*. Retrieved October 28, 2003, from http://www.pewtrusts.org/grants/grants_item.cfm?image=img3&program_area_id=6

Pickeral, T., & Peters, K. (1996). *From the margins to the mainstream: The faculty role for advancing service-learning on community colleges*. Mesa, AZ: Campus Compact National Center for Community Colleges.

Putnam, R. (2000). *Bowling alone: The collapse and revival of American community*. New York, NY: Simon & Schuster.

Ramaley, J. (2000, March). Embracing civic responsibility. *AAHE Bulletin, 52*(7), 9-13.

Rodgers, R. F. (1980). Theories underlying student development. *Student Development in Higher Education* [ACPA, Student Personnel Series], *27*, 10-95.

Romer, R., & Education Commission of the States. (1996, April). What research says about improving undergraduate education. *AAHE Bulletin, 48*(8), 5-8.

Rosaen, C. (1999). Enhancing teaching and student learning through collaborative inquiry. In A. Driscoll & E. Lynton, *Making outreach visible: A guide to documenting professional service and outreach*. Washington, DC: American Association for Higher Education.

Rouche, J. E., Baker, G. A., III, & Rose, R. R. (1989). *Shared vision: Transformational leadership in American community colleges*. Washington, DC: Community College Press.

San Jose/Evergreen Community College District. (2002). *Board priorities for 2002-2003*. Unpublished Document.

Scannell, T., & Roberts, A. (1994). *Young and old serving together: Meeting community needs through intergenerational partnerships.* Washington, DC: Generations United.

Schechter, P. (1999). Collaborations: The Portland YWCA and women's history, 1901-2001. In A. Driscoll & E. Lynton, *Making outreach visible: A guide to documenting professional service and outreach* (p. 28). Washington, DC: American Association for Higher Education.

Schroeder, C. C. (1993, September/October). New students—new learning styles. *Change, 25*(4), 21-26.

Schulz, A. J., Parker, E. A., Israel, B. A., Becker, A. B., Maciak, B. J., & Hollis, R. (1998). Conducting a participatory community-based survey: Collecting and interpreting data for a community intervention on Detroit's east side. *Journal of Public Health Management and Practice, 4*(2), 10-24.

Shulman, L. S. (1999, July/August). Taking learning seriously. *Change, 31*(4), 11-17.

Sigmon, R. (1994). *Linking service with learning.* Washington, DC: Council of Independent Colleges.

Silcox, H. C. (1995). *A how to guide to reflection* (2nd ed.). Holland, PA: Brighton Press.

Smith, V. (1998, June). *Comments on a national project on civic responsibility and higher education.* Paper presented at the Florida State University/American Council on Education Conference on Higher Education and Civic Responsibility, Tallahassee, FL.

Spanier, G. (1999). *The engaged university: Best practices in outreach and public service.* University, PA: Pennsylvania State University.

University of Southern Mississippi. (1999, Spring). *A national university for the Gulf South, Strategic Plan.* Hattiesburg, MS: Author.

Unsigned editorial. (2001, August 23). *Star Tribune.*

Vaughn, P. M. (2002). *Enhancing student development in service-learning with performance-based assessment rubrics.* (Doctoral dissertation, Arizona State University). AAT 3043835.

Ward, K. (1998). Addressing academic culture: Service-learning, organizations, and faculty work. In R. A. Rhoads & J. Howard (Eds.), *Academic service-learning: A pedagogy of action and reflection* (pp. 73-80). San Francisco, CA: Jossey-Bass.

West, C. (1989). *The American evasion of philosophy: A genealogy of pragmatism.* Madison, WI: University of Wisconsin Press.

Whitehead, A. N. (1929). *The aims of education.* New York, NY: Macmillan.

Wood, R. J. (1990). Changing the educational program. In D. W. Steeples (Ed.), *Managing change in higher education* (pp. 51-58). San Francisco, CA: Jossey-Bass.

Worrall, L. (2001, March). *Bringing it home: Linking foreign and domestic study through language immersion and service-learning.* Unpublished grant proposal to the Fund for the Improvement of Post-Secondary Education.

Yanikoski, R. (1986). DePaul University: Urban by design. *Current Issues in Catholic Education, 6*(2), 5-8.

Zlotkowski, E. (Ed.). (1997-2002). *Service-learning in the disciplines.* Washington, DC: American Association for Higher Education.

Zlotkowski, E. (Ed.). (1998). *Successful service-learning programs: New models of excellence in higher education.* Bolton, MA: Anker.

Zlotkowski, E. (1999). Pedagogy and engagement. In R. G. Bringle, R. Games, & E. A. Malloy (Eds.), *Colleges and universities as citizens* (pp. 96-120). Boston, MA: Allyn & Bacon.

Zlotkowski, E. (2000, Fall). Service-learning research in the disciplines. *Michigan Journal of Community Service-Learning* [Special issue], 61-67.

Index